The AUTHENTICITY of FAITH

The AUTHENTICITY of FAITH

The varieties and illusions of religious experience

RICHARD BECK

Abilene Christian University

Abilene Christian University Press

THE AUTHENTICITY OF FAITH
The varieties and illusions of religious experience

Copyright 2012 by Richard Beck

ISBN 978-0-89112-350-7

LCCN 2011045532

Printed in the United States of America

The following North Park University students provided collaborative assistance with this work: Robin Spencer, Yoonhee Kim, Amanda Hasse, Michelle Ness, Heather Yanul, and Krissa Harwood

LIBRARY OF CONGRESS CATALOGING-IN-PUBLICATION DATA
Beck, Richard Allan, 1967-
The authenticity of faith : the varieties and illusions of religious experience / Richard Beck.
    p. cm.
Includes bibliographical references (p. 267).
ISBN 978-0-89112-350-7
1. Personality--Religious aspects--Christianity. 2. Typology (Psychology)--Religious aspects--Christianity. 3. Apologetics. I. Title.
BV4597.57.B43 2012
248.2--dc23

    2011045532

Cover design by Nicole Weaver, Zeal Design Studio
Interior text design by Sandy Armstrong

For information contact:
Abilene Christian University Press
1626 Campus Court
Abilene, Texas 79601

1-877-816-4455
www.abilenechristianuniversitypress.com

12 13 14 15 16 17 / 7 6 5 4 3 2 1

For Brenden and Aidan

It has long been known that need and desire play a part
in the shaping of beliefs. But is it true, as modern psychology
often claims, that our religious beliefs are nothing but attempts to
satisfy subconscious wishes? That the conception of God is merely a
projection of self-seeking emotions, an objectification of subjective
needs, the self in disguise? Indeed, the tendency to question the
genuineness of man's concerns about God is a challenge no less
serious than the tendency to question the existence of God. We are
in greater need of a proof for the authenticity of faith
than of a proof for the existence of God.

—Abraham Joshua Heschel

CONTENTS

Part 1
The Illusions of Religious Experience

Part 2
The Varieties of Religious Experience

Part 3
Varieties and Illusions: Four Case Studies

Acknowledgments

Special thanks to Leonard Allen and ACU Press for the invitation to write this book. Also, a heartfelt thanks to Robyn Burwell for all her work shepherding this book through the editing and design process. Thanks to Sandy Armstrong for her creative and steady hand. You've produced a beautiful looking book. Thanks also to Duane Anderson, Seth Shaver, Ryan Self, and Lettie Morrow for their work to promote this publication.

I would also like to thank the readers of my blog *Experimental Theology* where early drafts of this material first appeared. I'm blessed to have one of the most intelligent and thoughtful readerships on the Internet. A warm thank-you to my readers for your many helpful comments, feedback, and encouragement. You were the first to let me know that this material deserved a wide audience.

I would like to thank Dan McGregor, Brooke Woodrow, Andrea Haugen and Kyna Killion, my coauthors on the research discussed in Chapter 10. Thanks also to Sara Taylor, my coauthor on the research I discuss in Chapter 11.

Thanks to Anne Briggs for her assistance in securing image permissions and to Tim Lowly for the use of *Carry Me* in Chapter 10.

A great deal of this book summarizes my theoretical and empirical research which has previously appeared in the *Journal of Christianity and Psychology* and the *Journal of Theology and Psychology*:

Chapter 6:

Beck, R. (2006). Communion and complaint: Attachment, object-relations, and triangular love perspectives on relationship with God. *Journal of Psychology and Theology, 34*, 43–52.

Beck, R. (2007). The winter experience of faith: Empirical, theological, and theoretical perspectives. *Journal of Psychology and Christianity, 26*, 68–78.

Chapter 7:

Beck, R. (2004). The function of religious belief: Defensive versus existential religion. *Journal of Psychology and Christianity, 23*, 208–218.

Chapter 8:

Beck, R. (2006). Defensive versus existential religion: Is religious defensiveness predictive of worldview defense? *Journal of Psychology and Theology, 34*, 142–151.

Chapter 9:

Beck, R. (2009). Feeling queasy about the Incarnation: Terror management theory, death, and the body of Jesus. *Journal of Psychology and Theology, 36*, 303–312.

Chapter 10:

Beck, R., McGregor, D., Woodrow, B., Haugen, A. & Killion, K. (2010). Death, art and the Fall: A terror management view of Christian aesthetic judgments. *Journal of Psychology and Christianity, 29*, 301–307.

Chapter 11:

Beck, R. & Taylor, S. (2008). The emotional burden of monotheism: Satan, theodicy, and relationship with God. *Journal of Psychology and Theology, 36*, 151–160.

I was blessed to be able to work with Andrea Haugen as my graduate assistant during the year I wrote this book (and the year before when I wrote my first book *Unclean*). My research and collaboration with

Andrea has been one of the most rewarding experiences of my teaching career. Andrea read and edited the entire manuscript and was a constant source of encouragement. I can't thank her enough.

I'd also like to thank Bandit for keeping me company as I typed away at my laptop during the mornings I worked at home on this book. When writing a lot about existential anxiety having a dog around really helps.

Everything I think, research, or write about gets its first hearing with Jana. For twenty years of marriage, Jana has been my intellectual partner and companion. But mainly, she's my best friend. Everything I accomplish is a product of our love and partnership.

Finally, I've dedicated this book to my two wonderful sons, Brenden and Aidan. This book is about the messy and difficult journey toward a faith that is honest, truthful, and fearless. Any lessons I've learned about that journey I pass on to my boys.

A Note to Readers about the Use of Statistics

One audience for this book, although not exclusively so, is the social scientists interested in religious belief and experience. Consequently, at points in this book (particularly in Part 3) I use statistics to communicate various trends, observations, and findings. However, any readers unfamiliar with statistics should feel free to skip over the statistical material (which is confined to footnotes and parentheses).

Prelude

A NEW KIND OF APOLOGETICS

THE GOAL OF THIS BOOK IS TO ANSWER A QUESTION: WHY DO people believe in God? More specifically, this book is aimed at answering a particular form of this question, a nuance that emerged in the modern period through the work of thinkers such as Karl Marx, Charles Darwin, and, of particular importance for this book, Sigmund Freud. The shift in emphasis in "the God question" occasioned by these thinkers has rendered much of Christian theology and apologetics effectively useless in addressing many contemporary criticisms of religious faith. The playing field has shifted, and a new kind of apologetics is needed.

1.

How have things changed?

Simplifying, what we might call Classical Christian apologetics has tended to focus upon an *epistemological formulation* of the question "Why do people believe in God?" The classical, epistemological formulation asked the following of religious believers: "What are your *reasons* for believing in God?" This is an issue about evidence and rational justification. The question "Why do you believe in God?" boiled down, in classical apologetics, to "Do you have *good reasons* for believing in God? And if so, what are those reasons?"

No doubt, the classical questions of apologetics are still with us. People still question religious belief on issues related to empirical evidence and rational justification. The classic epistemological criterion of "justified true belief" is still applied to faith. Critics of religious faith, such as the New Atheists, often question if faith in God is reasonable or justifiable. The Christian response to these sorts of questions is both complex and varied. Outside of the academy, from the pulpits and pews, Christian believers have tended to respond in one of three ways.

First, there is a suite of metaphysical questions that science cannot address. The popular query "Why is there something rather than nothing?" is an example. Methodologically, science restricts itself to explaining empirical phenomena through an appeal to a naturalistic mechanism. Metaphysical questions are therefore, by definition, out of bounds for scientific inquiry. Given the self-imposed boundaries of science, religious believers find room for faith in the area beyond the territory marked off by empirical inquiry and evidence. And yet, while this move has a certain appeal, there are some concerns. One important concern is that if faith claims become radically decoupled from empirical evidence it becomes difficult to provide rational justification for either faith generally, or for the more particular faith claims associated with a faith tradition. For example, Christians are monotheists (even if Trinitarian). Hindus, by contrast, are polytheists. How, outside of empirical evidence, do believers within those religious traditions justify their belief in the Divine generally and, more specifically, their very particular claims about the number of gods? How are these general and particular beliefs *justified*?

A second strand of popular Christian apologetics attempts to address these questions by citing archaeological and historical evidence that supports the biblical narrative. Beliefs in God and about God, general and particular, are grounded in God's revelation to humanity. Consequently, if the Christian Scriptures are found to be trustworthy, historically speaking, Christian believers feel justified using the Bible as warrant for their faith claims. There is an enormous scholarly literature regarding the historical accuracy of the biblical witness, for both the Hebrew Bible and the New Testament. A review of that literature is beyond our purposes here. Suffice it to say, despite the historical support found for various biblical events and persons, many modern readers of the Bible continue to struggle with the metaphysical worldview found within the premodern societies of the biblical authors. Many, both inside and outside the Christian faith, agree with the assessment of the German theologian Rudolf Bultmann (1984):

> The world picture of the New Testament is a mythical world picture. The world is a three-story structure, with the earth in the middle, heaven above it, and hell below it. Heaven is the dwelling place of God and of heavenly figures, the angels; the world below is hell, the place of torment. . . . Can Christian proclamation today expect men and women to acknowledge the mythical world picture as true? To do so would be pointless and impossible. It would be pointless because there is nothing specifically Christian about the mythical world picture, which is simply the world picture of a time now past that was not yet formed by scientific thinking . . . it is impossible to repristinate a past world picture by sheer resolve, especially a *mythical* world picture, now that all of our thinking is irrevocably formed by science. . . . Experience and control of the world have developed to such an extent through science and technology that no one can or does seriously maintain the New Testament world picture. (pp. 1, 3–4)

No doubt, many Christian believers would disagree with Bultmann. Regardless, Bultmann's assessment makes an important point: while various aspects of the biblical narrative have empirical and historical support, the cosmological claims of the Bible, particularly when they butt up against modern science, are hotly contested and remain sources of disbelief and skepticism.

A final move common to popular Christian apologetics is to view the whole debate over justifiability as woefully misguided. In this view, faith is not reducible to *data* and *evidence*. The inherently scientistic criterion of justified true belief simply is not applicable to faith. It is an issue of apples and oranges. Terry Eagleton offers an example of this argument in a recent book about the misfires of the New Atheists. Regarding "justifying" faith on scientific grounds, Eagleton (2009) writes: "Believing that religion is a botched attempt to explain the world . . . is like seeing ballet as a botched attempt to run for a bus" (p. 50). We can see the move at work here. Asking if faith is true is like asking if Hamlet or Mozart is true. Religion is fundamentally about the human experience, about meaning, transcendence, value, beauty, and goodness. This point is well-intentioned, but this perspective struggles to justify why answers to these questions must be *religious* in nature, and why those answers might be preferable to other philosophies on offer. Couldn't a person find perfectly acceptable nonreligious answers to questions related to the good life, answers independent of religious dogma? If so, why should a religious account of the good life, with its freight of metaphysical baggage, be preferred?

The goal of this survey of popular Christian apologetics is not meant to be exhaustive and comprehensive. I merely wanted to sketch the shape of Christian apologetics, in its popular manifestations, when it is driven by the epistemological criterion of justified true belief. As I have tried to show, there are persuasive arguments on both sides of the issue, for faith and against it.

By and large, this territory is well-known. Importantly for Christian believers, we find in classical apologetics a suite of arguments that can be deployed to provide an epistemologically driven apology for faith. Christians can make appeals to evidence and argument giving warrant for their belief in God. These arguments may not persuade skeptics, but they suggest that faith might be *reasonable*. Epistemological arguments of this sort I have called "classical apologetics."

2.

But this book is not about classical apologetics. It is about a wave of questions directed at religious belief occasioned by the work of thinkers such as Sigmund Freud, Charles Darwin, and Karl Marx. These questions are radically different from those handled by classical apologetics. More, the questions here are so unique and peculiar we are finding that they cannot be effectively handled by Christian theology and classical apologetics as taught in the seminary. And because of this, the questions raised by Freud, Darwin and Marx are leaving the Christian community intellectually vulnerable and effectively defenseless. Again, a new kind of apologetics is needed.

What exactly changed with the work of Freud, Darwin, and Marx? How are criticisms of faith informed by their work, directly or indirectly, any different from those encountered in classical apologetics?

Consider Marx's famous formulation that religion is the "opiate of the masses." How is Marx's attack on faith any different from the epistemological questions found in classical apologetics? To start, note that Marx is not asking for religious believers to give an account. Marx is, rather, giving an account of religious believers. Marx is shifting away from the *reasons* for belief and focusing a spotlight upon the *functions* of religious belief: in this case, the sociological functions of religion (i.e., faith functions to keep the working class from seeking revolutionary change). This shift, from reasons to functions, is a radical and destabilizing change in the history of Christian apologetics. It has, effectively, changed the subject.

How so? The questions prompted by Freud, Darwin and Marx sweep past the issues involved in classical apologetics (i.e., rational justification) to ask questions about the biological, social, and psychological functions of religious belief. Specifically, might religion be doing some sort of useful biological, social, or psychological work for us? Perhaps religion aided in evolutionary survival as an adaptive trait handed down by our ancestors. Perhaps, as Marx suggested, religion is helpful in keeping political order. Or perhaps, following Freud, religion is a defense mechanism, a way of repressing our existential fears in the face of an unpredictable existence and an eventual death. Maybe, in short, religion has a function: a biological, social, and/or psychological role that explains its existence and ubiquity. Religion exists not because of its *justifiability* but because of the function it serves. Of course, religious believers will offer justifications for their faith ad nauseam, but the *real* reason people believe in God, so this new argument goes, is to be found a level lower, at a more foundational and functional level, in the ways religion helps us survive and thrive—physically, socially, and psychologically. And this argument is, as they say, a whole new ballgame.

Let me give an example of the relevant contrast here, albeit somewhat crudely. In classical apologetics, Christians might have been asked to justify their beliefs that Jesus of Nazareth was resurrected from the dead. What justifies that belief? By contrast, in the wake of the work of thinkers such as Freud, the question morphs and becomes something a bit different, something like this: Why would someone be attracted to the idea of life after death? That is a different kind of question, a question that moves past the propositional contents of faith and begins to investigate the underlying, often subterranean, motivations behind belief-formation itself. These questions are highly destabilizing because few of us are able to plumb the depths of our unconscious motivations. Is it possible that I believe in the Resurrection because I am motivated by a deep and unconscious fear of death? Honest people admit that this may be a very real possibility. If so, hasn't my faith been rendered to be an illusion, a psychological system that helps me cope with an unsettling reality? Suddenly, we are no longer talking about evidence, argument, and reasonableness. We are talking about psychological motivations, often *unconscious* motivations. And if those motivations are called into question (plausibly so, for who does not want to live forever?), how are we to respond? The tools of classical apologetics are impotent here. Neither is the Bible nor theology of any help.

3.

In sum, the task of apologetics has been complicated by the rise of functional accounts of religion. In these accounts religious belief exists not because of evidence but because it serves some other function (e.g., helps us cope with death). The particular intellectual content of faith (e.g., the Christian creeds or the doctrines of a particular faith community) can be ignored as mere epiphenomena, post hoc rationalizations pulled along by deeper psychological, biological, and sociological forces. Why people *really* believe in God is to be found at this deeper, functional level.

This account of religion is disruptive in two ways. First, functional accounts of religion are inherently *reductionistic* in a way the earlier, classical debates were not. By positing an underlying mechanism giving rise to religious belief, a functional account threatens to explain faith. The contents of faith are explained by a reductionistic appeal to a deeper level of analysis. For instance, it might be claimed, as it was by Freud, that a person believes in God and heaven because they fear death and nonexistence. Beliefs in the afterlife are explained here in functional terms, as a means of coping. And once this functional account is offered, beliefs in the afterlife are thus explained; this is the reason for their existence.

This reductionistic move is highly deflationary when it comes to religious belief. For example, in a debate about the afterlife the reductionistic account could deflate in the following way: "You say you believe in an afterlife, but the real reason you believe that is because you are afraid of dying." Fear of death is offered here as an explanation for belief-formation. The conversation has shifted to a lower level, away from the contents of belief (i.e., is there actually an afterlife?) to motivations, or how the belief is being adopted and deployed to assuage existential anxiety. And once the conversation shifts to this motivational level it is hard to know how to proceed. The explanation possesses a certain face validity, and a denial from the believer would appear defensive, rhetorically speaking. An appeal, say, to the argument from design (a classic argument for the existence of God) is revealed to be of little help here.

A second reason functional accounts are destabilizing is that they make unclear how Christian intellectuals and defenders of the faith should respond. Christian theologians are trained to handle the content and warrants of the faith. They are not, as a rule, well versed in how religion might be implicated in social control or as a means to repress death anxiety. In short, criticisms based upon Darwin, Marx, and Freud have left the Christian theological community largely flat-footed and flummoxed. It is true that Christian thinkers have resisted the reduction of faith to biology, sociology, or psychology, but much of this resistance is mere hand waving. Why do I say this? Because the questions shaped by Freud, Marx, and Darwin, as we have seen, often go to issues regarding human motivation. And issues related to human motivation, particularly unconscious motivation, cannot be settled with armchair speculation or biblical analysis. Nor will introspection, even erudite and sophisticated introspection, move us forward. These issues, ultimately, boil down to human psychology. To make any headway with these new criticisms of faith, to show, for example, that faith is more than wishful thinking, a person is going to need to know a bit about how religious belief functions in the mind of believers. Apologetics has shifted to the social sciences.

4.

So this book is about a new kind of apologetics, an apologetics aimed at examining the functional accounts of religious belief. While both Darwin and Marx will be discussed, our treatment will focus upon the account of religious faith offered by Freud (1927/1989) in his seminal work *The Future of an Illusion*. The reason for focusing upon Freud is that his account of religious faith remains one of the most influential accounts regarding the origins of religious belief, particularly in the heated contemporary debates about the legitimacy of faith. Freud's basic claim that faith is a form of wishful thinking in the face of an unsettling existence is widely known and often deployed, with devastating and deflationary effect, in cultural conversations about the cogency of the Christian faith.

In light of all this, our procedure will be as follows. In Part 1, we will dig deeper into the logic of functional accounts of religious belief to understand how they work. While there are a variety of functional accounts on offer—biological, sociological, and psychological—they share a similar structure. Grappling with that structure will help illuminate the particular challenge functional accounts pose and highlight the need for fresh approaches within Christian apologetics. After this survey we will examine Freud's account of religious belief in his seminal book *The Future of an Illusion*. After taking the measure of Freud's argument we will step back and ask the obvious questions: Was Freud right? How does the evidence stack up?

This issue of empirical support is important for this book because the challenge of, say, a Freud, is that these questions are no longer theoretical or theological. Functional accounts of faith, like Freud's, are making a set of empirical claims about the psychology of religious belief. Consequently, psychological methods will be needed to assess the accuracy of Freud's theory. This new sort of apologetics will be as interested with the laboratory as it is with theology.

At the end of Part 1, as we finish our examination of Freud and *The Future of an Illusion,* we will want to find an alternative formulation of the religious experience, one suggesting that faith cannot be reduced to a defense mechanism as Freud suggested. We will find our rival model with William James and his seminal work *The Varieties of Religious Experience*. These two books, *The Future of an Illusion* and *The Varieties of Religious Experience*, remain two of the most influential books in religious studies literature. They are required reading for those interested in scientific approaches to religious belief. By placing these two works into conversation, we will create a sort of "Clash of the Titans." In Part 2, *The Future of an Illusion* and *The Varieties of Religious Experience* will be treated as rival models and hypotheses regarding the functions and origins of religious belief. That is, we will set up Freud and James as debating partners—"illusions versus varieties" will become our shorthand. And then, in Part 3, we will examine empirical evidence from a variety of case studies regarding their respective positions. How do illusions versus varieties explain a variety of features within the Christian experience, from doctrine, to the problem of suffering, to the experience of the body, to aesthetic judgments? What we will find, in the end, is that while Freud's model explains a significant portion of the religious experience (there are religious illusions), his account cannot explain the full range of religious experience. James's notion of religious varieties appears to be the better fit.

Overall, the goal of this new kind of apologetics will be to address functional accounts of religious belief, such as Freud's in *The Future of an Illusion*, on their own terms: assessing the viability of these functional accounts as functional accounts, as explanations of religious belief and experience. This is new and perhaps unexpected terrain. It may seem odd that psychological science is required to assess criticisms of the faith. But that is the only road ahead of us if we wish to grapple directly with deflationary functional accounts of faith. A new kind of apologetics is needed to complement the old. The assessment of Abraham Heschel (1955, pp. 35–36) cited on the frontispiece summarizes the situation well. In light of the Freudian worries that "God is merely a projection of self-seeking emotions," we find ourselves today "in greater need of a proof for the authenticity of faith than of a proof for the existence of God."

In the end, though, this book will not offer a proof for the authenticity of faith. If our apologetical approach is going to lean on psychological science the outcome cannot be determined a priori. The data will be what it will be. So, there is real risk in this approach. Freud, we could find, might have had it right. In fact, we will find that Freud had a great deal of it right. Much of what we will discover in the chapters ahead will prove to be disconcerting to many Christian believers. This book will not argue that faith is *necessarily* authentic. It will only, in the end, conclude that faith *can be* authentic—that an authentic faith, while rare, is possible. We are looking for some elbow room.

Does it exist?

PART 1

THE ILLUSIONS OF RELIGIOUS EXPERIENCE

Chapter 1

MASTERS OF SUSPICION

1.

SO, WHY DO PEOPLE BELIEVE IN GOD?

In the Prelude, I described a seismic shift in the landscape of apologetics in which conversations regarding the validity and nature of religious belief have turned away from a consideration of reasons to an examination of functions. The focus of classical apologetics was mainly upon reasons, the warrants for religious belief given the available evidence. By contrast, a focus on the function of religious belief tends to downplay the contents of belief (e.g., Did Jesus rise from the dead?) to ask questions about how religious beliefs, such as a belief in a life after death, might have originated and spread.

When we raise the question of function we ask if religious belief has some utility that might explain its existence and universal appeal. Perhaps, it is argued, belief in God has some biological, sociological, or psychological function, purpose, or role. And it is this function that explains why religion originated and became a staple of human culture. This function becomes the real reason people believe in God. Identifying the function of religious belief is, thus, considered to be the process of locating its underlying cause, providing then a reductionistic explanation for belief in God. For example, if the function of religious belief is, say, to help fend off existential anxieties (e.g., the terror of death) then the function of religious belief is revealed to be a mechanism for existential coping. Such a functional account reshapes the apologetical conversation in two ways.

First, functional accounts take belief out of the hands of the believer. In the existential formulation just sketched, faith is used to cope with an unsettling existence; this is faith's function. Fearing our finitude and ultimate extinction, we posit an afterlife with blessed reunions with loved ones long deceased. The issue here is less about the warrants of faith—the intellectual reasons for why we believe these things—than it is about our deep existential needs and fears. And yet, for these beliefs to work (i.e., actually repress our existential anxiety), we need to convince ourselves that these beliefs are not adopted as a means of coping. We need to believe that these beliefs are true and adopted for good, solid, justifiable reasons. In short, for the beliefs to work we need to engage in a bit of self-deception. We must convince ourselves we have good reasons for belief when, in fact, our beliefs are being driven by subterranean and unconscious fears. The reason this formulation is destabilizing, if this is not already obvious, is that the functional account suggests that religious believers do not know their own minds, cannot fathom their true motivations, and cannot, as a consequence, really answer (at the deepest level) the question about why they do believe in God. As I said, these functional accounts take belief out of the hands of the believers.

A second reason functional accounts of religious belief are destabilizing is that, as mentioned before, they dismiss a consideration of reasons (i.e., the effort to create justified true belief). This effectively shelves the entire Christian apologetical project, a massive and intellectually sophisticated edifice built up from the earliest days of the church. This is a breathtaking move. How is it accomplished?

Functional accounts of religious belief take their cue from David Hume (1739/2001) and argue that reason is, at root, the slave of the passions. The passions—our felt convictions (e.g., the belief in God)—are not produced by reason, evidence, or argument. In this view, we do not actually reason ourselves into a belief in God. Rather, we begin with a felt conviction and look for reasons or evidence to support or bolster our worldview. Rational arguments are ad hoc justifications for the preexisting commitments we already hold.

Some psychological research might be illuminating on this point. Consider below four moral situations from a study conducted by the psychologist Jonathan Haidt (Haidt, Koller, & Dias, 1993). As you read each scenario, make a normative evaluation: Is there anything wrong with this situation?

1. A woman is cleaning out her closet, and she finds her old American flag. She doesn't want the flag anymore, so she cuts it up into pieces and uses the rags to clean her bathroom.

2. A family's dog was killed by a car in front of its house. Family members had heard that dog meat was delicious, so they cut up the dog's body and cooked it and ate it for dinner.

3. A brother and sister like to kiss each other on the mouth. When nobody is around, they find a secret hiding place and kiss each other on the mouth.

4. A man goes to the supermarket once a week and buys a dead chicken. But before cooking the chicken, he has sexual intercourse with it. Then he thoroughly cooks it and eats it.

In the study, the researchers asked participants if they felt anything was morally or normatively amiss in a given scenario. The answers, as you might expect, were yes. Participants felt very strongly that a moral principle was being violated in each of the four scenarios. The researchers then proceeded to ask the participants to provide a moral warrant for their judgments. What moral principle was being violated in a given case? (In light of your own reactions to the scenarios you might try this yourself.) More often than not, the researchers found that the participants struggled with this task, often resorting to recasting their judgments as warrants in a classic example of circular reasoning. For example, the judgment that "a brother and sister shouldn't kiss" is justified with the warrant "because brothers and sisters' kissing is wrong." When pushed as to why this activity is wrong people tend to get stuck, saying, in effect, "just because it is."

Haidt et al. (1993) calls this phenomenon "moral dumbfounding." Moral dumbfounding occurs when we make strong normative judgments but struggle with providing rational warrants to support those judgments. The four scenarios above produce a strong, almost visceral response, a clear judgment that a moral principle is being violated. Something is wrong. And yet we struggle with articulating the warrant for this feeling. An affective experience—the feeling of a normative violation—appears to exist independently of and prior to any rational justification. As David Hume suggested, passion seems to precede reason. We make affective judgments of right versus wrong and then go in search of warrants to justify, in an ad hoc fashion, those initial judgments. This seems to be the reverse of what we think should happen in normative judgment. We tend to think, when faced with ethical dilemmas, that we work through a moral calculus, weighing the issues of right versus wrong. Then, having worked through this calculus, we render a considered moral verdict. Following this verdict our emotions respond: we feel righteous anger, contempt, or moral revulsion. The passions, we think, should follow our reasons. And yet, in light of the moral dumbfounding research, the reverse often appears to be the case. Righteous anger seems to come first, prompting a search for a reason as to why I feel the way I do. And sometimes I have difficulty finding that reason. Still, I am upset and morally outraged.

To be clear, there is a continuing debate between the moral traditions associated with Immanuel Kant (reason over passion) and David Hume (passion over reason) regarding the exact relationship between reason and emotion in normative judgments. But most agree that the moral-dumbfounding research demonstrates that emotion is an important and powerful factor in the formation of normative judgments. Of course, normative judgments are not the same as religious beliefs. Yet religious belief and normative evaluations, as least in the Christian tradition, overlap to a considerable extent. Religious belief shapes how we feel we ought to live and what in life is worthy of moral approbation or censor. In light of this, functional approaches to religious belief suggest that something akin to moral dumbfounding occurs when individuals offer warrants for the contents of their faith. Rather than warrants producing belief, it is argued by skeptics of religion that the warrants for faith are offered in an ad hoc manner, as a justification for a felt conviction. Knowing in their bones that God exists, believers, in a manner similar to what is seen in the moral dumbfounding research, go in search for warrants to explain or justify the existence of those feelings. Not surprisingly, David Hume (1779/1947) articulated this view in his *Dialogues Concerning Natural Religion*:

> It is my opinion . . . that each man feels, in a manner, the truth of religion within his own breast; and from a consciousness of his imbecility and misery, rather than from any reasoning, is led to seek protection from that Being, on whom he and all nature is dependent. . . . For is it necessary to prove, what every one feels within himself? It is only necessary to make us feel it. (p. 193)

According to Hume each person feels the truth of religion within himself, making rational proof unnecessary. These feelings are independent from any reasoning. It is only necessary to feel it.

This, then, is the second reason functional accounts of religious faith are destabilizing. Similar to what is observed in moral dumbfounding, functional accounts of religious belief suggest that the arguments and evidence associated with classical apologetics, the need to justify faith on rational grounds, is at root an ad hoc justification attempting to defend a preexisting conviction. The felt conviction, in this model, precedes and is independent of any apologetical account. As Hume claims, why is it necessary to prove what we already feel to be true within ourselves?

The practical implication of this account, if it is true, is that no argument of any kind can alter the felt convictions of true religious believers. And make no mistake: this is the working assumption of many who are hostile to religious faith. It is assumed by many that religious believers are immune to rational argument and empirical evidence. Consequently, should functional accounts prove to be persuasive, critics can cast religious believers as acting in bad faith, as too intellectually compromised to be objective and rational conversation partners.

2.

So, functional accounts are destabilizing in two related ways. First, by appealing to subterranean mechanisms (sociological, biological, or psychological), functional accounts take belief out of the hands of believers. Given that our deepest motivations are often hidden, distorted, or opaque, believers are considered not to have access to the real reasons associated with their belief in God. At the very least, believers are viewed as unreliable reporters regarding their true motivations. So the believer's testimony is treated with the utmost skepticism, if not rejected outright. Second, functional accounts, following David Hume and the moral-dumbfounding research, cast doubt on the entire apologetical enterprise. To be clear, this is not a commentary upon the intellectual quality of classical apologetics. Rather, this is a psychological observation regarding the relationship between religious convictions and their associated warrants, about the relationship between passion and reason. Religious believers will tend to assert that their warrants, their reasons and evidence for faith, precede and produce their convictions, that their faith is the product of objective and rational deliberation. Functional accounts will call this story into question, suggesting that religious convictions *precede* the formulation of warrants and rational justifications. Apologetics, in this view, is an ad hoc effort to make it appear that religious belief is not arbitrary or irrational. Recall that in some functional accounts for the beliefs to work their true purpose must be hidden from view. Classical apologetics helps with this obfuscation and illusion. By giving the believer warrants, evidence, and argument, classical apologetics helps the believer conclude, with some relief, that there are good reasons for faith and that these reasons are *the* reasons for belief.

Again, what we see in all this is how functional accounts effectively change the subject. The focus shifts away from the *beliefs* to the *believers*, to dwell upon their motivations, their ability for honest introspection, or their psychological needs. Belief is no longer taken at face value. Something else is wriggling beneath the surface.

What this means, in the end, is that functional accounts import a hermeneutics of suspicion into discussions about religious belief. The contents of belief—Is there a God? Is there an afterlife?—are no longer examined on their own terms. Rather, beliefs are surface-level symptoms of a deeper phenomenon. Today when warrants for faith are offered, suspicion is often expressed by critics of religion. These critics regularly assume that the stated reasons for faith are not, in fact, the real reasons. Moreover you, the believer, are likely to be unaware of what those real reasons might be. Your faith has been rendered cryptic.

3.

As mentioned in the Prelude, these functional and suspicious accounts of religion gained prominence in the wake of the Enlightenment. Paul Ricoeur (1970) has identified Freud, Marx, and Nietzsche as the great "school of suspicion" when it comes to the modern stance toward the sacred. Of course, as a school there are many family resemblances regarding their criticisms of religious belief. And of these three, Freud gave the most sustained account of religion. Consequently, by engaging Freud's extended account of religion we can address much of the whole, then and now. Modern accounts suspicious of religious belief have not improved upon Freud's seminal work on religious belief, most clearly articulated in his *The Future of an Illusion*. In sum, by taking up Freud's account of religious belief we will have firmly grasped the nettle.

But before moving onto Freud in the next chapter, I would like to take the remainder of this chapter to examine the true source of these functional accounts within modern thought. Ricoeur aside, I think the school of suspicion was not founded by Freud, Marx, or Nietzsche. The great "master of suspicion," whose work influenced all three of these thinkers, was Charles Darwin. It is true that Darwin was not hostile to religious belief, but Darwin's theory of natural selection created the theoretical tools used by subsequent thinkers to create suspicious functional accounts of religious belief. By wrestling with Darwin before turning to Freud, we will gain insight into how functional accounts operate and how they render faith cryptic.

4.

How did Darwinian evolution help create the theoretical tools for the hermeneutics of suspicion? I have made the claim that suspicions are raised about religious belief when functional accounts are in play. So what is the association between functional accounts and suspicion?

It might be assumed by many Christians that the most disruptive aspect of Darwin's (1859/2003) *On the Origin of Species* was its assault on a literal reading of the creation story in Genesis 1 and 2. No doubt this is a part of the story, but the most provocative aspect of Darwin's theory of natural selection was that it was able to provide an account of biological design without recourse to a Designer. Darwin's great insight was not evolution per se. Many before Darwin had posited evolution (in fact, Darwin's grandfather Erasmus Darwin believed in evolution). What Darwin discovered was the *mechanism* for evolution: natural selection.

The mechanism of natural selection was provocative to religious believers in Darwin's day (as well as today) as it provided an explanation for how complex and beautiful biological structures—from the human brain to the zebra's stripes to the peacock's tail—could have evolved from a random and dumb process: reproduction and differential survival, or what we call (a bit inaccurately) "the survival of the fittest."

Before and during Darwin's life, the most powerful argument for the existence of God was the argument from design, or what is known in classical apologetics as the teleological argument. William Paley published his famous watchmaker version of this argument in 1802, fifty-seven years before *Origin*. According to Paley (1802/2010), creation—physical and biological—displayed the complex and intricate design of a mechanical watch. And if we were to stumble upon a watch on the beach we would, naturally and rationally, posit an intelligent creator and designer: a watchmaker.

The provocative nature of natural selection was that it could account for design (watches) without positing a designer (a watchmaker). All natural selection needed was time, lots of time. Order does not randomly form out of whirlwinds. But order could emerge slowly and accumulatively through natural selection.

But our interests here are not how natural selection affected the argument from design in classical apologetics. Our interest is in how natural selection, by providing a functional account for biological design, created the tools used in the hermeneutics of suspicion.

Specifically, in the wake of *Origin* the natural world was rendered cryptic. Suddenly, the function of the peacock's tail (to take one example) was no longer obvious. Before Darwin, the purpose and function of the peacock's tail seemed clear: it revealed the power and benevolence of the watchmaker. But after *Origin*, the peacock's tail appeared to have some other role, purpose, or function. And that underlying function was the real reason the peacock's tail was so large and colorful.

It is not too much of an exaggeration to say that *Origin* turned the peacock's tail into a hermeneutical problem. What was the meaning behind the peacock's tail? If the peacock's tail was not for the delight of God and humanity, then what was it for?

The answer, according to Darwin, had to do with function: specifically, with how the peacock's tail functioned in the processes of natural selection—reproduction and differential survival. Once we identify the function of the tail, we have in hand the reason for why it is the way it is. And what I am trying to show in this analysis is how natural selection, by introducing functional accounts into biology, created a hermeneutical challenge. Suddenly, the peacock's tail was rendered cryptic. The stated surface-level function of the tail—that humans found it beautiful and that it gave witness to the Creator—was called into question. People became suspicious about the religious account for the peacock's tail, for Darwin's theory suggested that the true answer to the mystery of that plumage was to be found elsewhere: with the biological function of the tail and how the peacock's feathered display aided in natural selection.

This is, we have observed, the same kind of argument offered by functional accounts of religious belief. Faith might be like the peacock's tail. Classical apologetics displays complex and beautiful intellectual plumage. But what is faith's true function? In the wake of Darwin we have been encouraged to ask these questions, to become suspicious of surface-level accounts that might have nothing to do with the reality of the situation. During modernity, faith, like the peacock's tail, has been rendered cryptic and mysterious. And the answer to these mysteries, if we follow Darwin, is to be found down at the functional level, with how the trait in question helps the organism survive and thrive.

Functional accounts have this Darwinian structure. The hermeneutics of suspicion suggest that the surface-level account is to be rejected because the real reason for the phenomenon is found elsewhere. Consider, as an example, feminist theory in reading cultural texts such as the Bible. Using a hermeneutics of suspicion, feminist scholars refuse to take the use of the masculine pronoun in reference to God (God as "He") at face value. Rather, they see in the use of the masculine pronoun an exercise of *power*: of men, through the use of symbols, marginalizing women. Note how, in this analysis, a functional account is used to create suspicion about the text. On the surface, the text might be an expression of praise or trust as found in Psalm 23: "He leads me beside still waters." (NKJV) However, the feminist reading suggests that the function of the text, its true and deeper purpose, is something else entirely (e.g., preserving male hegemony through the use of the pronoun "He"). Suddenly, the functional account renders the text cryptic. What does it really mean? What is its true function?

5.

In the wake of *Origin*, these functional accounts began to emerge in all of the life sciences—social, psychological, and biological—and in the humanities. The race was on to identify the deeper function of a host of biological, psychological, and sociological phenomena. Darwin taught us that appearances are deceiving, that the truth lies elsewhere. More, the truth was often much darker and more sinister than we had guessed. Natural selection plays out against the backdrop, as Tennyson wrote, of "Nature, red in tooth and claw." In a similar way, when Marx examined class relationships throughout history he did not see a Divine Plan and a Celestial Order. What Marx (1843/1970) found was class struggle and oppression, with religion functioning as the "opium of the people." Also following Darwin, Freud suggested that the mind was a location of conflict driven by primal sexual and aggressive urges. Through the illuminations of Darwin, Marx, and Freud we see sinister forces at work, the dark mechanisms behind biological evolution, class struggle, and human motivation.

In light of all this, it was not long until functional accounts of religion began to emerge. Unsurprisingly, these functional accounts tended to have many of the features we have noted: namely, a suspicious reading of religious belief that posited underlying psychological or sociological mechanisms at work. For example, Marx (1843/1970) suggested that religion existed to soak up and dissipate the anger of the lower classes:

> The struggle against religion is, therefore, indirectly the struggle against that world whose spiritual aroma is religion. Religious suffering is, at one and the same time, the expression of real suffering and a protest against real suffering. Religion is the sigh of

the oppressed creature, the heart of a heartless world, and the soul of soulless conditions. It is the opium of the people. The abolition of religion as the illusory happiness of the people is the demand for their real happiness. To call on them to give up their illusions about their condition is to call on them to give up a condition that requires illusions. The criticism of religion is, therefore, in embryo, the criticism of that vale of tears of which religion is the halo. (p. 131)

Most are familiar with Marx's formulation that religion is the opium of the masses, but some might be surprised here by the nuanced vision Marx expresses in this passage. Specifically, Marx claims that religion is "the expression of real suffering and a protest against real suffering." Religion captures and gives voice to the cries of oppressed people, then as now. But in the end the consolation religion provides is an illusion. What the masses need to do is reject religion as an "illusory happiness" and to raise a "demand for their real happiness." Religion, in short, inhibits revolutionary fervor, keeping the masses focused on a future promise of happiness in an afterlife and thus unwilling to agitate for change here and now in this life and in this world. Religion in this view, while poignant and soaked with the tears of the oppressed, is in the end serving a sinister function: it is keeping the masses docile and leaving oppressive class structures intact. According to Marx, the function of religion is sociological in nature: a mechanism to preserve the status quo by keeping oppressed people focused upon attaining a future bliss in heaven. The peacock's tail is not what we think it is.

But perhaps the most potent and influential account of religious belief as illusion was offered by Sigmund Freud (1927/1989) in his theory regarding the origins of religious belief in *The Future of an Illusion*. As evidence of the contemporary relevance of Freud's argument in *The Future of an Illusion*, one only needs observe how often the New Atheists appeal to the work. Christopher Hitchens (2007a, 2007b) includes a selection of *The Future of an Illusion* in his edited work *The*

Portable Atheist and cites the work multiple times in his book *god is not Great*. Sam Harris (2004) references Freud in his book *The End of Faith* and Daniel Dennett (2006) begins a section on defining religion in *Breaking the Spell* with a quote from *The Future of an Illusion*. A recent essay in the *New York Times* noted the influence of Freud's analysis in *The Future of an Illusion* on the contemporary arguments of the New Atheists:

> A good deal of the antireligious polemic that has recently been abroad in our culture proceeds in the spirit of Freud's earlier work. In his defense of atheism, "God Is Not Great,"[*sic*] Christopher Hitchens cites Freud as an ally who, he believes, exposed the weak-minded childishness of religion. Sam Harris and Richard Dawkins come out of the same Enlightenment spirit of hostile skepticism to faith that infuses "The Future of an Illusion." (Edmundson, 2007, ¶ 2)

The powerful functional analysis found in *The Future of an Illusion* continues to disturb and provoke. We turn, now, to wrestle with Freud's seminal analysis.

Chapter 2

THE FUTURE
OF AN ILLUSION

IF YOU HAD PICKED UP A *NEW YORK TIMES* IN LATE DECEMBER
of 1927, you would have encountered this headline (Gay, 1988, p. 535):

RELIGION DOOMED / FREUD ASSERTS

Says It is[*sic*] at Point Where It Must Give Way Before Science

Curiously, this claim was nothing new. Ever since the Enlightenment,
beginning with the work of thinkers such as Spinoza, Hume, and
Voltaire, it had been asserted that science had ushered in a new era of
human consciousness and progress. Religious superstition was to be left
behind in the infancy of humankind. A new age of rational and skeptical adulthood had pushed fairy tales and religious myth to the side. In
the words of Dietrich Bonhoeffer (1997), the world had "come of age."

But while it might have seemed that this claim was no longer news,
there has always been something alluring and provocative about the life
and work of Sigmund Freud. So it is not surprising that the *New York
Times* would have given Freud's assessment of religion such prominence

and notoriety—such was the international reaction to the publication of *The Future of an Illusion*.

1.

Not much has changed. Freud still makes headlines. In 1999, Freud was named by *Time* as one of the "Top 100" most influential individuals of the 20th Century. In his essay honoring Freud for *Time*, Peter Gay (1999) observed:

> There are no neutrals in the Freud wars. Admiration, even downright adulation, on one side; skepticism, even downright disdain, on the other. . . . But on one thing the contending parties agree: for good or ill, Sigmund Freud, more than any other explorer of the psyche, has shaped the mind of the 20th century. The very fierceness and persistence of his detractors are a wry tribute to the staying power of Freud's ideas. (p. 1)

Harold Bloom (1986) has called Freud the "greatest modern writer." Bloom argues that Freud's ideas have so shaped our world that Freud's view of the human psyche and culture has become the implicit mythology of modern intellectuals, and even the person on the street. Whether we know it or not, we are all, to some degree, Freudians:

> [Freud's] conceptions are so magnificent in their indefiniteness that they have begun to merge with our culture, and indeed now form the only Western mythology that contemporary intellectuals have in common. As with every true mythology, a diffused version of psychoanalysis has become a common possession of most people in middle-class Western society, who may not be particularly intellectual, and doubtless are not always aware that psychoanalysis has provided the psychology in which they can believe without continual reflection or conscious effort. (p. 2)

Bloom goes on to argue that we cannot contemplate our everyday lives without consulting Freud:

No 20th-century writer—not even Proust or Joyce or Kafka—rivals Freud's position as the central imagination of our age. We turn to Freud when we wish to read someone absolutely relevant on any matter that torments or concerns us: love, jealousy, envy, masochism, cruelty, possessiveness, fetishism, curiosity, humor or what we will. (p. 3)

And beyond our workaday lives, Bloom goes on to argue that "Freud has contaminated every 20th-century intellectual discipline": history, art, law, political science, literature, film, sociology, biology, psychology, philosophy, theology, and on and on. All have been influenced by the work and thought of Sigmund Freud.

In light of Freud's impact upon the modern world, it is then not so surprising that Freud's views on the origins and nature of religious belief would have attracted so much attention, then and now. In fact, this state of affairs goes a fair way in explaining the lasting influence of Freud's views on religion. The cogency, persuasiveness, and continuing appeal of *The Future of an Illusion* may be due to the fact that the modern mind has been thoroughly shaped by psychoanalytic thought and theory.

2.

Interestingly, it was Freud's atheism that fueled his interest in religious belief. As Peter Gay (1989) has noted,

[Freud's] professional interest in the phenomenon of religion was anything but abstract. It was fueled by his principled, highly aggressive, anti-religious stance. Except for a brief spell during his university career, when one of his professors, the persuasive philosopher Franz Brentano, lured him into a tentative flirtation with theism, Freud was a convinced, uncompromising atheist. . . . As a true heir of the Enlightenment, Freud saw history as a great war between science and religion and rejected all compromise between the two contending forces. (p. 685)

The Future of an Illusion was not Freud's first engagement with religion. Nor was it his last. In *Totem and Taboo*—published in 1913—Freud makes an appeal to the Oedipus complex to account for the origins of religious ritual. However, the anthropological account in *Totem* (which posits a primal and original patricide) is highly speculative and, as a result, *Totem* has not achieved any lasting influence. Still, *Totem* revealed Freud's early interest in providing a scientific account of religious belief. Two years after the publication of *The Future of an Illusion*, in 1929, Freud's furthered his analysis of religion in *Civilization and Its Discontents* (Chapter 2 in particular). We will turn to this analysis shortly. Finally, in the year of his death, 1939, Freud published his final engagement with religion in *Moses and Monotheism*, a speculative and psychohistorical rereading of the Exodus story that attempted to provide an account of the rise of Hebrew monotheism.

The seed that eventually grew into the analysis at the heart of *The Future of an Illusion* (and *Civilization and Its Discontents*) was first planted in 1907 in an essay Freud published entitled "Obsessive Actions and Religious Practices." In this essay Freud attempted to make a connection between the repetitive actions of obsessive-compulsives and the rituals and ceremonies observed among religious groups. Freud notes that obsessive-compulsive rituals share a variety of similarities with religious rituals. For example, both are infused with anxiety. People suffering from obsessive-compulsive disorder (OCD) experience an inner anxiety that prompts a compulsive act (e.g., a fear of contamination can prompt the repetitive washing of hands). Religious persons are often motivated to engage in sacred rituals from an anxiety rooted in a god's displeasure. More, for those suffering from OCD and for religious persons, the successful enactment of the ritual leads to anxiety reduction. Freud also noted that OCD sufferers and religious participants will not countenance any deviation, however minor or trivial, to the ritual. According to Freud, the root cause for these anxiety-infused ceremonies, for both obsessive-compulsives and the religious, is an unconscious experience of guilt. That is, both groups fear being punished if they fail to execute the ritual properly. The ritual is conducted then as, quoting Freud (1989), "an action of defense or insurance, as a protective measure" (p. 433). Freud's summary analysis, then, is that religious ritual is serving a prophylactic function, as a defense mechanism to fend off neurotic anxiety:

> The sense of guilt of obsessional neurotics finds its counterpart in the prostrations of pious people that they know that at heart they are miserable sinners; and the pious observances (such as prayers, invocations, etc.) with which such people preface every daily act, and in especial every unusual undertaking, seem to have the value of defensive or protective measures. (p. 433)

More, Freud goes on to suggest that obsessive compulsions and religious rituals are motivated to control instinctive impulses felt to be socially or morally out of bounds. This impulse is experienced as a temptation, and the compulsion or ritual channels this illicit impulse into a fabricated conscientiousness used to combat, dissipate, or offset the impulse. In this, both obsessives and the religious use ritual to combat illicit, often sexual, impulses. Further, the religious might use rituals as a means of penance to cope with the guilt and anxiety associated with moral failure and sin. Overall, then, we find in religious rituals functions similar to those found in OCD: behavioral routines that must be strictly and conscientiously adhered to producing anxiety reduction and the management of illicit impulses. In light of these similarities, and in anticipation of *The Future of an Illusion*, Freud (p. 435) brings the argument to its conclusion with the assessment that religion is "a universal obsessional neurosis" (p. 435).

3.

Before turning to *The Future of an Illusion*, a few summary comments about the essay "Obsessive Actions and Religious Practices" would be helpful before going forward.

First, note the functional thrust of the analysis given in the essay. Freud never takes up an analysis of the contents of religious belief or ritual. For Freud, the theological particulars are quite beside the point. These rituals could be pagan, Christian, Jewish, Buddhist, or Islamic. Freud's analysis is trying, by working at a deeper level of analysis, to provide a functional account for each and every one of these rituals. The move is inherently reductionistic, and by appealing to naturalistic processes, asks the reader to accept the account as scientific. Freud's functional account is implicitly saying: here is the scientific explanation for religious belief and ritual—its real origin, function, and cause. This functional appeal is the source of the essay's deflationary power.

Second, note how the functional account creates a hermeneutic of suspicion. On the surface, the religious ritual is involved in sublime and sacred mysteries. But according to Freud, the reality is much more mundane and workaday. Worse, it is neurotic and potentially diseased.

The above observations are about the metalevel features of Freud's theory, which are found in most functional accounts. Consequently, "Obsessive Actions" is an illustrative case study clearly showing how functional accounts are both reductionistic and inherently suspicious.

With these observations duly noted, the issue going forward now shifts to the plausibility of the functional account. If a deflationary and suspicious functional account is not plausible or persuasive, we have little to worry about. Worries only accrue when the account is reasonable, persuasive, and backed by empirical evidence. In that case, in the face of a plausible and powerful functional account, the deflationary implications of the theory will be acutely felt.

In short, we need now to turn from the metalevel features of functional accounts, how they operate generally and generically, to examine the particulars of Freud's theory along with the associated evidence. In light of this narrower focus, what, exactly, did Freud think about the nature and function of religious belief?

In the essay "Obsessive Actions and Religious Practices," we have already caught a glimpse of the overall shape of Freud's fuller account found in *The Future of an Illusion*. Specifically, as we have seen, Freud argued that religious belief and ritual is "an action of defense" motivated by neurosis. In more contemporary language we would say that religion is motivated by anxiety and its management. Religion is a defense against anxiety. In "Obsessive Actions and Religious Practices," Freud locates this anxiety in illicit, unconscious impulses. However, in *The Future of an Illusion* this account shifts in important ways. Anxiety in *The Future of an Illusion* is less neurotic than existential. This existential turn in psychoanalytic thought, initiated by Freud in his later work, was completed in the years after *The Future of an Illusion* by thinkers such as Otto Rank, Rollo May, and Ernest Becker. But that is getting a bit ahead of ourselves. The point for now is that we can see the overall shape of Freud's functional account: religion is an action of defense against anxiety.

4.

As Peter Gay (1989, p. xxiii) has noted, "Freud was a convinced, consistent, aggressive atheist" and *The Future of an Illusion* was, for Freud, the "culmination of a lifelong pattern of thinking" on the phenomenon of religion. *The Future of an Illusion* is divided into ten small chapters. In Chapters 1 and 2, Freud opens with comments about the rise and function of civilization. At the start of the treatise, Freud (1927/1989) describes a two-fold function for civilization:

> [Civilization] includes on the one hand all the knowledge and capacity that men have acquired in order to control the forces of nature and extract its wealth for the satisfaction of human needs, and, on the other hand, all the regulations necessary in order to adjust the relations of men to one another and especially the distribution of the available wealth. (p. 6)

Chapter 1 focuses upon the former: the technological functions of civilization, and Chapter 2 discusses the latter: the social, moral and political functions of civilization. Religion is most strongly associated with these latter functions and now, having come to the threshold of his subject, Freud opens Chapter 3 with the following question: "In what does the particular value of religious ideas lie?" (p. 18) Let us pause and consider the form of this question as it starkly illustrates the shift we have been discussing in Christian apologetics. Freud's question, the issue at the heart of his analysis, focuses upon the function of religious belief. The question is not, "Is religious belief true?"—a question from classical apologetics. Rather, Freud asks if religious belief has a particular value. In light of his discussions regarding the functions of civilization—technological and social—Freud wonders if religion is serving a related function.

According to Freud (1927/1989), the technological and social innovations of civilization have helped protect humanity from the ravaging forces of the natural world: cold, hunger, predation, disease, and natural disaster. And while some people (those chaffing against the constrictions and consumerism of modern life) might long for a return to an Edenic "state of nature," Freud is keen to throw cold water on that romantic impulse:

> But how ungrateful, how short-sighted after all, to strive for the abolition of civilization! What would then remain would be a state of nature, and that would be far harder to bear. It is true that nature would not demand any restrictions of instinct from us, she would let us do as we liked; but she has her own particularly effective method of restricting us. She destroys us—coldly, cruelly, relentlessly, as it seems to us, and possibly through the very things that occasioned our satisfaction. It was precisely because of these dangers with which nature threatens us that we came together and created civilization, which is also, among other things, intended to make our communal life possible. For the principal task of civilization, its actual *raison d'être* [sic], is to defend us against nature. (pp. 18–19)

Beyond technology and social coordination, a part of this defense against nature is psychological. Nature is terrifying and death mocks human pretensions. A basic and existential anxiety about our vulnerabilities in the face of nature is a universal feature of the human experience:

But no one is under the illusion that nature has already been vanquished; and few dare hope that she will ever be entirely subjected to man. There are the elements, which seem to mock at all human control: the earth, which quakes and is torn apart and buries all human life and its works; water, which deluges and drowns everything in a turmoil; storms, which blow everything before them; there are diseases, which we have only recently recognized as attacks by other organisms; and finally there is the painful riddle of death, against which no medicine has yet been found, nor probably will be. With these forces nature rises up against us, majestic, cruel and inexorable; she brings to our mind once more our weakness and helplessness, which we thought to escape through the work of civilization. (p. 19)

Despite all the advances of modern civilizations, our victories against nature have proven to be fragile and fleeting as our recent global experiences with hurricanes, tsunamis, famine, earthquakes, and pandemics can well attest. More, even if natural disasters are avoided there remains the specter of death "against which no medicine has yet been found."

And while these abstract and global reflections are terrifying in their own right, these struggles with nature and death are also very much close to home. Every human life is riddled with personal and intimate experiences with grief, loss, terminal illness, and tragedy:

For the individual, too, life is hard to bear, just as it is for mankind in general. The civilization in which he participates imposes some amount of privation on him, and other men bring him a measure of suffering, either in spite of the precepts of his civilization or because of its imperfections. To this are added the injuries which untamed nature—he calls it Fate— inflicts on him. . . . [So] how does he defend himself against the superior powers of nature, of Fate, which threaten him as they threaten all the rest? (Freud, 1927/1989, pp. 19–20)

According to Freud, our technological and political defenses against nature are temporary, ineffective, or illusory. Consequently, "life is hard to bear." Anxiety crackles beneath the surface of modern life. This anxiety can prove debilitating and disorienting if allowed personal or collective expression. To keep civilization on track, technologically and socially, a psychological mechanism needs to come alongside these efforts: a means of consolation to attenuate our existential fear. This consolation will have two interrelated features, one cognitive, the other emotional: "Man's self-regard, seriously menaced, calls for consolation; life and the universe must be robbed of their terrors; moreover his curiosity, moved, it is true, by the strongest practical interest, demands an answer" (p. 20).

Emotionally, consolation must involve anxiety reduction: "life and the universe must be robbed of their terrors." Cognitively, we are perplexed by the cosmos generally and suffering specifically. We want to know why these things are happening to us. We want to know why the world seems to be spinning out of control. Why *this* death? Why *this* cancer diagnosis? Why *this* tragic car accident? We live with an acute "curiosity" that "demands an answer."

According to Freud (1927/1989), the need for anxiety reduction and the associated metaphysical answers eventually coalesces in religious belief. In most religious systems, and specifically with our focus on Christianity, nature is no longer seen as malevolent, random, and ending in death. Rather, nature is ultimately benevolent and providential, and beyond death there is a blessed existence in an afterlife. According to Freud, each facet of this religious worldview is involved in reducing basic human insecurities—emotional and cognitive—in the face of nature, Fate, and death. Freud summarizes the basic religious stance:

> And thus a store of ideas is created, born from man's need to make his helplessness tolerable. . . . Here is the gist of the matter. Life in this world serves a higher purpose. . . . Everything that happens in this world is an expression of the intentions of an

intelligence superior to us, which in the end, though its ways and byways are difficult to follow, orders everything for the best that is, to make it enjoyable for us. Over each one of us there watches a benevolent Providence which is only seemingly stern and which will not suffer us to become a plaything of the over-mighty and pitiless forces of nature. Death itself is not extinction, is not a return to inorganic lifelessness, but the beginning of a new kind of existence which lies on the path of development to something higher. . . . In the end all good is rewarded and all evil punished, if not actually in this form of life then in the later existences that begin after death. In this way all the terrors, the sufferings and the hardships of life are destined to be obliterated. (pp. 23–24)

Given the function of these beliefs in the human psyche, the religious worldview becomes central and vital to the human experience. These beliefs speak to the deepest mysteries and allow us to create meaning out of an existence that, without religious consolation, would become random, meaningless, incoherent, and absurd. These beliefs are so vital that a life without them would be deemed not worth living:

Ideas which are religious in the widest sense are prized as the most precious possession of civilization, as the most precious thing it has to offer its participants. It is far more highly prized than all the devices for winning treasures from the earth or providing men with sustenance or preventing their illnesses, and so forth. People feel that life would not be tolerable if they did not attach to these ideas the value that is claimed for them. (pp. 24–25)

And given that these beliefs are as vital as life itself, Freud felt that it would be psychologically impossible for the believer to rationally examine and question his belief system. And even if believers were successful in this endeavor, the result might cause more harm than good: "The

51

believer will not let his belief be torn from him, either by arguments or by prohibitions. And even if this did succeed with some it would be cruelty" (p. 62).

Freud is not engaging in hyperbole. I have heard my students and people at church make earnest declarations of just this sort:

"If there is no God," they say, "life would not be worth living."

5.

Freud (1927/1989) goes back to his psychoanalytic bread and butter in Chapters 4–10 of *The Future of an Illusion*, connecting religious belief to childhood neurosis, oedipal projections, and wish fulfillment. But as we will see, Freud's more straightforward existential analysis in Chapter 3 has proven to be the more durable and influential aspect of the work. And in light of Chapter 3 we have in hand the answer to Freud's question: What is the particular value, the function, of religious belief?

Similar to his earlier analysis in "Obsessive Actions and Religious Practices," Freud argues in *The Future of an Illusion* that religion is driven by an attempt to defend against anxiety. But the frame has shifted slightly, although some continuity is also evident. In "Obsessive Actions" and in the latter half of *The Future of an Illusion*, Freud's analysis focuses on anxiety stemming from childhood neuroses, an anxiety rooted in primal feelings of helplessness. But in the early part of *The Future of an Illusion*, Chapter 3 in particular, the anxiety is more basic, less neurotic and infantile. Our anxiety in the face of nature and death is less oedipal than existential. This shift to an existential formulation will be the subject of the next chapter. Regardless, the function of religion—managing anxiety—is the same. And Freud summarizes this function in a famous metaphor, echoing Karl Marx: "The effect of religious consolations may be likened to that of a narcotic" (p. 62).

According to Freud, the function of religion, its particular value, is similar to the analgesic, anxiolytic, and euphoric functions of narcotics. As an analgesic, religion reduces the experience of pain. Religion also reduces anxiety, an anxiolytic effect. Finally, beyond attenuating psychic pain and anxiety, religion also produces euphoric states—feelings of peace, contentment, joy, and even ecstasy.

6.

Freud's assessment of the narcotic function of religion remains influential. It is almost a given that any comprehensive criticism of religious belief will, in some form or another, deploy the argument Freud made in *The Future of an Illusion*. Examples abound, but consider this one, the argument Sam Harris (2004) makes in his best-selling book *The End of Faith*. In Chapter 1 of *The End of Faith* Harris, in a section with the Freudian-inspired title "Death: The Fount of Illusions," states that

> [W]e live in a world where all things, good and bad, are finally destroyed by change. The world sustains us, it would seem, only to devour us at its leisure. Parents lose their children and children their parents. Husbands and wives are separated in an instant, never to meet again. Friends part company in haste, not knowing that it will be for the last time. This life, when surveyed with a broad glance, presents little more than a vast spectacle of loss. (p. 36)

In light of this terrifying predicament Harris, following Freud, suggests that religion helps us overcome our existential dread:

> But it seems that there is a cure for all this. If we live rightly . . . we will get everything we want after we die. When our bodies finally fail us, we just shed our corporeal ballast and travel to a land where we are united with everyone we loved while alive. . . . This is wondrously strange. If one didn't know better, one would think that man, in his fear of losing all that he loves, had created heaven, along with its gatekeeper God, in his own image. (p. 36)

What is particularly insidious about this line of argument is that it suggests religion is a form of cowardice or, at the very least, emotional immaturity. Given that religion is aimed at hiding harsh realities to help us cope with fear, it can be suggested that those who eschew the comforts of religious consolation are acting like rational adults. True, the argument goes, there is an emotional price to pay for facing life honestly, but at least we are being grown-ups about it, biting the bullet and being truthful. Refusing to ingest the existential narcotic is seen as heroic and noble when contrasted with religious illusions. Freud (1927/1989) explicitly makes this claim in the final chapters of *The Future of an Illusion*:

> [Individuals who have given up religious consolation] will, it is true, find themselves in a difficult situation. They will have to admit to themselves the full extent of their helplessness and their insignificance in the machinery of the universe; they can no longer be the center of creation, no longer the object of tender care on the part of a beneficent Providence. They will be in the same position as a child who has left the parental house where he was so warm and comfortable. But surely infantilism is destined to be surmounted. Men cannot remain children forever; they must in the end go out into "hostile life." We may call this *education to reality*. Need I confess to you that the sole purpose of my book is to point out the necessity for this forward step? (pp. 62–63)

According to Freud (and the New Atheists), to give up religious illusion is to grow up, to become educated to reality. We cannot remain children forever. True, when we leave the tender care of God's warm and comfortable house we will be in a difficult situation facing a hostile life, now fully aware of our helplessness and insignificance. But what options do we have? Surely "infantilism is destined to be surmounted" by courageous persons. In his *Letter to a Christian Nation*, Sam Harris (2008) makes a similar move, only much more aggressively:

> Mommy claims to know that Granny went straight to heaven after she died. But Mommy doesn't actually know this. The

truth is that Mommy is lying—either to herself or to her children—and most of us have agreed to view this behavior as perfectly normal. Rather than teach our children to grieve, and to be happy despite the reality of death, we nourish their powers of self-deception. (pp. 111–112)

The implication is clear. Rather than "teach our children to grieve," allowing them, in the words of Freud, to become educated to reality, we tell them consoling lies. Rather than helping our children find a difficult but honest path toward happiness—"to be happy despite the reality of death"—religious believers nourish powers of "self-deception." And these childish illusions continue to persist into adulthood.

So Freud is still very much with us. The arguments made in *The Future of an Illusion* are ubiquitous. More, they are cogent, plausible, and persuasive. As Freud observed in *The Future of an Illusion*, it is highly suspicious, to the point of damning, that the very thing we dearly wish for—for example, to see Granny again in heaven—is the very thing we believe. Such a close association cannot be mere coincidence. The correlation is, in Harris's mocking tone, "wondrously strange." Is it not more rational to assume that these beliefs are not true but merely an expression of wishful thinking?

Much of this book will be focused on just that question. But before turning to that question and the data associated with its various answers, we need to see how the analysis offered by Freud in *The Future of an Illusion* made a fully existential turn in the decades after his death. For it is the existential formulation of Freud's critique of religion, begun but not completed in *The Future of an Illusion*, that has proven to be the most influential aspect of his thought.

Chapter 3

THE EXISTENTIAL TURN

1.

IN *THE FUTURE OF AN ILLUSION*, WE FIND FREUD OFFERING AN existential analysis regarding the origin of religious belief. Humanity grows anxious in the face of death, nature, and the vast emptiness of the cosmos (as Blaise Pascal [1669/1958] wrote: "The eternal silence of these infinite spaces strikes me with terror.") Thus, in *The Future of an Illusion* and in his later work, we see Freud's thinking take an existential turn. Still, Freud never fully broke with his oedipal framework, suggesting as he does in *The Future of an Illusion* that our existential terrors simply remind us of our childhood oedipal experiences, our feeling of smallness and powerlessness in the encounter with powerful parental figures, the father in particular. But, even during Freud's lifetime and continuing after, an influential, existential strain began to emerge within the Freudian psychoanalytic tradition. Thinkers such as Otto Rank, Rollo May, Viktor Frankl, Irvin Yalom, and Ernest Becker took many of the features of Freud's psychodynamic theory and created social, psychological, and cultural theories that placed existential concerns at the heart of the human experience. These were thinkers who fused the insights of Freud with the rich existential tradition in philosophy, literature, and art. While our story begins with Freud, our analysis of religious belief will begin to follow the thinkers who, inspired by Freud, made this existential turn.

This turn toward existentialism is warranted for two reasons. First, the move was anticipated by Freud in *The Future of an Illusion* and his existential analysis within that work has, as we saw in the last chapter, proven to be more influential than his somewhat forced oedipal framing of that account. Second, as we will see later in this chapter, the existential psychodynamic accounts have, since the 1990s, been gaining a great deal of impressive empirical and laboratory support. The burgeoning field of experimental existentialism has taken the airy and angst-filled abstractions of Søren Kierkegaard and Albert Camus and put them to the test in the laboratory. Consequently, any analysis of the existential functions of religious belief will not only have to wrestle with theoretical accounts such as in *The Future of an Illusion* but also with the impressive empirical literature that now supports those accounts. The way ahead is, perhaps surprisingly, both more existential and more empirical.

2.

There are structural similarities between the classic Freudian understanding of anxiety and how anxiety is understood by the existential thinkers influenced by the Freudian tradition. These similarities are important to note as they demonstrate how both the classical and existential psychodynamic traditions understand the function of religious belief to be the management of anxiety, as Freud argued in *The Future of an Illusion*. As Irvin Yalom (1980) has noted, the classical and existential psychodynamic traditions are structurally similar and differ mainly in how they understand the contents of psychic struggle, the source of our fundamental anxieties. But first, a comment on that word "struggle."

Yalom (1980) notes that the Greek word *dunasthi*, the etymological root of the word "dynamic," means to have force, strength, or power.

Consequently, psychodynamic theories of mental functioning, which Freud pioneered, understand mental life to be characterized by forces (e.g., instincts, drives, motivational states) that often come into conflict or work in tension with each other. As Yalom observes:

> Freud's major contribution to the understanding of the human being is his dynamic model of mental functioning—a model that posits that there are forces in conflict within the individual, and that thought, emotion, and behavior, both adaptive and psychopathological, are the resultant of these conflicting forces. Furthermore—and this is important—these forces exist at varying levels of awareness; some, indeed, are entirely unconscious. (p. 6)

Existential theories differ from classical psychodynamic theories in how they understand the nature of these conscious and unconscious forces, motives, and conflicts. According to Freud, anxiety was produced by unconscious drives, often of an oedipal nature, that are experienced as illicit (personally or socially). The anxiety is the neurotic fear that these illicit motives, should they be admitted into consciousness or acted upon, will provoke punishment or stigma (intra- and interpersonally). To cope with this anxiety and the illicit impulse that occasions it, the psyche represses, transforms, or redirects the impulse and anxiety. These psychic responses are collectively called defense mechanisms. For example, through sublimation, illicit sexual or aggressive impulses might be transformed into activities related to work or creative expression. This is an example of how a defense mechanism could be involved in adaptive and useful work. However, defense mechanisms can be maladaptive as well. For example, aggressive impulses might be repressed which could adversely affect physical health (e.g., ulcers, high blood pressure) or prompt unhealthy means of coping (e.g., heavy drinking). Schematically, here in Figure 1, we can sketch the psychodynamic processes of classical Freudian theories this way:

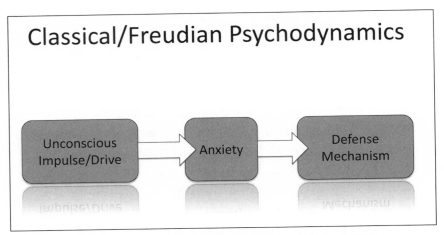

Figure 1. Classical-Freudian psychodynamics. Adapted from Yalom, I. D. (1980) *Existential Psychotherapy*. New York, NY: Basic. p. 9.

Existential theories share similarities with classical psychodynamic formulations. The main difference is the source of anxiety. Where classical psychodynamic perspectives believe that illicit unconscious drives are the source of anxiety, the existential perspectives see existential realizations as the source of the psychic anxiety. See Figure 2.

According to Freud, neurotic anxiety was caused by unconscious drives that, due to their sexual and aggressive content, were experienced as illicit. Defense mechanisms were thus deployed to repress, transform

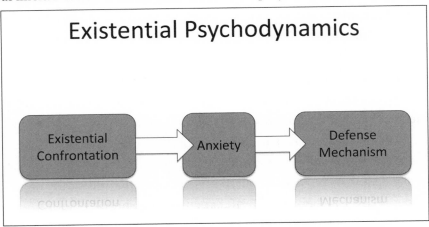

Figure 2. Existential Psychodynamics. Adapted from Yalom, I. D. (1980) *Existential Psychotherapy*. New York, NY: Basic. p. 10.

or manage these primal impulses. But according to existential models neurotic anxiety is caused by existential confrontations: being thrown up against the various terrors inherent in finite human existence. For example, we grow anxious when we contemplate our death and the prospect of nonexistence. This anxiety can become debilitating if left unchecked. Thus, defense mechanisms are deployed to repress, transform, or manage these existential fears. In sum, the structure of both the classical and existential psychodynamic theories is broadly the same. The only difference is the source of the anxiety: illicit oedipal impulse versus existential confrontation.

3.

According to Yalom (1980), existential confrontations can be grouped into four broad categories. We can consider this to be a summary and distillation of the concerns that preoccupied existential philosophers such as Søren Kierkegaard, Martin Heidegger, Jean-Paul Sartre, and Friedrich Nietzsche and writers such as Fyodor Dostoevsky, Leo Tolstoy, Franz Kafka, and Albert Camus. Yalom groups the four types of existential confrontations this way:

1. **Death:** We are finite creatures. Time moves us inexorably toward death, dissolution, and nonexistence.

2. **Meaning:** Life is not inherently or intrinsically meaningful. When we experience something as devastating as a natural disaster or a cancer diagnosis, the cosmos refuses to answer the question, "What does this *mean?*" Consequently, meaning must be constructed by individuals and their society, moment by moment and day by day. But this process of socially constructing meaning makes meaning fragile and infuses it with a sense of artificiality, shallowness, and arbitrariness.

3. **Freedom and Responsibility:** The moment by moment experience of life involves making choices and accepting the burden of responsibility for these choices. Yet that

burden can become so overwhelming that we attempt to avoid or deny the weight of our responsibility. Courage is required to assume the ultimate and sole responsibility for the shape of one's existence.

4. **Isolation:** Try as we might, we cannot borrow the life of another. Our existence is a singularity, uniquely and wholly our own. Although we may try to understand, love, and support each other we can only go so far. In the final analysis, we are alone. Our existence is only fully available to ourselves.

When we encounter these existential realizations we experience anxiety. The existential literature is full of descriptions attempting to describe the various forms this anxiety might take—anomie, angst, alienation, despair, terror, sickness, dread, nausea. While few of us experience these emotions in our workaday lives they do lurk in the background, at times creating the sense that our struggles, strivings, and strainings are pointless and futile. We devote so much time and effort in life to accomplishing . . . what, exactly? Building castles of sand? Leading lives, as Thoreau said in *Walden*, of "quiet desperation"? And while we might think that these worries are unique to our modern, technological world, few have improved upon the words of Ecclesiastes 3:19–20:

> Surely the fate of human beings is like that of the animals; the same fate awaits them both: As one dies, so dies the other. All have the same breath; humans have no advantage over animals. Everything is meaningless. All go to the same place; all come from dust, and to dust all return.

Building upon the reflections in Ecclesiastes, we might say that death renders life absurd (or, in the language of Ecclesiastes, "vanity," a "chasing after the wind"). That which renders life meaningful suddenly appears, in the face of death, impotent, fragile, and fleeting. Charles Taylor (2007), in his book *A Secular Age*, describes how our worries over the fragility of meaning creep into our everyday lives:

> Almost every action of ours has a point; we're trying to get to work, or to find a place to buy a bottle of milk after hours. But we can stop and ask why we're doing these things, and that points us beyond to the significance of the significances. The issue may arise for us in a crisis, where we feel that what has been orienting our life up to now lacks real value, weight. . . . [We come to feel that these orienting] answers are fragile, or uncertain; that a moment may come where we no longer feel that our chosen path is compelling, or cannot justify it to ourselves or others. There is a fragility of meaning. (p. 308)

Few of us, however, take the time to contemplate or worry about our existential predicaments. We are, after all, busy people with jobs. We might, actually, need to swing by the store today on the way home from work to buy some milk. We just do not have the time or energy to fiddle with this existential nonsense. But according to the existential psychodynamic tradition, this trick, this ability to carry on in the face of our existential predicament, is largely an act of repression and denial: we are employing a defense mechanism. To be clear, these defenses are largely adaptive. Most of us would be hard-pressed to carry on with daily tasks if we were asked to stop and contemplate our existential situation at every moment of every day, to ponder, as Taylor writes, the legitimacy of the significance behind the significances. Excessive ruminations of this sort would become debilitating, producing anxiety, depression, or some other neurotic symptomatology. To carry on with life, we have to set existential worries to the side, and a host of psychological and cultural variables help us accomplish this. And one of them, as Freud argued in *The Future of an Illusion*, is religion.

It should be obvious how religious belief, both broadly speaking and regarding Christianity in particular, can aid in repressing existential anxiety. Consider how faith neatly steps in to address each existential predicament:

1. **Death:** Death is not, in fact, the cessation of existence. There will be a blissful and eternal afterlife.

2. **Meaning:** Despite appearances, life is inherently meaningful. Meaning comes from beyond this life, an infusion from the Creator. Meaning and significance is granted by God and your particular existence is a part of a Providential plan and design.

3. **Freedom and Responsibility:** While it is true that we must take responsibility for our lives, we are given assistance and clear guidance. We can "set out a fleece" and pray for signs so that God can tell us what we should do. We are not to choose so much as to follow a preordained path set before us.

4. **Isolation:** We are not alone. More, we are fully known and understood by another—God. And God created this world for our benefit. We are at home in the universe.

At each step religion helps attenuate the existential dilemma. In the face of death we can think of heaven. In the face of tragedy we can look for God's plan and purposes. In our loneliness we can turn to God. And in the face of difficult life choices we can pray for signs. This is Freud's argument in *The Future of an Illusion*: how our wishes—to avoid death, to make sense of pain, to feel at home in the universe, to have someone take us by the hand when choices are hard—create our beliefs. The match, it seems, is perfect. For every existential worry there is a consoling religious belief. Consequently, it is argued, this is the function of religious belief. Religious belief is a form of psychological consolation that represses existential anxiety, a defense mechanism that allows us to carry on with our daily lives and buy milk on the way home from work.

4.

To pause for a moment, I think it is important to point out that these observations are not lost upon many religious people. Thoughtful

Christians have always wondered about how religious belief was functioning in the minds of fellow believers. The fact is that Freud's basic claims have face validity. Who does not want to live forever in a blissful existence? It seems clear that the vast majority of individuals would be attracted to this idea, for no other reason than that the belief makes us feel better. This attractiveness (what Freud called a "wish") seems to explain, for many at least, everything that needs to be explained about the origin of religious belief. People wish it to be so and thus believe it to be so.

Many religious thinkers have worried about this dynamic within the religious experience. Freud, they argue, should not be dismissed too quickly. In fact, he should not be dismissed at all, because he clearly placed his finger upon a pervasive force within religious belief. It is true, as we will see, that Christian thinkers part ways with Freud when he claims that *all* religious belief is motivated by a need for consolation. But most thoughtful people, even religious believers, agree that Freud had discerned a real dynamic in the origin and maintenance of religious belief. People can, and often do, use religious belief to assuage existential anxiety. Religion can, and often is, deployed (consciously or unconsciously) as a defense mechanism.

Consider, as an example, the analysis of Arthur C. McGill (1987) in his book *Death and Life: An American Theology*. McGill observes that "Americans like to appear as if they give death hardly any thought of all" (p.7). The American ethic is, thus, "for people to create a living world where death seems abnormal and accidental. . . . [Americans] must create a living world where life is so full, so secure, and so rich with possibilities that it gives no hint of death and deprivation" (p. 18). We accomplish this feat, according to McGill, through acts of avoidance. Americans live with "the conviction that the lives we live are not essentially and intrinsically mortal" (p. 27). But this, says McGill, is a "dream," an "illusory realm of success" (p. 35). Americans accomplish this illusion by devoting themselves

to expunging from their lives every appearance, every intima-
tion of death. . . . All traces of weakness, debility, ugliness and
helplessness must be kept away from every part of a person's
life. The task must be done every single day if such persons
really are to convince us that they do not carry the smell of
death within them. (p. 26)

What we see in all this is how the American success ethos, the cultural
push to be fine, is being driven by an underlying existential fear. A collective pretending is going on, a psychic game that allows us to avoid
a direct confrontation with our own mortality. Through these acts of
avoidance "Americans," writes McGill, "are able to shield themselves
from the awfulness of life, from the torment and destination which
always threaten to overwhelm their sensitivity" (p. 41). To shield ourselves from the "awfulness of life," we create illusions to protect us.
McGill's analysis of these illusions is very similar to Freud's:

This whole realm of successful life (even for the people who
live by it) is only a dream, only an illusion, only an imaginative
creation like a work of art. . . . Americans know, at some deep
level, that every generation will suffer like its predecessors and
will die like them. Foam rubber mattresses, anesthetics, fast
airplanes, and color TVs—these do not enhance the quality of
inner life. These do not make human life any less a plaything for
death. But these do help to create an illusory realm of success
and happiness: a realm without pain, without failure, without
destitution and death; an illusory realm so centered in life that
on Sunday afternoons in the fall, the spectacle of twenty-two
adult men running around after a bag of air is enough to provide
millions of people with zest and joy. The optimism is known to
be an illusion. But, like a work of art, it is serious and important because it is a work of imagination. This illusory world is
critical, in fact, because it performs an absolutely important
function for the American people. It helps them conceal the

horror of life which they half know to be there. In order for these sensitive Americans psychically to endure their existence at all, they have to interpose between themselves and actual life a dream world of success and cleanliness and health and beauty and perpetual youth. (p. 35)

McGill goes on to note that vast portions of American Christianity are aimed at propping up these illusions, giving religious sanction to American death avoidance through the success ethos. McGill contends that "It is the Christian God who helps veil the horror," it is the Christian God who is "the crucial figure in the illusory world . . . [helping] us veil and endure this nightmare world" (p. 39).

The point in all this is that reflective and honest Christians see within much of what passes for Christian belief and practice the very same dynamics described by Freud in *The Future of an Illusion*. Following McGill, it seems clear that Christian belief can function as an illusion, as a wall we can interpose between real life and a dream world we construct for ourselves. This dream world is created to help us psychically endure the existential predicament of our existence.

5.

Perhaps the most influential treatment integrating the Freudian and existential tradition was offered by Ernest Becker (1973) in his Pulitzer-prize winning book *The Denial of Death*. Becker's analysis has been influential for three reasons. First, the ideas in *The Denial of Death*, as we will see, provided the foundational insights of what is called terror management theory. Since the 1990s terror management theory has become one of the most influential paradigms guiding the empirical research that is seeking to examine, in the laboratory, the nature of existential anxiety and its associated defense mechanisms. Understanding *The Denial of Death* will help us grapple with the empirical research to come.

A second reason Becker's work has proven influential is attributable to how Becker sees existential anxiety as a powerful creative force, both psychologically and culturally. This is an important development as the analysis of existential defensiveness offered by Freud (and others) has tended to see existential repression as a form of infantilism. The assumption made by Freud in *The Future of an Illusion* is that modern persons are able to grow up and face reality honestly, eschewing religious consolation. But Becker's analysis in *The Denial of Death* suggests that Freud might have overstated how easy that process might be. Specifically, while it is true that many modern persons have rejected religious belief, that rejection does not mean that they have not replaced religion with some other cultural worldview or life project that renders their life meaningful, significant, and comprehensible. Such worldviews and projects are also involved in death repression and transcendence, and are open to the same criticisms Freud leveled at religious belief in *The Future of an Illusion*. As Paul Tillich argued, we all have an ultimate concern that is an object of faith. From this existential vantage everyone is, in fact, religious. Here is Tillich (1999) on this point:

> Faith is the state of being ultimately concerned: the dynamics of faith are the dynamics of man's ultimate concern. Man, like every living being, is concerned about many things, above all about those which condition his very existence, such as food and shelter. But man, in contrast to other living beings, has spiritual concerns—cognitive, aesthetic, social, political. Some of them are urgent, often extremely urgent, and each of them as well as the vital concerns can claim ultimacy for human life or the life of a social group. If it claims ultimacy it demands the total surrender of him who accepts this claim, and it promises total fulfillment even if all other claims have to be subjected to it or rejected in its name. (p. 13)

One only needs to look at the life of Freud and his life work—psychoanalysis—to find an example of a person driven by an ultimate concern. Freud staked the ultimate meaning of his life on establishing psychoanalysis as a mainstream scientific approach to the mind. In realization of that dream, psychoanalysis hardened into a quasi-religious movement with disciples, a rigid orthodoxy, and a few high-profile heretics who rejected the work of the master (e.g., Carl Jung, Alfred Adler).

The point for Ernest Becker in *The Denial of Death* is how our ultimate concerns, religious or not, are, at root, attempts to manage existential anxiety. For example, Camus (1955) opens *The Myth of Sisyphus* with this provocative assessment:

> There is but one truly serious philosophical problem, and that is suicide. Judging whether life is or is not worth living amounts to answering the fundamental question of philosophy. . . . I therefore conclude that the meaning of life is the most urgent of questions. How to answer it? (pp. 3, 4)

Becker's argument is that this is not a question reserved for philosophers. It is a question that has to be answered by every individual within our quotidian existences. Cultures, according to Becker, aid in this effort by handing their members a set of ready-made and time-tested ultimate concerns that, because of the cultural consensus supporting them, appear to give prima facie evidence that one is leading a meaningful and admirable life.

This brings us to the third and final point of interest in Becker's theory. By helping its members assuage or transcend existential anxiety, cultures can harness and channel this psychic energy, directing it toward objectives the culture deems valuable. What Becker is suggesting is that existential anxiety—the desire to answer Camus's question "Why is life worth living?"—is the engine of culture, the source of its origin, maintenance, evaluation, and elaboration. This is a bold and ambitious claim as it suggests that existential anxiety is the taproot, the motive force, beneath human existence. But this analysis is no more ambitious than Freud's own attempt to see the whole of civilization as the outworking of primal psychodynamic forces (see *Civilization and its Discontents*). Becker's accomplishment in *The Denial of Death* was his ability to create a similar scheme regarding the origins of culture but from an existential vantage point. In this sense, *The Denial of Death* represents the final movement in the existential turn within psychodynamic thinking. What this account allows us to see is how existential defensiveness, while neurotic, becomes a powerful and creative cultural force. As we pursue our ultimate concerns, seeking to create a meaningful life as a butcher, baker or candlestick maker, we create cultural goods that are shared and accumulated. More, our private experience of self-worth and self-esteem is produced by how effective we are, in our own estimation and in the estimation of others, in traveling the various paths of ultimate concern borrowed from our cultural matrix. We are more or less successful in life as measured by what our culture values and pursues. And if these values and pursuits are, as the existentialists argue, involved in death repression and transcendence then we find, perhaps surprisingly, that self-esteem itself is pushed and pulled by existential anxiety. Culturally or psychologically, publically or privately, a fear of death rumbles beneath it all.

6.

Before turning to the empirical literature inspired by the work of Ernest Becker, it will be helpful to review the major themes of *The Denial of Death* and its sequel *Escape from Evil*. Becker centers his analysis on our need for self-esteem, our craving for our life to be significant and meaningful to both ourselves and to others. Becker (1973, p. 1) describes this as a striving for heroism, suggesting that "our central calling, our main task on this planet, is the heroic." This heroism, this path toward significance, is achieved by navigating the cultural pathways and symbols that mark a life, within any given culture, as both admirable and well lived:

> [T]his is what a society is and always has been: a symbolic action system, a structure of statuses and roles, customs and rules for behavior, designed to serve as a vehicle for earthly heroism. Each script is somewhat unique, each culture has a different

hero system. What the anthropologists call "cultural relativity" is thus really the relativity of hero-systems the world over. But each cultural system is a dramatization of earthly heroics; each system cuts out roles for performances of various degrees of heroism. . . . It doesn't matter whether the cultural hero-system is frankly magical, religious, and primitive or secular, scientific, and civilized. It is still a mythical hero-system in which people serve in order to earn a feeling of primary value, of cosmic specialness, of ultimate usefulness to creation, of unshakable meaning. They earn this feeling by carving out a place in nature, by building an edifice that reflects human value: a temple, a cathedral, a totem pole, a skyscraper, a family that spans three generations. The hope and belief is that the things that man creates in society are of lasting worth and meaning, that they outlive or outshine death and decay, that man and his products count. (pp. 4–5)

We achieve a sense of significance by living within and comparing ourselves to these symbolic structures. We all strive to be heroic, to achieve self-esteem, in lesser or greater ways.

But what is motivating this need for heroism? Becker's (1973, p. 11) second move is to suggest that cultural heroics are fundamental attempts to cope with the terror of death: "heroism is first and foremost a reflex of the terror of death." In *Escape from Evil* Becker (1975, p. 125) notes that "cultures are fundamentally and basically styles of heroic death denial." According to Becker, our higher cognitive and symbolic capacities make our workaday lives existentially unbearable. The specter of death looms over all, making a mockery of our life projects. Our primal instincts for self-preservation are brought up short in the face of our cognitive capacities that inform us death is unavoidable. This clash—the instinct for self-preservation with an ever-present death awareness—creates an extreme burden of anxiety that other animals are spared:

The knowledge of death is reflective and conceptual, and animals are spared it. They live and they disappear with the same thoughtlessness: a few minutes of fear, a few seconds of anguish, and it is over. But to live a whole lifetime with the fate of death haunting one's dreams and even the most sun-filled days—that's something else. It is only if you let the full weight of this paradox sink down on your mind and feelings that you can realize what an impossible situation it is for an animal to be in. (p. 27)

This experiential burden threatens madness or despair. How do we make life count in the face of death? It is at this point where cultural hero systems step in to provide paths toward death transcendence, a means toward a symbolic immortality. Life achieves significance and meaning by participating in these greater goods that can outlive or transcend our finite existence. Culture, then, provides us with routes toward significance by providing us means to achieve death transcendence. We can create a life that matters through reaching for symbolic, if not literal, immortality. My life is deemed meaningful because my children outlive me or I wrote the book you have in your hands or I made a difference in the life of a young person or if I built a company. At the very least, we can purchase a block of granitite, inscribe our name upon it, and place it over our grave. We do not want our passing out of existence to go unnoticed and unremembered. So we etch our name on life, even on rocks if necessary.

The upshot of this analysis—that we strive for a heroic existence and that cultural hero systems are helping us face the terror of death—is that our very sense of self is being driven by mechanisms that are helping us cope with our fear of death. This is largely achieved through the defense mechanisms of repression and sublimation, pushing our awareness of death out of consciousness or redirecting it into our creative life projects.

This is, perhaps, a startling conclusion. In this view, self-esteem, the bedrock of personality, is revealed to be a form of denial, an existential-defense mechanism, an illusion to help us avoid the full force of our existential predicament. This is why Becker calls human character—our personal route toward cultural heroics—a *vital lie*. Character is a lie as it is a fundamental dishonesty, in the moment, about our true existential situation. Yet such dishonesty is vital as this daily obfuscation is necessary for the human animal to continue on in the face of death. Again, the existential burden death places upon humans is impossible. So culture helps us bear this burden, largely through repression and sublimation, by providing us routes of character formation via cultural heroics. Here is Becker (1973) in *The Denial of Death* on these dynamics:

> We called one's life style a vital lie, and now we can understand better why we said it was vital: it is a *necessary* and basic dishonesty about oneself and one's whole situation. . . . We don't want to admit that we are fundamentally dishonest about reality, that we do not really control our own lives. We don't want to admit that we do not stand alone, that we always rely on something that transcends us, some system of ideas and powers in which we are embedded and which support us. This power is not obvious. It need not be overtly a god or openly a stronger person, but it can be the power of an all-absorbing activity, a passion, a dedication to a game, a way of life, that like a comfortable web keeps a person buoyed up and ignorant of himself, of the fact that he does not rest on his own center. All of us are driven to be supported in a self-forgetful way, ignorant of what energies we really draw on, of the kind of lie we have fashioned in order to live securely and serenely. Augustine was a master analyst of this, as were Kierkegaard, Scheler, and Tillich in our day. They saw that man could strut and boast all he wanted, but that he really drew his "courage to be" from a god, a string of sexual conquests, a Big Brother, a flag, the proletariat, and the fetish of money and the size of a bank balance. The defenses that form a person's character support a grand illusion, and when we grasp this we can understand the full drivenness of man. He is driven away from himself, from self-knowledge, self-reflection. He is

driven toward things that support the lie of his character, his automatic equanimity. (pp. 55–56)

[T]he armor of character was so vital to us that to shed it meant to risk death and madness. It is not hard to reason out: If character is a neurotic defense against despair and you shed that defense, you admit the full flood of despair, the full realization of the true human condition, what men are really afraid of, what they struggle against, and are driven toward and away from. (p. 57)

It can't be overstressed, one final time, that to see the world as it really is is devastating and terrifying. It achieves the very result that the child has painfully built his character over the years in order to avoid: it *makes routine, automatic, secure, self-confident activity possible.* (p. 60)

In day-to-day life, our secure and self-confident activity moves along fairly smoothly. I do not know about you, but my life projects, selected and approved by my culture, keep me pretty busy. So rarely do I look up to confront my full existential situation. Yet moments of existential awareness can crack into our daily awareness. When these moments come, when we glimpse the seeming absurdity of the human rat race and hear the cry of Ecclesiastes about the vanity and meaninglessness of our life ambitions in the face of death, we, in a moment of terror, face the abyss of the human predicament. Irvin Yalom describes one of these moments (as cited in Greenberg, Solomon, & Pyszczynski, 1997):

Not too long ago I was taking a brief vacation alone at a Caribbean beach resort. One evening I was reading and from time to time I glanced to watch the bar boy who was doing nothing save staring languidly out to sea—much like a lizard sunning itself on a warm rock, I thought. The comparison I made between him and me made me feel very snug, very cozy. He was simply doing nothing—wasting time. I, on the other hand was doing something useful, reading, learning. I was, in short, getting ahead. All was well, until some internal imp asked the terrible question: Getting ahead of what? How? And (even worse) why? (p. 63)

Reflective people are well acquainted with these moments of existential awareness. Suddenly, the cultural armor, our means of getting ahead, is stripped away and we find our entire life, all our dreams and aspirations and accomplishments, to be built on a foundation of sand. We, in a paralyzing instant, feel the full force of the opening words of Ecclesiastes:

"Meaningless! Meaningless!" says the Teacher.
"Utterly meaningless! Everything is meaningless."
What do people gain from all their labors at which they toil
   under the sun? (Ecclesiastes 1:2–3)

But these moments quickly pass. The cultural armor eventually reasserts itself. And we get back to life. Back to mowing the lawn. Or to our job. Or to our favorite hobby. Or to writing this book. Back to getting ahead.

7.

What we find in Becker's work is the completion of the existential turn, begun with Freud himself, within the psychodynamic tradition. Becker offers an account that suggests human personality and culture is built atop neurotic anxiety: not due to oedipal- or libidinal-sexual instincts but as the result of existential awareness. Human personality and culture are inherently about *the denial of death*, about helping the human animal achieve day-to-day equanimity in the face of our existential burden and helping us manage our instinct for self-preservation in the face of a cognitive awareness that we are bound for death, that we cannot run away or escape our fate. Death activates a fight or flight response in us, but we have nowhere to run. No one to fight. So the anxiety just sits there, churning away. To handle this anxiety, we repress death awareness or sublimate the anxiety it causes by working on projects our culture deems significant and valuable. Through these efforts we attach our life stories to goods that can outlive us. And by doing so, we achieve both self-esteem and a symbolic immortality. We feel that we made a difference. And our culture declares our life meaningful.

However, this is a fragile and precarious business. As we saw in Yalom's comparisons with the bar boy, our cultural hero systems can be called into question. When this happens, the bedrock of meaning we have built our lives upon no longer seems to be eternal, timeless, and stable. Suddenly, we wonder if our hero systems are arbitrary, relativistic, and fickle. Why is *this* life worthwhile and significant when compared to others? In these moments we have misgivings about the values of our culture, questioning its routes toward self-esteem and success. Opinions about what constitutes getting ahead can vary.

This has become an acute problem in modernity. As our world grows smaller and more pluralistic, we are confronted with a bewildering diversity of values, customs, ethical systems, and religious beliefs. We live in world where gay and straight, atheist and theist, and Christian and Muslim work side by side. This daily exposure to alternative hero systems threatens our belief that our particular cultural heroics, our way of life, are eternal and timeless. As noted earlier, in our modern, pluralistic society there is a fragility of meaning. We see now that this is largely due to the clash of worldviews we encounter on a daily basis. Pluralism hints that worldviews are relative and not timeless and eternal. And if this is so, is *anything* to be counted on? Where am I to find meaning, truth, and significance in the face of death if the foundations have all turned to sand?

The fear inherent within modernity, the anxiety that the ideological Other calls my worldview into question, is one explanation for the rise of fundamentalism in the modern era. For example, Peter Berger and Anton Zijderveld (2009) argue in their book *In Praise of Doubt* that recent history has refuted the central premise of secularization theory which predicted that as modernity advanced people would give up religious belief and become secular. This was, incidentally, the very view

Freud espoused in *The Future of an Illusion*. But Berger and Zijderveld note that, empirically speaking, secularization theory has been falsified. Modernity has not run faith out of the building. If anything, faith is experiencing a renaissance in modernity. What has happened in modernity, argue Berger and Zijderveld, has not been secularization but plurality or what Charles Taylor (2007) has called "the nova effect," a massive proliferation of worldviews and ideologies. Modern peoples have not become less religious. They have been, rather, asked to choose from among a host of competing belief systems. Protestant or Catholic? Atheist or Christian? Buddhist or Muslim? Wiccan or Mormon?

Consequently, in light of all these choices, religion within a pluralistic society is fragile. As noted, the mere existence of ideological Others will call your faith system into question. How do you know you have the Truth when everyone around you believes something different, and believes they have the Truth as well? Why are you so special?

Religious and ideological fundamentalism, then, appears within modernity (perhaps paradoxically) as a defense against these questions. Fundamentalism, of all stripes, is the individual and collective effort to defend the truth of your worldview against the relativization inherent in the existence of the Other. Becoming a true believer is one way to defend against the existential predicament of modern day pluralism. And this leads to a surprising conclusion. Rather than making humanity less religious, as Freud believed, secularism is driving an increase in religious fundamentalism and often violent fundamentalism (one way to deal with the existential threat posed by ideological Others is to kill them). Modernity is shaping up to be less an age of reason than a violent battle between ideologies, ways of life, and worldviews.

So what is fueling the anxiety behind fundamentalism? According to Becker, it is existential terror. We defend our worldviews because they are existentially vital. Our worldviews grant us ultimate significance. Thus, we will defend to the death their status as eternal truth. This is the argument Becker makes in *The Escape from Evil*, his sequel to *The Denial of Death*.

According to Becker, the great tragedy of human existence is this. Our lives are significant because we create cultural hero systems. These hero systems are vital, the location of our ultimate significance, individually and collectively. And yet, this hero system will come into conflict with other hero systems, other cultural worldviews. This encounter with the ideological Other calls our entire worldview into question, threatening to reveal that what we hold most dear and holy is merely an illusion. A lie. A vital lie, but a lie nonetheless. Not surprisingly, in the face of this threat we double down on our worldview and come to see the Other as a devil and a monster, as an enemy to be defeated or eliminated. Sadly, what we see in all this is how that which makes us feel happy, secure, and significant—our cultural hero system—is also that which makes us violent and prone to evil, killing Others to protect our way of life, our nation, and our God. Here is Becker (1975) in *Escape from Evil*:

> The thing that feeds the great destructiveness of history is that men give their entire allegiance to their own group; and each group is a codified hero system. Which is another way of saying that societies are standardized systems of death denial; they give structure to the formulas for heroic transcendence. History can then be looked at as a succession of immortality ideologies, or as a mixture at any time of several of these ideologies. We can ask about any epoch, What are the social forms of heroism available? (pp. 153–154)
>
> [C]ultures are fundamentally and basically *styles of heroic death denial*. We can then ask empirically, it seems to me, what are the costs of such denials of death, because we know how these denials are structured into styles of life. These costs can be tallied roughly in two ways: in terms of the tyranny practiced within the society, and in terms of the victimage practiced against aliens or "enemies" outside it. (p. 125)
>
> Each person wants his life to be a marker for good as his group defines it. Men work their programs of heroism according

to the standard cultural scenarios. . . . It is as Hegel long ago said: Men cause evil by wanting heroically to triumph over it, because man is a frightened animal who tries to triumph, an animal who will not admit his own insignificance, that he cannot perpetuate himself and his group forever, that no one is invulnerable no matter how much of the blood of others is spilled to try to demonstrate it. (p. 151)

Cultures give us routes to significance in the face of an indifferent and hostile cosmos. And yet for this process to work, our value systems must appear to us eternal and timeless. Only in that way will our life projects, guided by these values, be able to outlast us. But when worldviews collide, as they do in pluralistic societies, our hero systems are relativized and called into question. This undermines the existential armor we need to achieve a workaday equanimity in the face of death. And when facing this prospect, it is much easier to cope with this existential anxiety by *defending* the worldview against ideological Others. Mildly, these Others are believed to be in error or mistaken. They simply worship the wrong god (or whatever is believed to ground the cultural worldview). In more severe cases, ideological Others are believed to pose threats that can prompt social marginalization and even potentially escalate into physical violence.

8.

Having taken stock of the work of Ernest Becker, we are now ready to approach the research emerging from the literature of experimental existentialism. And while it might seem in this chapter that we have wandered away from *The Future of an Illusion*, we have simply deepened, broadened, and extended the argument that was first offered by Freud. Specifically, while Freud suggested that religion and religion alone was involved in existential repression, we find through the work of Ernest Becker that culture itself, of which religion is only a part, is involved in the denial of death. In fact, cultural heroics need not involve religion at all. The prime example of this was Freud himself and the way he made the legacy of psychoanalysis his existential lifeboat. As Becker (1975) observed in *Escape from Evil*:

> It was no news to Freud that the ability to love and to believe is a matter of susceptibility to illusion. He prided himself on being a stoical scientist who had transcended the props of illusion, yet he retained his faith in science—in psychoanalysis—as his particular hero system. This is the same as saying that all hero systems are based on illusion except one's own, which is somehow in a special, privileged place, as if given by nature herself. . . . It means that Freud, too, was not exempt from the need to fit himself into a scheme of cosmic heroism, an immortality ideology that had to be taken on faith . . . *the* hero system that guaranteed him immortality. (p. 157)

So everyone, ultimately, is involved in some form of death denial, some form of heroism we feel to be a route to significance and death transcendence. Of course, these cultural heroics may involve religious faith, but that need not be the case.

Still, Freud's point in *The Future of an Illusion* remains. In fact, his central argument has been significantly strengthened. While religion is not alone in providing existential consolation, Becker's work comes alongside Freud in fundamental agreement. Religion is a form of death-denying cultural heroics, a route to meaning, significance, and immortality. As Becker (1973) writes in *The Denial of Death*:

> When man lived securely under the canopy of the Judeo-Christian world picture he was a part of a great whole; to put it in our terms, his cosmic heroism was completely mapped out, it was unmistakable. He came from the invisible world into the visible one by the act of God, did his duty to God by living out his life with dignity and faith. . . . In turn he was justified by the Father and rewarded with eternal life in the invisible dimension.

Little did it matter that the earth was vale of tears, of horrid sufferings, of incommensurateness, of torturous and humiliating daily pettiness, of sickness and death, a place where man felt he did not belong. . . . Little did it matter, because it served God and so would serve the servant of God. In a word, man's cosmic heroism was assured, even if he was as nothing. This is the most remarkable achievement of the Christian world picture: that it could take slaves, cripples, imbeciles, the simple and the mighty, and make them all secure heroes, simply by taking a step back from the world into another dimension of things, the dimension called heaven. (pp. 159–160)

Thus while it might be comforting to see Freud, in his atheism, as in the same boat as the religious believer he criticized in *The Future of an Illusion*, his overarching diagnosis remains in place: the function of religious belief is to offer existential consolation. Religion is a death-denying form of heroics used to repress awareness of our existential predicament. Freud suggested that faith is a kind of *existential narcotic*. And while the picture has been nuanced and expanded by the existential psychologists, nothing much has changed about Freud's basic claim regarding the function of religion belief.

Chapter 4

TERROR MANAGEMENT

1.

SO NOW IT IS TIME, HERE AT THE END OF PART 1, TO CONSIDER the evidence. Although the theories of Freud and existential thinkers such as Ernest Becker may be persuasive on the surface, these theories remain, well, theories. After taking it all in we might simply choose to disagree, to adopt some other, rival theoretical model for the origin and function of religious belief. In the end, who can say if Freud was correct? Perhaps Freud was wrong.

But at the end of the day, these issues are not, in point of fact, theoretical. Freud's entire argument in *The Future of an Illusion* (and Becker's expansion in *The Denial of Death*) is a theory about human motivation, about why and how religious belief is adopted and deployed in the face of life experience. And human motivation is an empirical phenomenon that is routinely studied in psychological laboratories throughout the world. So Freud is not simply offering a theory; he is articulating a set of empirical predictions that can be tested in psychological experiments. The ultimate arbiter regarding the argument in *The Future of an Illusion* is not going to be philosophy or theology. The issues here are empirical.

The fate of *The Future of an Illusion*, as a theory of religious belief, will be decided in the laboratory. So, does the empirical data support Freud's theory regarding the function of religious belief? That is the question going forward.

Now it might seem to those outside the social sciences that it would be near impossible to put Freud's theories regarding religious belief to the test, particularly in their existential guise. How could you possibly determine if religious belief was involved in existential consolation? That faith is functioning as an unconscious defense mechanism involved in repressing death anxiety? If these dynamics are unconscious, how could we put any of this to the test?

Perhaps, it is assumed, the psychological dynamics in question here are too large, complex, and abstract to investigate in the laboratory. In fact, for decade after decade this was the working assumption within the field of psychology, that there was an unbridgeable divide between the abstract concerns of the existential psychologists and the empirical concerns of the experimental psychologists. Greenberg, Koole, and Pyszczynski (2004) describe the historical situation well:

> For most of the relatively short history of scientific psychology the mere idea of an experimental existential psychology would have been considered oxymoronic—in fact, such a juxtaposition of experimental and existential psychology was probably never considered at all. Although experimental psychology has flourished for well over 100 years, and existential ideas have made their way into the theories of clinically oriented theorists and therapists for most of the 20th century, these two approaches have traditionally been thought of as opposite ends of the very broad and typically finely demarcated field of psychology. Experimental psychologists applied rigorous research methods to relatively simple phenomena, usually with the intention of discovering the most basic building blocks of human behavior. Existential psychologists, on the

other hand, speculated about the human confrontation with very abstract questions regarding the nature of existence and the meaning of life—ideas that typically are considered far too abstruse and intractable to be fruitfully addressed by the scientific method. For the most part, experimentalists and existentialists acknowledged the existence of each other only when pointing to the fundamental absurdity of what the other was trying to accomplish. (pp. 3–4)

And yet, despite the historical standoff, the last few decades have seen a remarkable surge in interest regarding what is called *experimental existentialism* within psychology: the application of empirical methods to study the human confrontation with our existential situation. This is as it should be. Existentialism, even at its most philosophical, has always been preoccupied with human psychology, with how humans make meaning, particularly in the face of life's absurdities. So it is not so surprising that psychological research methods would, eventually, turn to illuminate the psychological processes that so interested thinkers such as Kierkegaard, Sartre, Kafka, and Dostoevsky.

For our purposes, the work in experimental existentialism is of great interest as this literature is providing some of the first empirical examinations of the psychological dynamics involved in religious belief. As noted above, in *The Future of an Illusion* Freud was making a series of empirical claims, namely about the motivations (largely unconscious) behind the adoption of religious belief. Consequently, it will prove important to determine if the data stack up in Freud's favor. For if Freud's claims have empirical support, then his account of religious belief grows more potent and persuasive. In that event, Freud could not be dismissed as a simple critic of religion. Freud would rather be describing something fundamentally true about the nature of religious belief. And any Christians ignoring this truth (with its associated data) would simply confirm Freud's thesis: that religious belief is, at root, a denial of reality, an illusion.

And so we turn to the research of experimental existentialism to see how this research has begun to illuminate the nature and function of religious belief.

2.

Our focus for the rest of this chapter, and for most of this book, will be upon what is called terror management theory (TMT; Greenberg, Solomon, & Pyszczynski, 1997; Pyszczynski, Solomon, Greenberg, 2003; Solomon, Greenberg, and Pyszczynski, 2004), one of the most influential paradigms within the experimental existentialism literature. Developed in the mid-1980s by Sheldon Solomon, Jeff Greenberg, and Tom Pyszczynski, TMT closely follows the work of Ernest Becker. Having reviewed the major themes of Becker's thought, the overall structure of TMT should be easy to grasp.

At the outset, Solomon et al., (2004, p. 14) focused TMT on two questions:

1. Why are people so intensely concerned with their self-esteem?
2. Why do people cling so tenaciously to their own cultural beliefs and have such a difficult time coexisting with others different than themselves?

As we know, Ernest Becker gave an answer to the first question in *The Denial of Death* and an answer to the second in *Escape from Evil*. TMT follows Becker, suggesting we are intensely concerned with self-esteem because it guides us through cultural worldviews that give life meaning and significance in the face of death. Solomon et al., (2004) summarize the core axioms of TMT, relating self-esteem to success in upholding cultural worldviews in order to achieve death transcendence:

> TMT posits that humans share with all forms of life a biologi-
> cal predisposition to continue existence, or at least to avoid
> premature termination of life. However, the highly developed

intellectual abilities that make humans aware of their vulnerabilities and inevitable death create the potential for paralyzing
terror. Cultural worldviews manage the terror associated with
this awareness of death primarily through the cultural mechanism of self-esteem, which consists of the belief that one is a
valuable contributor to a meaningful universe. Effective terror
management thus requires (1) faith in a meaningful conception
of reality (the cultural worldview) and (2) belief that one is meeting the standards of value prescribed by the worldview (self-
esteem). Because of the protection from the potential for terror
that the psychological structures provide, people are motivated
to maintain faith in their cultural worldviews and satisfy the
standards of value associated with their worldviews. (p. 20)

Given our review of Becker's work these ideas should be familiar. But
it was the particular genius of Solomon, Greenberg, and Pyszczynski
to use this theory to create testable hypotheses for the psychological
laboratory. Two of their most influential hypotheses have been the self-
esteem as an anxiety-buffer hypothesis and the mortality-salience and
worldview-defense hypothesis.

If cultural hero systems are defenses against the terror of death,
and self-esteem helps mark our progress through these hero systems,
then it seems clear that a part of self-esteem's function is to protect us
from existential anxiety. Self-esteem buffers us from existential terror.
Early tests of this self-esteem as an anxiety buffer hypothesis provided
empirical evidence for this mechanism. For example, Greenberg, Simon,
Pyszcynski, Solomon, and Chatel (1992) manipulated self-esteem in
participants and then exposed them to an existentially disturbing stimulus—autopsy footage. According to TMT, if self-esteem functions as an
anxiety buffer then increasing self-esteem prior to watching the autopsy
footage should attenuate anxiety during the exposure to the existentially
troublesome stimulus. This is, in fact, what Greenberg et al. observed.
Participants who had their self-esteem artificially increased (by giving

positive, but false, feedback after taking a personality assessment and an IQ test—who does not like to be told they are charming and smart?) prior to watching the autopsy footage reported less anxiety after the viewing than those in the control condition. This pattern of results is consistent with the notion that self-esteem is involved in protecting us from existential anxiety.

If self-esteem is, as it seems, involved in managing existential anxiety, Ernest Becker pointed out in *Escape from Evil* that the cultural worldviews that support our self-esteem are vulnerable to the critique of Otherness. The mere existence of alternative cultures, worldviews, religions, and value systems threatens the assumption that one's own values, culture, or beliefs are timeless and eternal sources of meaning. Otherness threatens our self-esteem at the deepest level. So in the face of this threat, we demean, denigrate or destroy ideological Others. We protect our existential equanimity by lashing out at difference. In the language of TMT, we engage in worldview defense. Worldview defense occurs when we display "vigorous agreement with and affection for those who uphold or share our beliefs (or are similar to us) and equally vigorous hostility and distain for those who challenge or do not share our beliefs (i.e., are different from us)" (Solomon et al., 2004, pp. 20–21). TMT suggests that worldview defense is most likely to occur in the face of an existential threat. When we feel existentially unsettled or worried our tendency will be to bolster and protect our cultural worldview. As it is our location of ultimate meaning and significance, we want to experience our worldview as sturdy and durable in the face of death. Consequently, we defend our worldview by siding with those who share our values and attacking those who do not. According to TMT, one situation in which this occurs is when our mortality is made salient, when we are forced to ponder our eventual death. Thus, according to the mortality-salience hypothesis, worldview defense should occur when we are confronted with our death. When death awareness is elevated, we will display increased in-group favoritism along with an increased tendency to denigrate out-group members. By engaging in these largely unconscious defensive processes, we secure our cultural hero systems in the face of the existential threat posed by Otherness.

In the TMT literature, the mortality-salience and worldview-defense dynamics are often assessed by assigning some participants to a mortality-salience condition. In this condition, participants can be asked to write a brief essay about the experience of dying (The common prompts are: "Please briefly describe the emotions that the thought of your own death arouse in you," along with "Jot down, as specifically as you can, what you think will happen to you as you physically die."); or be exposed to death-themed stimuli (e.g., autopsy footage); or priming (e.g., completing a death-anxiety questionnaire). By having death brought to mind, overtly or subtly, the participants in the mortality-salience condition have existential material pulled into consciousness. Mortality, in being brought to mind, is made salient and accessible.

After this manipulation, participants are then usually asked to engage in a task in which they are evaluating or interacting with in-group and out-group targets: those who support the participant's worldview and those who call that worldview into question (either by violating norms, questioning norms, or simply being an out-group member). For example, in early tests of the worldview-defense hypothesis two different studies (Greenberg et al., 1992; Harmon-Jones et al., 1997) had college participants rate two different student essays about impressions regarding America. The writer of one essay expressed clear pro-American sentiment, praising the United States for its political system, freedoms, safety, and opportunities. The writer of the second essay expressed the view of a foreign student who was critical of America for its economic inequalities, materialism, and lack of sympathy for those outside of its borders. In short, one essay was supportive of the American hero system and the other was, as an outsider, skeptical of that worldview. After reading these essays, participants were asked to rate the quality of each essay as well as the personality and intelligence of the essayists. In both studies, the participants in the mortality-salience condition displayed worldview defense. Participants who were asked to contemplate their own death prior to reading the essays rated the pro-America essay as better written than the anti-American essay. More, they rated the pro-American essayist, as a person, as more intelligent and possessing more positive personality traits (e.g., honesty, kindness, patience, warmth, humanity). By contrast, the foreign essayist was rated as less intelligent and possessing more negative personality traits (e.g., arrogance, insensitivity, obnoxiousness, self-centeredness, hypocrisy). This pattern of results is consistent with the mortality-salience hypothesis: when existentially threatened we defend our cultural worldviews (our path toward meaning and significance in the face of death) by favoring in-group members and denigrating out-group members.

This is the tragic dynamic described by Ernest Becker (1975) in *Escape from Evil*: those things which are most important and vital to us—our values, way of life, religion—are the very things that make us prone to evil as we protect our worldview against Otherness. What is very important for our purposes here is that this theory has received significant laboratory support. The ghost of Ernest Becker, I suspect, is very pleased.

3.

As just noted, the importance of the TMT research is that it provides empirical evidence supportive of the work of the existential psychologists who have suggested that culture and self-esteem are involved in repressing and managing our existential anxieties. Consequently, this research is of interest given Freud's claims regarding the function of religious belief in *The Future of an Illusion*. If Freud was correct that the function of religious belief is existential consolation, then TMT research techniques should be able to provide the supporting data. In fact, such data is very much expected as we know that religious belief is woven deeply into the fabric of cultural worldviews and value systems. Thus, in light of the reality of worldview defense as revealed in the TMT literature, we should fully expect that religious belief would be deeply implicated in existential repression—providing meaning, significance, and cultural heroics in the face of death. And with this supporting empirical data in hand, Freud's case in *The Future of an Illusion* grows that much more persuasive.

Beyond a general focus on cultural worldview, TMT research has in fact explicitly examined the role of religion in worldview defense. In an early study that will prove important later on in this book, Greenberg et al. (1990) examined the reactions of Christian undergraduate participants in the face of a mortality-salience manipulation. After either a mortality-salience or control manipulation, the Christian participants were asked to evaluate the personality profiles and social-attitude questionnaires of two (fictional) students. These two profiles were different but counterbalanced across the participants (i.e., for each new participant the profiles were switched so that any biasing effect regarding the actual content of the profile was averaged out). The only difference in the two essays (after counterbalancing) was that one fictional student self-identified as Christian and the other as Jewish. After reading the personality and social attitude profiles of either the Jewish or Christian targets, the Christian participants rated each target across a variety of personality descriptors (e.g., honest, cheerful, reliable, trustworthy, argumentative, intelligent, warm, patient, kind, ambitious). Importantly, the researchers also added a variety of stereotypical personality descriptors found within the anti-Semitic literature: stingy, manipulative, arrogant, snobbish, and obnoxious.

In sum, what Greenberg et al. (1990) had set up was a worldview-defense study with a uniquely religious flavor and focus. Specifically, do anti-Semitic attitudes among Christians have an existential basis? When existentially composed, we should expect that Christians would evaluate individuals in an unbiased and evenhanded fashion. We would predict that the Christian participants in the control condition of Greenberg et al. would, for the most part, ignore the religious affiliation of the two profiles. However, what will happen in the mortality-salience condition? If the Christian belief system is involved in existential repression then we should expect the Christians in the mortality-salience condition to engage in worldview defense. Feeling existentially unsettled by the death priming, the Christian participants should favor the in-group member—their fellow Christian—and denigrate the Jew, the out-group member.

This is, in fact, what Greenberg et al. (1990) observed. While the Christian participants in the control condition did not show any bias, the Christian participants in the morality-salience condition rated the Christian target more favorably relative to the Jewish target. Moreover, when the Christian target was rated first, the Jewish target was rated as higher on stereotypical anti-Semitic traits in the mortality-salience condition. That is, in the death-awareness condition the Jewish individual was rated as more stingy, manipulative, arrogant, snobbish, and obnoxious when an explicit comparison with Christians was available. In short, in the face of death Christians became anti-Semitic in their attitudes and judgments. This is the pattern of results we would expect if religious belief was involved in existential repression and consolation.

Strengthening this case, additional TMT research (for a review see Vail et al., 2010) has shown that, in the face of a death reminder, belief in the afterlife and in supernatural beings (e.g., angels) increases. Mortality-salience manipulations have also increased belief in (ostensibly) scientific articles purporting to show the causal efficacy of prayer. Finally, challenges to religious belief, like pointing out inconsistencies within the Bible, create greater death-thought accessibility. When the foundations of faith are shaken, worries about mortality and death appear to float to the surface of consciousness. These findings, combined with the findings of Greenberg et al. (1990), provide strong empirical evidence that religious belief, as proposed by Freud in *The Future of an Illusion*, is deployed as an anxiety buffer: a repressive, largely unconscious, defense mechanism that protects us from existential terror. *Existential solace and consolation*—this is the function, if we accept this evidence, of religious belief.

4.

So where does all this leave us? Well, for religious believers, in a somewhat difficult place. So here at the end of Part 1, let us step back, take stock, and locate where we are.

Freud's thesis regarding the origins of religious belief in *The Future of an Illusion* presents a unique challenge to Christian apologists, for Freud's arguments are not merely influential. In many ways the work of Freud, along with thinkers such as Marx and Darwin, signaled a new era, a new challenge, a radical reconfiguration of the debate regarding the nature of religious belief. Where classical apologetics had focused on the contents of religious belief, we are now considering the function of religious belief. What are the dynamics—biological, sociological, or psychological—behind the origin and maintenance of religious belief?

This shift in the debate is difficult for two related reasons. First, functional approaches to religious belief, as we have seen, are inherently reductionistic and deflationary; they are attempts to explain faith away. With the functional explanation in hand, the suspicion grows that the reason behind faith has less to do with justified true belief than, say, biological adaptations, psychological fears, or sociological pressures. Second, the tools of this debate—evolutionary biology, sociology, and psychology—are unfamiliar to most theologians and philosophers trained in the great and rich literature of classical apologetics.

Freud's specific functional account in *The Future of an Illusion* was that religious belief is an existential narcotic that provides believers existential consolation and solace in the face of death and an indifferent and hostile cosmos. In the decades after Freud, existential psychologists greatly expanded upon Freud's early work. These existential psychodynamic thinkers agreed with Freud that conscious life in modernity was only possible through an act of repression and sublimation. However, these thinkers replaced Freud's oedipal instincts with existential confrontations. What we repress in our workaday lives are not illicit libidinal instincts but existential awareness and anxiety. We are engaged, individually and collectively, in a denial of death. As we have seen, the work of Ernest Becker has been particularly influential in this area, namely because of his impact upon the laboratory work of experimental existentialism, in particular TMT.

One feature of the existential development of Freud's thought was how it expanded Freud's narrow focus on religion to include culture generally. Human culture, as the taproot of human meaning and significance, is inherently religious, a means for death transcendence and immortality. Such an analysis fits Freud's own pursuit of the heroic. Eschewing religious belief, Freud poured his life into securing the scientific legacy of psychoanalysis. Psychoanalysis was Freud's faith, his ultimate concern, the means by which Freud felt his life would matter, existentially speaking.

Still, while this existential formulation may have placed Freud in the same boat along with the religious believer, this does not affect the heart of Freud's theory. If anything, the existential turn within the psychodynamic tradition strengthened the suspicion that religion, so deeply woven into the fabric of our cultural worldviews, is very much involved in existential repression. In fact, the laboratory research of TMT has emerged to provide empirical evidence supporting Freud's contention in *The Future of an Illusion*. As we observed, Christians deploy worldview defense in the face of death, showing favoritism toward fellow Christians and denigrating out-group members from other world religions. This finding is what we would expect if religious belief was functioning as an anxiety buffer, a means of existential repression and consolation.

What this means is that, supported by the findings of the TMT research, *The Future of an Illusion* cannot be dismissed by religious believers. Let me be clear: religious belief is implicated in existential repression. While data may have been necessary to convince some, reflective religious persons have always known this to be the case. For example, in Chapter 3 we discussed the work of Arthur McGill, a

Christian theologian who both recognized and wrestled with the death-denying functions of Christian belief.

So where does this leave us? If religious belief is, as seems clear, used as an existential defense mechanism, a buffer we place between ourselves and death, can we conclude that religious belief is an illusion as Freud contended? How are we to think about the nature of religious belief in light of these revelations?

This, it seems to me, is new and uncharted territory. The ground has shifted and the road ahead seems uncertain. Christian theologians and philosophers can no longer dismiss Freud on theoretical grounds. Freud's thesis has received and is receiving increasing laboratory support.

This is why we need a new kind of apologetics. Here at the end of Part 1, in the wake of Freud and the existential psychologists, we are left with a situation aptly described by Abraham Joshua Heschel (1955):

> It has long been known that need and desire play a part in the shaping of beliefs. But is it true, as modern psychology often claims, that our religious beliefs are nothing but attempts to satisfy subconscious wishes? That the conception of God is merely a projection of self-seeking emotions, an objectification of subjective needs, the self in disguise? Indeed, the tendency to question the genuineness of man's concerns about God is a challenge no less serious than the tendency to question the existence of God. We are in greater need of a proof for the authenticity of faith than of a proof for the existence of God. (pp. 35–36)

A new challenge now faces us. In the modern debates about religion, debates shaped by the functional accounts of religious belief, it seems that we are less in need of an argument for the existence of God than for an argument that religious believers are not, at some deep level, deluding themselves—that religious belief is not a fear-based, childish, naïve, or wishful illusion.

What is needed today is a "proof for the authenticity of faith."

PART 2

THE VARIETIES OF RELIGIOUS EXPERIENCE

Chapter 5

THE TWO FAMILIES OF GOD

IN 1898, WILLIAM JAMES, THE FAMOUS HARVARD PSYCHOLO-gist and philosopher, was invited to give the Gifford Lectures at the University of Edinburgh. The Gifford Lectures were prestigious but relatively new, established in 1885 by the will of Adam Lord Gifford for four Scottish universities—the Universities of Edinburgh, Aberdeen, Glasgow, and St. Andrews—to host lectures on the topic of "natural religion": the attempt to explore religion scientifically and investigate the intersections between faith, belief, and science. Considered now one of the highest honors a scholar can receive, the Gifford Lecturers have included luminaries such as the theologians Reinhold Niebuhr and Karl Barth as well as Nobel laureates in science such as Werner Heisenberg and Niels Bohr. Now over 100 years old, the Gifford Lectures, it could be argued, owe a bit of their continuing influence to what Williams James did with his lectures in Edinburgh, lectures culminating in the work we know as *The Varieties of Religious Experience*. *The Varieties of Religious Experience* secured, for history, the fame of both William James and every Gifford lecturer who would follow. And with that work, James set the standard against which every Gifford lecturer would forever be compared.

James's Gifford Lectures were given across two years. Ten lectures were given in 1901 and a second set of ten given the following year in 1902. Those lectures were then combined to create the twenty chapters of *The Varieties of Religious Experience*, published in 1902. The actual lectures were a rousing success, warmly received by the audiences in attendance in Edinburgh, and the book became a bestseller, establishing practically on its own the field of religious studies. To this day, *The Varieties of Religious Experience* remains required reading in religious-studies classes. As Robert Richardson (2006) observes in a list enumerating the reasons behind the continuing legacy and influence of William James:

> James is the author of *The Varieties of Religious Experience*, the founding text of the modern study of religion, a book so pervasive in religious studies that one hears occasional mutterings in the schools about King James—and they don't mean the Bible. (pp. 5–6)

1.

When reading *The Varieties of Religious Experience*, one is immediately struck by how different James's approach is compared to Freud's in *The Future of an Illusion*. Freud's great obsession was to reduce all mental phenomena to psychodynamic mechanisms. In all of Freud's work, he believed he was explaining, causally and reductionistically, the inner workings of the human mind. This approach is clearly on display in *The Future of an Illusion*, in which we have seen how Freud attempts to explain the origin and function of religious belief.

James's approach to religion, by contrast, is more descriptive than explanatory. In *Varieties*, James acts as a cartographer, mapping a vast and uncharted realm—the length, width, and depth of the human religious experience. One gets the sense in reading James, and this is consistent with all his psychological work, that the mind is too complex, mysterious, and unruly to be captured by any reductionistic scientific theory. The very title of his book, highlighting religious *varieties*, displays a radical departure from Freud's approach. Where Freud attempted to stuff the genie of religious experience into a single, tight, psychodynamic bottle, James sets out to open up a Pandora's box.

2.

One reason for the lasting influence of *Varieties*, and what continues to make it a great read, is the testimonial approach used by James in his Gifford Lectures. James's method, in his attempt to map the terrain of religious experience, was to collect, sort, organize, and interpret first-person testimonials. Across the pages of the *Varieties*, James appears as a butterfly collector, a bird watcher, or a field botanist collecting specimens. In each lecture, James marshals a chorus of voices giving us, page after page, first-person autobiographical accounts of religious experience. We hear from religious mystics, poets, philosophers, and people on the street. In one chapter, the famous Lectures 16 and 17 on Mysticism, we hear from 55 different individuals. Richardson (2006) nicely describes the approach and argumentative style of *Varieties*:

> [James's] approach, his strategy for presenting the material, was [that] for each major point he provided a series of examples; each example was a quotation, often lengthy, from a personal account. The effect on the hearer is of an ever-swelling crowd of witnesses, a growing accumulation of firsthand testimony, all with the authority of personal conviction. The lectures, as given and as printed, are, as a whole, a large democratic assembly of voices, some very well known and some very obscure. . . . James gives a courteous hearing to great saints, famous poets, itinerant preachers, illiterate converts, street mission workers, anonymous responders to questionnaires, and Victorian gentlemen with three names. . . . [T]he practical result of presenting a wide

sampling of voices is to give these lectures an authority no logical argument could match for immediacy, conviction, personal
intensity, and sheer range of articulated experience. . . . Such a
mass of testimony is not easily talked down by general propositions. (pp. 396–397)

James gathers these experiences under broad headings, categories of
religious experience that still shape current research: religious conver-
sion, mystical experience, and the fruits of saintliness (the products
of the religious geniuses among us). And if James is interested in the
diversity of religious experience, he is also interested in experience as
experience. This accounts for a second reason *Varieties* has such widespread contemporary influence and appeal. It could be argued that
James was the first person to give an account of faith in the modern
era. It is almost a given that modern persons make distinctions between
organized religion and spirituality, with the claim that a person can be
spiritual but not religious. William James was one of the first, if not the
first, to introduce this demarcation into the modern consciousness as
he builds his entire approach within *Varieties* upon this distinction.

James's focus is upon first-person experience. By focusing on
religious experience James ignores religious doctrine, dogma, belief,
theology, creeds, ritual, ecclesiology, philosophy, cosmology, and metaphysics. James's approach is phenomenological rather than theological. James has little interest in the question of whether religious belief
is true, metaphysically speaking. Rather, he is interested in describing
the subjective, emotional, and private encounter with the Divine. And
despite the differences, we see in this something similar to what we
observed with Freud: a marginalizing of the theological and doctrinal
aspects of faith. The truth of religious belief has less to do with classical Christian apologetics than how belief is functioning in the lives
of religious believers. We move, once again, from theology and biblical studies to a psychological analysis. James (1902/1987) makes this
move in Lecture 2 when he distinguishes between institutional and

personal religion (the modern distinction being between religion and spirituality):

> At the outset we are struck by one great partition which divides the religious field. On the one side of it lies institutional, on the other personal religion. . . . Worship and sacrifice, procedures for working on the dispositions of the deity, theology and ceremony and ecclesiastical organization, are the essentials of religion in the institutional branch. . . . In the more personal branch of religion it is on the contrary the inner dispositions of man himself which form the centre of interest, his conscience, his desires, his helplessness, his incompleteness. (p. 34)

In light of this distinction, James contends that subjective religious experience is "more fundamental than either theology or ecclesiasticism" (p. 35). Organized religion, with this doctrines and rituals, "lives at second-hand" upon the primary religious experiences of the founders of the faith. The encounter with the Divine precedes any theologizing.

3.

Before turning to the theme in *Varieties* that will most engage us for the rest of this book, it will be worth pausing to note important areas of agreement between James and our discussions from Part 1 concerning functional accounts of religious belief and the relationship between reason and the passions. Specifically, given James's assertion that religious experience is primary and precedes theology, doctrine, ritual, and dogma, it should not be surprising that James agrees with many of the observations noted in Part 1.

Recall from Chapter 1 the research on moral dumbfounding. This research suggested that when we make normative judgments our affective judgments of right versus wrong often precede intellectual arguments. We feel something to be wrong and then go, in an ad hoc fashion, looking for intellectual warrants to support or defend our initial reactions, and we often come up empty-handed. And yet that outcome does not affect our deeply felt conviction that something is indeed very wrong. The moral-dumbfounding research appears to suggest that Hume was at least partly right in his treatise on human nature when he said that reason is the slave of the passions. And if not the slave, reason can at times at least be bossed around and bullied by the passions.

This aspect of human psychology—passion pushing around reason—sits behind Freud's view of religion in *The Future of an Illusion*. Our emotional needs for solace, comfort, and consolation create religious belief. Psychology is producing theology. According to Freud, the wish (psychological need) precedes the belief (theology, metaphysics).

In *Varieties*, James (1902/1987) makes a similar observation, suggesting that our psychological needs, desires, and predispositions make religious belief (or any belief) more or less likely:

> Your whole subconscious life, your impulses, your faiths, your needs, your divinations, have prepared the premises, of which your consciousness now feels the weight of the result; and something in you absolutely *knows* that the result must be truer than any logic-chopping rationalistic talk, however clever, that may contradict it. This inferiority of the rationalistic level in founding belief is just as manifest when rationalism argues for religion as when against it. . . . The truth is that in the metaphysical and religious sphere, articulate reasons are cogent for us only when our inarticulate feelings of reality have already been impressed in favor of the same conclusion. . . . Our impulsive belief is here always what sets up the original body of truth, and our philosophy is but its showy verbalized translation. The immediate assurance is the deep thing in us, the argument is but a surface exhibition. Instinct leads, intelligence does but follow. (pp. 73–74)

This assessment of James is almost exactly what we find in the moral-dumbfounding research, and it underscores the modern shift away from classical apologetics and theology ("the rationalistic level") toward psychological considerations: the realm of instincts, needs, and desires. Psychology leads and intelligence, logic, reasons, and "logic-chopping rationalistic talk" follow.

The point here is that with *Varieties* we find ourselves back in some well-covered territory from Part 1. James is fully aware that religious belief might be adopted to assuage anxiety or to create a sense of well-being. James notes that religious belief can be a mode of "producing happiness, wonderful inner paths to a supernatural kind of happiness," and that "the happiness which a religious belief affords [is] proof of its truth" (p. 77). Why? James continues: because "[i]f a creed makes a man feel happy, he almost inevitably adopts it." This is, essentially, what Freud argued 25 years later in *The Future of an Illusion*.

Yet James eventually parts company with Freud in ways that will prove important in the chapters to come. A part of this is due to the different epistemologies adopted by Freud and James. While both men were scientists, James was one of the fathers of American pragmatism in contrast to Freud's more positivistic approach. Freud wanted beliefs to be verified by science and empirical evidence. This caused him to be dismissive of metaphysics generally and religious belief in particular. By contrast, the pragmatic tradition, whose founders include Charles Sanders Peirce and John Dewey along with William James, viewed the truthfulness of a belief to be a matter of practical consequences. What mattered for the pragmatists had less to do with evidence than if the belief worked, practically speaking. Truth was practical, useful, and pragmatic. Truth, simply put, gets stuff done.

James's pragmatism allowed him to be more open to religious belief than Freud. For James, the truth of religion had less to do with scientific verification than with its practical outcomes. Did religion work for people? Lectures 14 and 15 in *Varieties* on "The Value of Saintliness" are preoccupied with this question. From these, James's ultimate conclusion is that religion is a mixed bag. For some, religious belief is associated with a host of positive outcomes—social, psychological, and moral.

And these outcomes should be taken very seriously. But for others, religion is associated with pathology and dysfunction. James's assessment here rings true when we look out upon the religious landscape and observe the various activities of religious believers of all stripes, from heroic saints to violent extremists.

So a point of contrast between Freud and James is that James is willing to admit that religious belief can be true on pragmatic grounds. And James is willing in *Varieties* to admit that this seems to change the subject in a way that thinkers such as Freud would disapprove of:

> Abstractly, it would seem illogical to try to measure the worth of a religion's fruits in merely human term of value. How *can* you measure their worth without considering whether the God really exists who is supposed to inspire them? (p. 300)

Yet James asserts this is the only mode available to us for scientifically evaluating religious belief. With these objections duly noted, James sets out his pragmatic criteria for examining the truthfulness of religious belief:

> What I then propose to do is, briefly stated, to test saintliness by common sense, to use human standards to help us decide how far the religious life commends itself as an ideal of human activity. If it commends itself, then any theological beliefs that may inspire it, in so far forth will stand accredited. If not, then they must be discredited, and all without reference to anything but human working principles. (p. 303)

No doubt this leaves many unanswered questions and can seem, to some, a vast missing of the point. But it should be noted that a great deal of the debate between Christian believers and atheists is often waged around the pragmatic criteria set out by James. For example, in 2010 former British prime minister Tony Blair and Christopher Hitchens (author of *god is not Great: How Religion Poisons Everything*) debated if Christianity has been, historically, a global force for good.

That was not a debate about metaphysics or theology. It was a debate about Jamesian criteria, about the fruits of religion. It illustrated how, once again, Christian apologetics has shifted away from theology to the social sciences.

James's pragmatism is also on display in how he approaches the reductionistic threat posed by functional accounts. Recall in Part 1 how functional accounts tend to be deflationary. By pointing to an underlying cause or mechanism, religious belief is explained. We saw this move at work in how Darwin's account explained the beauty of the peacock's tail by pointing out its function: how it aided in sexual and natural selection. James is keen in *Varieties* to address similar functional moves in approaching religious belief. He mainly focuses on biological and medical accounts of the origin of religious belief. For example, in Lecture 1, his most sustained argument along these lines, James criticizes what he calls "medical materialism," the attempt to explain religious belief by appealing to some underlying physical, neurological, or medical condition:

> Medical materialism finishes up Saint Paul by calling his vision on the road to Damascus a discharging lesion of the occipital cortex, he being an epileptic. It snuffs out Saint Teresa as an hysteric, Saint Francis of Assisi as an hereditary degenerate.... And medical materialism then thinks that the spiritual authority of all such personages is successfully undermined. (p. 19)

While Freud's account of religious belief is more psychological than medical, James's description captures the general thrust of functional accounts as an attempt to undermine religious experience by suggesting that religious belief has its origins at some lower level of analysis, be that level biological or psychological. But James rejects these accounts in *Varieties*, largely because of his pragmatic focus. The origins of belief have little bearing upon the practical usefulness of faith. James calls this his "empiricist criterion" which he summarizes with the pithy formulation "By their fruits we shall know them, not by their roots" (p. 26).

4.

It is this focus on fruits over roots that marks the approach in *Varieties* as a very different one to that found in *The Future of an Illusion*. Freud was very much concerned about getting to the roots. That is what psychoanalysis is all about, after all. And, James's focus on fruits notwithstanding, having found the root of religious belief to be one of existential consolation, Freud felt that he had exposed religious belief to be the illusion he knew it to be. James would not have wholly disagreed with Freud on this point, noting in *Varieties* that religious belief can be adopted to produce happiness. The main difference for James was that he did not necessarily see that as a bad thing. Happiness, joy and optimism are, pragmatically speaking, very good outcomes. Sometimes illusions are helpful.

Yet the fruits versus roots debate between Freud and James will not be our main interest in the chapters to follow. Our focus will be upon the issues carried over from Part 1. Specifically, after reviewing a great deal of theory and laboratory research in Part 1, we reached the conclusion that religious belief is involved in assuaging existential anxiety. If we follow Freud, it appears that religion is functioning as an existential narcotic, a psychological drug to help us repress or sublimate death anxiety.

The question this understanding poses for us is as follows: Is existential consolation the *sole* function of religious belief? Phrased differently, does religious belief necessarily imply existential repression? No doubt, as the TMT research has shown, religion can be and often is involved in existential repression. But is this *always* the case? Can religious belief exist alongside existential awareness? Can religious belief refuse to play the part of existential narcotic? And if so, what might that religious belief look like? What is the experience associated with an existentially *unrepressed* faith?

The issue here is not if Freud was right in his account of religious belief. As noted in Chapter 4, there is laboratory research backing Freud. Religious belief *is* involved in existential consolation. We should have no debate with Freud on that score. But the question we are turning toward, led by William James, is if Freud's analysis is giving us the whole story. While it is true that many religious believers will adopt and deploy religious belief to attenuate and manage existential anxiety, might there be some religious believers who, perhaps even consciously so, refuse to use their beliefs as forms of existential consolation? Might there be religious believers just as educated to reality as Freud, along with his fellow atheists, claimed he was?

We get no hint from Freud of such a possibility. *The Future of an Illusion* comes to us as a totalizing account. *All* religious belief, it seemed to Freud, was involved in existential consolation. That is the sole purpose—the function—of religious belief. And as Freud saw it, if beliefs are not offering existential consolation why would you believe in these illusions? What would be the point?

And there is the rub. What is the purpose of religious beliefs if they provide no existential comfort? Religious believers might have a lot to say in response, pointing to the vast array of reasons and purposes, beyond existential comfort, for why they believe what they believe. In fact, Freud does seem to worry, late in *The Future of an Illusion*, that his totalizing account, his reduction of all religious belief to a single function, might be called into question. For a moment, Freud admits late in *The Future of an Illusion* that a religious faith that eschewed existential consolation would, momentarily, prove his case to be overstated. But Freud quickly moves on to suggest that these existentially unrepressed believers would fade away over time. These existentially unrepressed believers would, according to Freud, go on to drop their religious illusions. Thus Freud's account would be vindicated in the end:

> In the long run nothing can withstand reason and experience, and the contradiction which religion offers to both is all too palpable. Even purified religious ideas cannot escape this fate, so long as they try to preserve anything of the consolation of religion. No doubt if they confine themselves to a belief in a

higher spiritual being, whose qualities are indefinable and whose purposes cannot be discerned, they will be proof against the challenge of science, but then they will also lose their hold on human interest. (p. 69)

No doubt, religious belief devoid of existential consolation would lose a great deal of its human interest. But few religions have ever contended that authentic spirituality would be commonplace and marketable. More, the interest of faith is not always driven by personal experiences. Most reflective Christians will admit that their own faith is often fickle, fragile, shallow, cowardly, and even inauthentic. This is why the lives of the saints are so alluring and inspiring. While our own personal faith might be nothing to be proud of, we wonder if an authentic faith is possible. And does this authentic faith have to posit, as Freud suggested, an indefinable God whose purposes cannot be discerned? The point being, an authentic faith, a faith that was not used as an existential narcotic, may indeed be rare. But that rarity does not make us lose interest. If anything, such a faith, perhaps because of its rarity, becomes an object of interest, even the goal of the entire religious journey.

This is where William James's notion of religious varieties comes in. Our questions going forward have less to do with the validity of Freud's account than about the totalizing nature of that account. Might there, instead, be religious varieties? And, importantly for our purposes, might there be religious varieties that engage differently with our existential predicament? Are there religious varieties that use religion as existential consolation and religious varieties that do not? For if such varieties existed, we would have, in hand, one answer to the Freudian critique, that while existential consolation is often implicated in religious belief, that consolation is not religion's sole and necessary function. Faith could not be reduced to this function. The point going forward is to ask if Freud's account should be taken to be to the whole story. For while there are, indeed, religious illusions, we should go on to investigate if there might also be religious varieties.

5.

Perhaps nowhere is James's interest in religious varieties more on display than in Lectures 4–7 when James describes two religious types, two distinct sorts of religious experiences. In Lecture 4 of *Varieties*, James (1902/1987, p. 79) takes his cue for this typology from a quote by Francis Newman who wrote that "God has two families of children on this earth, *the once-born* and *the twice-born*." Lectures 4–5 deal with the once-born, the religious experience James will call "healthy-minded." In Lectures 6–7, James turns to the twice-born, the type he calls "the sick soul."

Our interest in these types is that James's description of the healthy-minded religious experience shares strong similarities to the religious experience described in Part 1. That is, while there are positive aspects involved in the healthy-minded experience, James suggests that a large part of this experience is a refusal to confront the more difficult aspects of our existence, death in particular. In this, we find James describing a religious experience that compliments Freud's treatment in *The Future of an Illusion* and much of what was described in Part 1 about religion as existential consolation.

In light of the parallel between James's healthy-minded type and Freud's view concerning the function of religious belief, our interest is piqued about the existence of a second type of religious experience, what James calls the sick soul. Here we encounter variety, a religious experience that Freud did not describe in *The Future of an Illusion*, a religious type that might be more existentially open and aware relative to the healthy-minded type. Consequently, in the sick soul we find James positing a rival model of religious experience in *The Varieties of Religious Experience* compared to Freud's treatment in *The Future of an Illusion*. Where Freud appears to have lumped all religious experience into the type James called healthy-minded, James goes on to describe religious experiences that are not captured by Freud's totalizing and reductionistic analysis. And the reason for this appears to be James's contention that there is a religious experience—the sick soul—that is not driven by a need for existential consolation. In this sense, the existence and experience of the sick soul functions as a sort of rebuttal to Freud's contention that religious belief is solely and necessarily involved in existential consolation. The sick soul appears to be a religious experience that Freud failed to notice, consider, or wrestle with. Perhaps this was due to his belief, as noted above, that such an experience would "lack human interest." And yet, if William James is to be believed, the sick soul is very much of interest.

6.

In *Varieties* James (1902/1987) begins his analysis of the two families of God with the analysis of the healthy-minded believer. According to James, the healthy-minded believer is positive and optimistic, willfully and intentional so. The healthy-minded believer actively ignores or represses experiences that are morbid, dark, or disturbing. James describes the experience he has in mind: "[W]e give the name of healthy-mindedness to the tendency which looks on all things and sees that they are good" (pp. 85–86). James goes on to distinguish between two different origins of healthy-mindedness. The first is a dispositional, trait-like healthy-mindedness, an optimism and positive affectivity that is rooted in the person's biology and innate psychological wiring. James calls this an "involuntary" healthy-mindedness, the sort of congenial good cheer many people seem to have. By contrast, there is a more systematic sort of healthy-mindedness that is more conscious and intentional, an active choice to see the world as good: "Systematic healthy-mindedness, conceiving good as the essential and universal aspect of being, deliberately excludes evil from its field of vision" (p. 86).

This congenital or intentional blindness to evil may seem pathological. James (1902/1987) admits that this trick may be "a difficult feat to perform for one who is intellectually sincere with himself and honest about facts" (p. 86), and yet, given James's pragmatic focus (fruits over roots), there are real benefits to healthy-mindedness. For example,

James discusses religious rapture where suffering and even death are transformed into something glorious and good:

> Suffering may actually be gloried in, provided it be for the ideal cause, death may lose its sting, the grave its victory. In these states, the ordinary contrast of good and ill seems to be swallowed up in a higher denomination, an omnipotent excitement which engulfs the evil, and which the human being welcomes as the crowning experience of his life. (pp. 87–88)

This, in many ways, is the allure of religion, the ability to transcend suffering, evil and death. Consequently, James concludes "the systematic cultivation of healthy-mindedness as a religious attitude is therefore consonant with important currents in human nature, and is anything but absurd. In fact, we all do cultivate it more or less" (p. 88).

That said, James does go on to describe healthy-mindedness as largely engaged in denial, obfuscation, and avoidance. The treatment here is very similar to Freud's. James (1902/1987) suggests that the happiness of healthy-mindedness manifests a "blindness and insensibility to opposing facts given as its instinctive weapon for self-protection against disturbance" (p. 86). This notion of religion as an "instinctive weapon of self-protection" against emotional disturbance sounds very Freudian. More, the mechanism of this self-protection is one of denial. In the face of evil and suffering, the healthy-minded believer "must ignore it" and "shut his eyes to it and hush it up" (p. 86). In Lecture 6, James summarizes the healthy-minded dynamic:

> [Healthy-minded] religion directs [the believer] to settle his scores with the more evil aspects of the universe by systematically declining to lay them to heart or make much of them, by ignoring them in his reflective calculations, or even, on occasion, by denying outright that they exist. (p. 121)

James goes on to suggest that this tendency toward "deliberately minimizing evil" (p. 124) can become almost delusional where "in some individuals optimism can become quasi-pathological" (p. 82). James even echoes Marx's infamous religion-as-narcotic formulation when he says that healthy-mindedness can appear to be "a kind of congenital anesthesia" (p. 82).

In summary, what we find in James' treatment of the healthy-minded religious experience is something we have already described in great deal in Part 1: religious belief as a form of instinctive self-protection against emotional disturbance. This protection is accomplished through repression and denial. It is an intentional form of blindness in the face of life to produce positive affect and existential equanimity.

7.

After describing the experience of healthy-mindedness, James turns in Lectures 6 and 7 to the experience of the sick soul. Here we encounter a religious experience that sounds very different from anything Freud considered in *The Future of an Illusion*. As such, the sick soul may be a black swan for Freud's totalizing account, a counter-example that suggests that religious experience is not necessarily involved in existential repression.

If the healthy-minded experience is typified by a blindness that seeks to minimize evil, the sick soul is a religious type involved in maximizing evil. According to James (1902/1987), the sick soul is driven "by the persuasion that the evil aspects of our life are of its very essence, and that the world's meaning most comes home to use when we lay them most to heart" (p. 124). Sick souls are those "who cannot so swiftly throw off the burden of the consciousness of evil," and consequently sick souls are "fated to suffer from [evil's] presence" (p. 126).

As we can see, there is an emotional cost to this existential awareness; the descriptor "sick" is used for a reason. Healthy-minded believers achieve their sanguine stance via denial and repression, so it stands to reason that we will suffer, psychologically, when we allow difficult existential material access to our conscious experience. As James describes in *Varieties*, "if we admit that evil is an essential part of our being and the key to the interpretation of our life, we load ourselves down with a difficulty that has always proved burdensome" (p. 124).

Importantly, in light of the issues raised in Part 1, James (1902/1987) considers the sick soul to be an example of existential awareness. For example, the sick soul lives with a constant awareness of death, that at the "back of everything is the great spectre of universal death, the all encompassing blackness" (p. 131). Given this death awareness, the sick soul knows that "all natural happiness thus seems infected with a contradiction" because "the breath of the sepulcher surrounds it." Where the healthy-minded type pushes death out of consciousness, the sick soul is preoccupied with these existential realizations. The issue here is not just about active suffering. No, the preoccupation of the sick soul is *the existential predicament* posed by our finite vulnerability in the face of death: "The fact that we can die, that we can be ill at all, is what perplexes us; the fact that we now for a moment live and are well is irrelevant to the perplexity" (p. 132). In the face of death, the sick soul eschews the existential oblivion of the health-minded. This means living with the awareness that death is an ever-present reality. As James writes:

> Let sanguine healthy-mindedness do its best with its strange power of living in the moment and ignoring and forgetting, still the evil background is really there to be thought of, and the skull will grin in at the banquet. (p. 132)

Here, then, is a religious experience unlike anything we find in *The Future of an Illusion*. There is no denial of death at work here. Here is a religious experience that seems intent on keeping death and evil firmly in view, an existentially aware and unrepressed religious experience.

And while there is an emotional cost involved in this existential awareness, James suggests that this existential honesty makes the sick soul resilient in the face of difficult life experiences. The illusions created by healthy-minded blindness may work in the short-term or when life is going smoothly, but such a religious stance is existentially vulnerable. Death and suffering can puncture the religion illusion. By contrast, the existential openness of the sick soul means that there is little in life or death that can surprise or upset. With death as a daily object in consciousness, there is little shock for the sick soul when death or tragedy shows up on life's doorstep. For the sick soul, death never shows up unannounced. This is why James (1902/1987) describes the sick soul as more profound than healthy-mindedness (p. 128); the sick soul experience is "a more complicated key" to the meaning of pain, fear and human helplessness. Here is James's final verdict on the existential resiliency of the two types:

> The method of averting one's attention from evil, and living simply in the light of good is splendid as long as it will work. . . . But it breaks down impotently as soon as melancholy comes; as even though one be quite free from melancholy one's self, there is no doubt that healthy-mindedness is inadequate as a philosophical doctrine, because the evil facts which it refuses positively to account for are a genuine portion of reality; and they may after all be the best key to life's significance, and possibly the only openers of our eyes to the deepest levels of truth. (p. 152)

The sick soul, by eschewing existential consolation, allows the shadow of death access to consciousness. This awareness comes with an emotional price tag. Again, James calls this religious experience "sick" for a reason—it is an existential sickness, what the existential philosophers call *angst*. Consequently, this is no easy path to travel for a religious believer, a path that seeks to maximize rather than minimize the most difficult aspects of life. So why do it? Why live religious life as a sick soul? Because, James suggests, such a path may be the only route to the "deepest levels of truth," the only way to obtain the "key to life's significance." Thus, in spite of the emotional price tag and cost, many religious believers appear to go in this direction—to pursue faith as a sick soul.

8.

Here, then, with the sick soul, we find something strange. At the very least Freud would have found it strange. Is it possible, as James suggests, that there are religious believers who, pace Freud, eschew existential consolation? Believers who, rather than denying death, seek to keep death firmly in view?

And even if we admit the theoretical possibility of the sick soul, is such an experience psychologically and theologically coherent? What does it mean to say a religious belief system is "existentially open" or "existentially aware"?

These are the questions that will occupy us for the rest of this book. For now, however, we simply want to note the intriguing possibility offered to us by William James in *The Varieties of Religious Experience*. Where Freud argued that religious experience was inherently involved in existential consolation, James suggests that some believers may eschew this consolation. Freud reduces religious experience to illusion while James posits religious varieties. James agrees with Freud that religious belief can be involved in existential repression. James's description of the self-protective functions of healthy-minded blindness anticipated key points of Freud's argument twenty-five years later in *The Future of an Illusion*. But where Freud restricts his account to these self-protective illusions, James goes on to posit another, more existentially aware type—the sick soul.

Given this contrast, critical to our discussions going forward, let me suggest that William James and Sigmund Freud are posing two rival hypotheses concerning the nature and function of religious belief: illusion versus varieties. Both thinkers agree that religious belief can be used as a form of existential repression and consolation. And, as we have seen in the TMT research, there is good experimental evidence supporting this case: religious believers do appear to deploy their beliefs to assuage, repress, or manage existential anxiety. But Freud and James differ regarding whether religious belief is solely or necessarily deployed as an existential defense mechanism, as an existential narcotic. James, in positing the experience of the sick soul, is suggesting in contrast to Freud that some religious believers are existentially open, unrepressed, and aware. While these sick souls pay an emotional price for this awareness, they appear to gain things as well (e.g., resiliency in the face of suffering or death).

Simplifying, we might represent the rival hypotheses of James and Freud by conceptualizing how they envision the overlap between existential illusion and religious experience. In Figure 3, we see how Freud views religious belief as wholly overlapping with existential illusion. Religious belief simply is an illusion. However, the relationship here is not an identity relationship as Freud might have suspected. Religious belief, following the existential work of thinkers like Ernest Becker, is best thought of as a *subset*, a type of existential illusion. All cultural worldviews, following Becker and the TMT research, whether religious or non-religious are implicated as forms of existential repression—routes to lives of significance and meaning in face of death. In short, on the left side of the figure we find a visual summary of the religious experience described in Part 1: religion as one of many existential illusions adopted and deployed to handle existential anxiety in daily living.

In comparison, on the right we find James willing to see religious experience as partly and perhaps even significantly overlapping with existential illusion. This is the area of religious experience James described as "healthy-minded," an experience parallel to Freud's account in *The Future of an Illusion*. However, as can be seen, James argues that religious experience is not wholly captured or reduced to existential illusion. The experience of the sick soul posits varieties, religious experiences that fall *outside* the domain of existential illusion, repression, and consolation.

In light of these rival models, how are we to proceed? Given our discussions in Part 1, we know there is evidence for Freud's contention that religious belief is involved in existential consolation. So how might we assess the thesis that there are religious varieties, some of which are less engaged in existential repression? Before getting a start on this

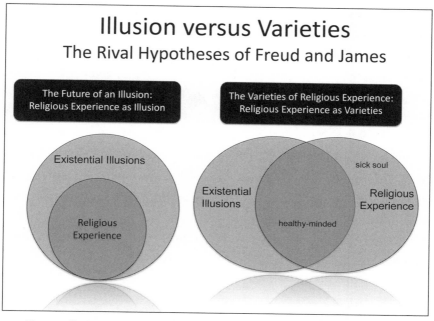

Figure 3. Illusion versus varieties: the rival hypotheses of Freud and James.

question we have to pause a bit to address a more fundamental question raised above. Specifically, before any comparing and contrasting of James's varieties begins, is the experience of the sick soul psychologically and theologically coherent? Some might argue that the sick soul is simply a theoretical entity, an idea with no real correspondence in the lives of actual religious believers. Can real-life religious believers, and our focus will be on the Christian experience, be characterized as sick souls? And if so, what might this existentially aware faith stance look like? Such questions will be the subject of the next chapter, the attempt to ground the sick soul experience within the lived experience of a particular faith tradition. Once this grounding has occurred, psychologically and theologically, we will be positioned, from a social-scientific stance, to create measures that can help us distinguish between the "two families of God" in a particular faith community. From there we can then proceed with comparing and contrasting the religious types (should they exist). Christianity will be our test case, our laboratory.

This process—grounding the sick soul within a particular faith tradition (Chapter 6), leading to assessment strategies (Chapter 7), followed by empirical comparisons of the religious types (Part 3)—will allow us to evaluate the rival theories of James and Freud. Specifically, if Freud is correct we would expect to see little if any difference between the religious varieties in tests assessing how the different types interact with existential stimuli. However, if James is correct, we should see subgroups emerge within the Christian population, each handling existential stimuli in very different ways. Such an outcome would signal diversity within the Christian faith, providing evidence for varieties over illusion.

So, to begin this process, we must wrestle with and ground the sick-soul experience within our religious test case—Christianity.

Chapter 6

SICK SOULS, WINTER CHRISTIANS, AND SAINTS OF DARKNESS

1.

ON SEPTEMBER 26, 1928, AGNES GONXHA BOJAXHIU, THEN 18, left her home in Skopje to join the Institute of the Blessed Virgin Mary in Ireland. In 1947, in a letter to her archbishop, Agnes recounted how the voice of Jesus had consistently come to her, asking for her to create the Missionaries of Charity to reach out to the poor of India. As Agnes recounted it, the voice asked and demanded the following:

> I want Indian Missionary Sisters of Charity—who would be My fire of love amongst the very poor—the sick—the dying—the little street children—The poor I want you to bring to me—and the Sisters that would offer their lives as victims of my love—would bring these souls to Me. You are I know the most unacceptable person, weak & sinful, but just because you are that I want to use you, for my Glory! Wilt thou refuse? (Kolodiejchuk, 2007, p. 49)

During the time of her calling, Agnes identified her experiences with Jesus as "so much union" (Kolodiejchuk, 2007, p. 83). Agnes described this mystical union with Christ as an experience of "love," "trust," "sweet-ness," and "consolation."

In 1948, on December 21, having finally obtained official approval for the establishment of the Sisters of Mercy, Agnes entered the slums of India to begin her work. After so much effort, petition and preparation, she, had finally fulfilled the call of God. She had obeyed the voice of Jesus. But suddenly, mysteriously, and painfully, that voice suddenly went silent.

For the next forty years, Agnes experienced a profound sense of loss and abandonment that shook the very foundations of her faith. Externally, the work of the Missionaries flourished and eventually gained international notoriety. Agnes herself became an iconic and inspirational figure, the very picture of Christ on earth. But internally, Agnes struggled with feelings of loss, spiritual grief, and desolation. Decades after decade she penned letters of confession to her spiritual supervisors, letters of heart-wrenching honesty:

July 3, 1959
In the darkness. . . .

Lord, my God, who am I that You should forsake me? The child of your love—and now become as the most hated one—the one You have thrown away as unwanted—unloved. I call, I cling, I want—and there is no One to answer—no One on Whom I can cling—no, No One.—Alone. The darkness is so dark—and I am alone.—Unwanted, forsaken.—The loneliness of the heart that wants love is unbearable.—Where is my faith?—even deep down, right in, there is nothing but emptiness & dark-ness.—My God—how painful is this unknown pain. It pains without ceasing.—I have no faith.—I dare not utter the words & thoughts that crowd in my heart—& make me suffer untold agony. So many unanswered questions live within me—I am afraid to uncover them—because of the blasphemy—If there be God,—please forgive me. (Kolodiejchuk, 2007, pp. 186–187)

September 1959
Part of My Confession Today
My own Jesus,

They say people in hell suffer eternal pain because of the loss of God—they would go through all that suffering if they had just a little hope of possessing God.—In my soul I feel just that terrible pain of loss—of God not wanting me—of God not being God—of God not really existing (Jesus, please forgive my blasphemies—I have been told to write everything). That darkness surrounds me on all sides—I can't lift my soul to God..

In my heart there is no faith—no love—no trust—there is so much pain—the pain of longing, the pain of not being wanted.—I want God with all the powers of my soul—and yet there between us—there is terrible separation.—I don't pray any longer. (Kolodiejchuk, 2007, pp. 192–193)

Much later, forty years after beginning her ministry, Agnes did begin to re-experience the presence of God. But as William James observed about the twice born, Agnes never fully returned to the bliss of her first encounter with God. Agnes's letters reveal that she began to experience the *absence* of God as a form of God's *presence*. For Agnes, the experience of God's loss and abandonment, the hole God had left in her life, became like a photographic negative. It was an inversion, a loss that hinted at God's existence. In all this, Agnes began to see her experience of abandonment as a mystical union with Christ in his experience of abandonment and god-forsakenness at Golgotha:

October 1961

No, Father [Neuner], I am not alone.—I have His darkness—I have His pain—I have the terrible longing for God—to love and not to be loved. I know I have Jesus. (Kolodiejchuk, 2007, p. 224)

Perhaps paradoxically, Agnes experienced God as pain and darkness, a longing to love but not being loved in return.

Late in life, Agnes, best known to the world as Mother Teresa of Calcutta, began to address the worldwide recognition that she was a living saint, and that, upon her death, she would become a candidate for sainthood within the Catholic Church. That Mother Teresa took this recognition in stride and with great humility is not surprising. But the way in which Mother Teresa chose to characterize her eventual sainthood is startling. Summing up, this exemplary Christian witness who had dedicated her life to serving the poorest of the poor, described her spiritual walk in the following words: "If I ever become a saint—I will surely be one of 'darkness'" Should read (Kolodiejchuk, 2007, p. 230).

2.

Many were startled when, after her death, a selection of Mother Teresa's private letters to her confessors was published in the book *Mother Teresa: Come Be My Light* (Kolodiejchuk, 2007). There was shock and confusion that this saint among saints, this iconic witness of the Christian faith, would have experienced such spiritual desolation and faith struggles. *Time* magazine (Van Biema, 2007) put Mother Teresa on its cover with the byline "The Secret Life of Mother Teresa." The article inside *Time* was titled "Mother Teresa's Crisis of Faith."

While the *depth* of Mother Teresa's dark night of the soul was startling, what was perhaps equally troubling was the duration of the experience. Religious believers expect to go through seasons of spiritual dryness. These might last for months or even a few years. But Mother Teresa's experience of darkness lasted for 40 years. It was hard for many to reconcile both the depth and duration of Mother Teresa's experience of god-forsakenness with the Nobel Laureate and spiritual hero we knew her to be. Was it possible that an exemplary Christian life, a life as close to the example of Jesus as we can imagine, could be characterized by doubt, spiritual darkness, and feeling unloved and abandoned by God?

3.

I have begun this chapter with the story of Mother Teresa for two rea-sons. The first reason has to do with engaging the question that ended the last chapter, the question concerning the spiritual coherence of William James's description of the sick soul experience. What would religious faith look like, experientially and theologically, if it were not engaged in existential repression or consolation? The experience of Mother Teresa helps us enter into this discussion. Our response of sur-prise upon hearing about Mother Teresa's spiritual struggles suggests that we find something paradoxical in her story. There seems to be a mismatch between her actions, the public life we knew and admired, and her private subjective religious experience of god-forsakenness. These two do not seem to go together. We expect religious belief to provide comfort, peace, and consolation. But we do not expect religious belief to be a source and location of distress and pain. Why believe if it is hurting you? We expect faith to reduce pain, not cause it. Overall, this feeling that something is paradoxical and amiss in the experience of the sick soul and Mother Teresa suggests that our working models, assumptions and and theories about the faith experience may be incom-plete or overly simplistic. Consequently, we may need to revisit some wrongheaded or simplistic assumptions about what the faith experi-ence actually looks like, experientially speaking. We need a model that can help us understand the full range of the faith experience, both of the healthy-minded and the sick souls. We need a model that helps us understand Mother Teresa's experience of darkness as a product of faith rather than as something paradoxical and strange.

The second reason for beginning this chapter with the story of Mother Teresa is that our discussions from here on out will make a clear turn toward the Christian faith experience. We will begin to focus a great deal upon Christian theology and belief, often referring to the faith experiences found in the Old and New Testaments. Up to this point our considerations have focused upon religious belief in the abstract.

While both Freud and James lived in Christian contexts, their treatments of religious belief in *The Future of an Illusion* and *The Varieties of Religious Experience* were generalized, although we can assume they had Christianity in their minds as the regulating exemplar of what they meant by religion. More, our treatment of the existential literature to this point has cast religion as a part of a cultural worldview. Again, this has been a generalized approach meant to encompass every world religion (along with any smaller religious sects that have or will ever exist).

But in what follows, we will move more deeply into the particularities of the Christian faith. As mentioned at the end of the last chapter, this grounding is necessary if we are to create specific empirical tests comparing the models of Freud and James, to learn if we are dealing with illusions or varieties. To generate testable predictions regarding the models proposed by James and Freud, we will need to describe, in great detail, the healthy-minded and the sick soul experience as they manifest themselves within a particular religious context. In our case, we will need to understand the Christian faith in enough detail so that we can understand how Christian belief might be deployed or rearranged to handle troubling existential material (e.g., death anxiety). These theological maneuvers will be highly particular to the religious tradition under consideration. We would not expect Muslim, Hindu, Buddhist, or Jewish persons to achieve existential consolation (if that is what is going on) in exactly the same way, theologically speaking.

Therefore, to understand how existential consolation may or may not operate within any given faith system, we need to immerse ourselves within particular faith experiences to understand belief from the *inside*. In this our task is somewhat anthropological. We ask: How do these particular people (Christians in our case) deploy their particular beliefs (Christian theology) to handle existential questions? Following William James, we will initially posit that the Christian population is not homogeneous in its religious experience. We will posit two families of faith: a Christian experience corresponding to James's healthy-mindedness and one corresponding to the sick soul. If James is correct, we should see some Christian believers deploy Christian belief in ways aimed at maximizing existential consolation. These would be Christians of the healthy-minded type. In contrast, if James is to be believed, we should also see Christian believers deploy Christian belief in a way that eschews existential consolation. These would be Christian believers of the sick soul type. To understand the nuances that might distinguish these two sorts of believers we will need to acquire a fair degree of facility in handling Christian belief and experience. This chapter and the next will be aimed at providing a description of the Christian faith that will allow us to unpack the healthy-minded and sick soul experiences within the Christian faith experience. And with these characterizations in hand, along with associated means of assessment, we will be poised to put the rival theories of Sigmund Freud and William James to the test.

4.

When we read about the faith experience of the sick soul in *The Varieties of Religious Experience* or read through the letters recounting Mother Teresa's faith struggles, many of us wonder if these experiences can be described as examples of faith. Again, there seems to be something paradoxical about a faith experience dominated by doubt and an experience of god-forsakenness. But it is possible, as mentioned above, that this paradox is produced by an overly simplistic model of faith, a model that fails to understand how negativity relates to faith and may actually be a sign of a mature and robust faith.

This failure to understand how negativity can relate to faith is somewhat curious for the Christian tradition as a biblical witness if full of expressions of negativity, complaint, lament, and protest. The Bible contains a chorus of sick souls. In light of this material, it is odd to find Christians surprised by Mother Teresa's faith journey or puzzled at William James's description of the sick soul, a faith experience that seems to maximize evil by focusing on the troubling, painful, and ambiguous aspects of life. Consider this assessment from the

Old Testament scholar Walter Brueggemann (1984) about how many Christian communities fail to use the psalms of lament and complaint in the book of Psalms to wrestle with and recognize that the world is often disordered, painful, violent, and unjust:

> It is a curious fact that the church has, by and large, continued to sing songs of orientation in a world increasingly experienced as disoriented. . . . It is my judgment that this action of the church is less an evangelical defiance guided by faith, and much more a frightened, numb denial and deception that does not want to acknowledge or experience the disorientation of life. . . . Such a denial and cover-up, which I take it to be, is an odd inclination for passionate Bible users, given the larger number of psalms that are songs of lament, protest, and complaint about an incoherence that is experienced in the world. . . . I believe that serious religious use of the lament psalms has been minimal because we have believed that faith does not mean to acknowledge and embrace negativity. (pp. 51–52)

What is interesting about Brueggemann's assessment is that it helps connect our prior discussions about existential defensiveness in Parts 1 and 2 with how a particular faith group, Christianity in this instance, rearranges its faith—its worship, its use of the sacred text, its theology—to accomplish existential repression, to achieve what James called the healthy-minded experience. An example of this, according to Brueggemann, is how biblical material (e.g., the lament psalms) is marginalized or ignored by the faith community. This avoidance of certain biblical material is motivated by "a frightened, numb denial and deception that does not want to acknowledge or experience the disorientation of life." What we see in this is how a faith community can manage its theology and reading of Scripture to avoid difficult existential confrontations, creating a "denial and cover-up" of a life that is painful and disordered.

In the Christian tradition, then, one symptom of existential defensiveness is an avoidance of experiences best captured in the psalms of lament, complaint, and protest, psalms that express a sense of god-forsakenness, the experience of the sick soul within the Christian tradition. These are the psalms of darkness that capture the journey of Mother Teresa. Consequently, following Brueggemann, when we see an avoidance of the experience of complaint, a refusal to admit to "incoherence that is experienced in the world," we can begin to suspect that the Bible is being used or deployed to achieve emotional and existential consolation. The background assumption of this move is that true faith "does not mean to acknowledge and embrace negativity." The motivating assumption is that doubt and complaint is antithetical to faith; the Bible must be used to answer questions and attenuate doubt rather than be used as a means to ask questions and express one's doubt. This model of faith is the underlying supposition that makes the experiences of the sick soul and of Mother Teresa seem so strange and paradoxical. Are not doubt and complaint symptoms of a loss of faith?

Perhaps not. Staying with Brueggemann (1984), we see that he goes on to push back on the assumption that negativity and faith are antithetical:

> We have thought that acknowledgement of negativity was somehow an act of unfaith, as though the very speech about it conceded too much about God's "loss of control." . . . The point to be urged here is this: The use of these "psalms of darkness" may be judged by the world to be *acts of unfaith and failure*, but for the trusting community, their use is *an act of bold faith*. (p. 52)

What we find in this analysis is something akin to James's description of the sick soul, a religious faith that acknowledges negativity, that embraces doubt, and that is honest about its experience of god-forsakenness. And yet these experiences are not symptoms of unfaith but are rather acts of a "bold faith."

Again, this juxtaposition—doubt and faith—might seem nonsensical or paradoxical. Such a notion might seem fine in theory, but experientially speaking can the two conditions be held together? To begin to make progress with this question we might simply start with an examination of the phenomenology expressed within the complaint psalms themselves.

5.

Walter Brueggemann (1984) suggests that the psalms provide a way to connect religious speech to religious experience. We can examine the psalms as a form of phenomenological data and observe how the words of the psalms capture, express, and describe a religious experience. Consequently, the psalms might provide some illumination for how complaint and faith might be held together, experientially speaking.

Overall, Brueggemann groups the religious experiences of the psalms under three broad categories: experiences of orientation, disorientation, and new orientation.

Psalms of orientation reflect a well-ordered and predictable world. This is largely because God is experienced as reliable and dependable. Moral symmetry is an indicator of this world. The good are rewarded and the wicked are punished. In this well-ordered and morally coherent universe, heartfelt praise and sense of well-being predominate. Psalms of orientation include 1, 33, 131, and 145. Psalm 1 is an excellent example of moral symmetry creating an existentially coherent experience:

> Blessed is the one
> who does not walk in step with the wicked
> or stand in the way that sinners take
> or sit in the company of mockers,
> but whose delight is in the law of the LORD,
> and who meditates on his law day and night.
> That person is like a tree planted by streams of water,
> which yields its fruit in season
> and whose leaf does not wither—
> whatever they do prospers.

Not so the wicked!
They are like chaff
that the wind blows away.
Therefore the wicked will not stand in the judgment,
nor sinners in the assembly of the righteous.
For the LORD watches over the way of the righteous,
but the way of the wicked leads to destruction.

The universe of Psalm 1 is existentially comfortable. God is present, reliable, and benevolent; he ensures that virtuous life projects are protected and reach fruition. Life, thus, is rendered coherent and meaningful. This then is a psalm that would be closely identified with the healthy-minded experience, a psalm of optimism and positivity, a psalm that maximizes goodness in the world.

To be clear, by linking this psalm to the healthy-minded experience, I am not saying that the experience of this psalm is inherently dishonest, existentially speaking. There are times in life, times of joy and prosperity, in which the speech of Psalm 1 is well suited and reflective of an objective reality. The issue here, as noted by Brueggemann, is when the experience of Psalm 1 and its use within Christian theology and worship is used as a "cover-up . . . a frightened, numb denial and deception that does not want to acknowledge or experience the disorientation of life." In some instances, Psalm 1 might be used as a form of existential repression, a theological assertion that the world is morally coherent when, in fact, the truth of the matter is that the wicked are doing quite well and the virtuous are getting trampled underfoot. Sung as a form of denial, Psalm 1 could help a Christian community pretend that the world is better than it really is.

The goal in using the psalm in this manner, as a way of hiding the world from view, would be to create a faith experience that buffers us from a harsh reality, creating a sense of comfort, peace, positivity, and well-being. Perhaps the best indicator of this repressive use of the psalms of orientation is not the use of these psalms per se, but rather their exclusive use. This gets to the heart of Brueggemann's criticism, the worry that if a faith community *exclusively* uses psalms of orientation they are failing to acknowledge that the world is full of brokenness and suffering. This is the use of the psalms of orientation that begins to look like "a frightened, numb denial."

In contrast to the psalms of orientation, there are religious experiences grouped under psalms of disorientation. The experience of disorientation involves a disintegration of the predictable structures in the world. Life here is rendered meaningless, incoherent, or absurd. In these experiences, God is encountered as absent or, in extreme cases, antagonistic. This is why these are psalms of complaint, lament, and protest. God is no longer present or willing to make life meaningful and coherent. Or, in extreme cases, it is God who is the destructive force, existentially speaking: making life absurd, incomprehensible or chaotic. In the psalms of disorientation, our ability to make sense or create meaning has disintegrated and God is held accountable for allowing this to happen. A sign that this existential disintegration has occurred is moral asymmetry: the wicked are flourishing and the righteous are suffering, even cruelly. The causal links between virtue and human flourishing have gone missing, creating the problem theologians call theodicy, the perennial question about why God allows evil and suffering in the world. These then are the psalms of the sick soul experience, psalms that maximize evil by focusing on the disorder, existential incoherence, and suffering in life.

Examples of complaint psalms are 13, 35, 86, and 88. I want to focus in on the phenomenology of these psalms as they help illustrate how complaint and faith can be held together in a unified faith experience. The psalms illustrate how, in the words of Brueggemann, complaint and doubt can be an act of bold faith. Consider Psalm 13:

How long, LORD? Will you forget me forever?
How long will you hide your face from me?
How long must I wrestle with my thoughts

and day after day have sorrow in my heart?
How long will my enemy triumph over me?
Look on me and answer, LORD my God.
Give light to my eyes, or I will sleep in death,
and my enemy will say, "I have overcome him,"
and my foes will rejoice when I fall.
But I trust in your unfailing love;
my heart rejoices in your salvation.
I will sing the LORD's praise,
for he has been good to me.

Stanzas one and two are expressions of complaint. Moral asymmetry is on display. The wicked, the enemy of the psalmist, is triumphant. And the psalmist takes his complaint to God, a God who should correct this moral situation and restore the moral symmetry. But suddenly, in the midst of this complaint, without preamble or transitional material, the psalmist moves, in the final stanza, into words of praise, faith, and trust. This shift in tone creates a kind of whiplash for the reader. As Brueggemann notes, this plea to praise movement, so common in the complaint psalms, is one of the most jarring, unexpected, and inexplicable transitions in the Bible: "This movement from *plea* to *praise* is one of the most startling in all of Old Testament literature" (1984, p. 56). Even when this movement is absent, as in extreme cases like Psalm 88 where no movement to praise concludes the psalm, the psalmist still prays; communion and connection with God is still sought after. Faith, as the desire for engagement, is still on display.

To be sure, social scientists would be hesitant to treat the plea to praise movement within the psalms of disorientation as conclusive data regarding the experiential coherence of the sick soul experience. Still, the psalms of disorientation raise the possibility that faith and complaint may not be, on closer inspection, antithetical. In fact, as Brueggemann suggested, there is a sort of heroic character, a boldness, about a faith emerging out of the depths of such darkness. Cast against the backdrop of her private faith struggles, Mother Teresa's life seems that much more amazing. Doubt and complaint can be incorporated into the faith experience. As Brueggemann concludes:

> [The] sequence of *complaint-praise* is a necessary and legitimate way with God, each part in its own, appropriate time. But one moment is not less faithful than the other. . . . In the full relationship, *the season of plea* must be taken as seriously as *the season of praise*. (1984, pp. 56–57)

6.

The psalms of disorientation suggest that the sick soul experience is known to the Christian tradition. More, the psalms of darkness suggest that, experientially speaking, faith and negativity can be held together. Faith and existential distress are not antithetical. Still the psalms, while suggestive, are not hard data. So we wonder if the coexistence of plea and praise is typical of ordinary Christian believers. To help shed some light on this issue, let us turn to some psychological research that I have been intimately involved with.

For many decades, psychology of religion researchers have intensively studied the Christian believer's relationship with God. Much of the recent work in this area has borrowed from object-relations (e.g., Hall, Brokaw, Edwards, & Pike, 1998; Hill & Hall, 2002) and attachment perspectives (e.g., Beck & McDonald, 2004; McDonald, Beck, Allison, & Norsworthy, 2005; Rowatt & Kirkpatrick, 2002) regarding the love relationship with God. To briefly summarize for those outside of the discipline of psychology, these theories use models of the child and caregiver experience, the emotional bonds that exist between parents and children, and apply them to the relationship with God. Might our early experiences with parents create relational and emotional schemas that go on to shape our experience with God? On the face of it, this seems plausible as the dominant metaphor in the Bible regarding relationship with God is a parent and child metaphor:

[God speaking to his people:] "As a mother comforts her child so I will comfort you." (Isaiah 66:13)

[God's people speaking to God:] "Yet, O Lord, you are our Father." (Isaiah 64:8)

[Jesus teaching his followers how to address God in prayer:] "Our Father in heaven, hallowed be your name." (Matthew 6:9)

[God comparing his love for his people with a mother's love for her child:] "Can a mother forget the baby at her breast and have no compassion on the child she has born?" (Isaiah 49:15)

[Jesus comparing his love for the people of Jerusalem to the protective behavior of a mother hen:] "O Jerusalem, Jerusalem . . . how I have often longed to gather your children together, as a hen gathers her chicks under her wings." (Luke 13:34)

[God comparing his love for his people to a parent teaching her child to walk:] "When Israel was a child, I loved him. . . . It was I who taught Ephraim to walk, taking them in my arms." (Hosea 11:1, 3)

[God comparing his love for his people to a parent raising a rebellious child:] "For the Lord has spoken: I reared children and brought them up, but they have rebelled against me." (Isaiah 1:2)

The argument here is that the attachment bond with parents creates an emotional and relational framework that allows us to understand how we can be in a love relationship with God. The influential childhood attachment researcher Mary Ainsworth (1985) delineated four features of the attachment bond. We might consider this to be the basic alphabet and grammar of human love relationships:

Proximity Maintenance: We wish to be near or close to our attachment figures.

135

Separation Anxiety: When separated from an attachment figure we experience distress.

Secure Base of Exploration: The attachment figure functions as an emotional "home" that confers confidence and risk-taking.

Haven of Safety: When hurt or fearful or distressed we go to the attachment figure for protection, healing, and comfort.

These four aspects of the attachment bond are readily seen in the parent and child relationship. And as Lee Kirkpatrick (1999) observed, there seem to be clear parallels with the God and believer attachment:

Proximity Maintenance:
Although God is not located in time or space, believers do express their relationship with God with spatial language. We can be close to God or feel distant from God. And, given this language, believers express the desire to be close, near, or intimate with God. Images of this intimacy often are understood as being held or embraced or touched by God.

Separation Anxiety:
In the New Tesatment (cf. Mark 15.34), Jesus cries out from the cross "My God, my God, why have you forsaken me?" Such a sentiment captures the distress experienced by believers when they feel separated from God. Generally, this distress is expressed in the language of lament, which captures the emotional devastation associated with being abandoned or orphaned by God.

Secure Base of Exploration:
God is often experienced as home, our True Home. Further, God is experienced as a source of strength and confidence that energizes the believer. "I can do all things through Christ who strengthens me." (Philippians 4:13)

Haven of Safety:
When in distress or in need of comfort believers turn to
God and seek out God's presence. And this presence, when
experienced, is generally found to be healing and a source of
peace and security. "Thy rod and thy staff they comfort me."
(Psalm 23:4b KJV)

The close parallels between the parent and God relationships found
in the attachment literature harkens back to Freud's argument in *The
Future of an Illusion* in which God is believed to be a projection of the
human parent, and as such, allows the believer to project insecurities
rooted in infantile helplessness onto a Cosmic Father. However, our
concern here has to do with how the attachment bond can be emotionally ambivalent. This becomes clearer when we consider how attachment researchers have used the early attachment bond with parents to
describe the love experience between romantic partners. During the
late '80 and early '90s, researchers began to assess aspects of the attachment bond in adulthood love relationships (Bartholomew & Horowitz,
1991; Hazan & Shaver, 1987, 1990), suggesting that the emotional schemas formed with childhood caregivers are imported into subsequent
love relationships. In the love relationships between romantic partners,
we continue to see the four features of the attachment bond: proximity maintenance, separation anxiety, secure base of exploration, and
haven of safety. And, perhaps not surprisingly, beyond the parent and
child metaphor the second most common metaphor used in the Bible
to describe the relationship with God is an adulthood love relationship,
the attachment between a husband and a wife:

[A description of God's love for his people:] "As a bridegroom
rejoices over his bride, so will your God rejoice over you."
(Isaiah 62:5)

[A description of God's relationship with his people:] "For
your Maker is your husband—the LORD Almighty is his
name." (Isaiah 54:5)

[An image of Jesus, the Lamb, marrying his people, the Church:] "'For the wedding of the Lamb has come, and his bride has made herself ready. Fine linen, bright and clean, was given her to wear.' Fine linen stands for the righteous acts of the saints." (Revelation 19:7–8)

[A continuation of the above image from the book of Revelation, where the people of God are compared to the New Jerusalem:] "I saw the Holy City, the new Jerusalem, coming down out of heaven from God, prepared as a bride beautifully dressed for her husband." (Revelation 21:2)

[The New Testament author, Paul, comparing marital love with Christ's love for his church:] "Husbands, love your wives, just as Christ loved the church and gave himself up for her. " (Ephesians 5:25)

We can take this even further, as it seems clear that the four features of the attachment bond—proximity, separation anxiety, secure base, haven of safety—are also intimately involved in the love relationship between friends. Following form, we find the Bible describing relationship with God using this third attachment metaphor: a love relationship between friends:

[Jesus to his disciples:] "I have called you friends." (John 15:15)

[A New Testament description of Abraham's relationship with God:] "And the scripture was fulfilled that says, 'Abraham believed God, and it was credited to him as righteousness,' and he was called God's friend.'" (James 2:23)

[A description of God's relationship with Moses:] "The LORD would speak to Moses face to face, as one speaks to a friend." (Exodus 33:11)

[Job describing his prior relationship with God:] "Oh, for the days when I was in my prime, when God's intimate friendship blessed my house. " (Job 29:4)

The point here is that the relationship with God is not solely or exclusively understood to be a parent and child relationship. Every aspect of human love—familial, romantic, friendship—has been used to describe the love the believer shares with God. And this is important to note because, across each of these relational domains, there are periods of stress, jealousy, strain, conflict, abuse, abandonment, and trauma. What the relationship with God literature in psychology has revealed is that relationship with God can be as complicated and conflicted as any human love relationship. Religious believers can feel jealousy or resentment toward God. God might be seen as more loving, responsive, communicative, and intimate with others than with me. Further, religious believers can fear commitment with God, anxious that God is not going to be a reliable partner in life. Believers can also fear emotional rejection from God. Believers, as we saw in the case of Mother Teresa, can also feel abandoned by God. And, in extreme cases, believers can feel abused by God. Consider the following descriptions of the God-relationship within the Bible:

Like a bear lying in wait,
like a lion in hiding,
he dragged me from the path and mangled me
and left me without help.
He drew his bow
and made me the target for his arrows. (Lamentations 3:10–12)
I have borne your terrors and am in despair.
Your wrath has swept over me;
your terrors have destroyed me.

All day long they surround me like a flood;
they have completely engulfed me. (Psalm 88:15b–17)

These are strong expressions of feeling abused by God. An extreme example of this sentiment is Jeremiah's description of his encounter with God, an encounter with strong overtones of sexual assault:

> You deceived me, LORD, and I was deceived;
> you overpowered me and prevailed. (Jeremiah 20:7)

For our purposes, the psychological literature regarding the God-attachment, and its parallels with the biblical experience of lament and complaint, suggest that the sick soul experience, the co-occurrence of plea and praise, is not rare or anomalous. In fact, these experiences appear to be a regular feature of any love relationship, human or divine. Love relationships of all sorts are full of conflict, ambivalence, abandonment, or even abuse. But none of this implies the extinction of the attachment bond. To be sure, relational distress can become so acute that the love relationship is terminated. In the God-relationship, we can assume that such a step is the beginning, if not the cause, of eventual apostasy, the loss of faith in God. But the presence of extreme relational distress is not a sign of a loss of faith or love. The experience of Mother Teresa provides one illustration of this.

The point here is that the recent research using human love relationships to describe relationship with God illustrates how complaint is not antithetical to faith. Negativity does not imply that the love relationship has dissolved. And most importantly, the psychological research suggests that these experiences with God are common to every believer and are not confused, anomalous, or paradoxical. Love relationships can be chaotic and conflicted. When relationship with God is understood to be an attachment bond, the experiences of the lament psalms—expressions of relational distress, pain, abandonment, and abuse—suddenly seem quite natural and expected.

7.

Some recent research of mine with these relational approaches to the God-relationship might clarify the dynamics on display even more.

Consider again how our initial reactions to the experience of Mother Teresa are those of paradox and confusion. As noted above, this sense of paradox comes from an underlying assumption, a model of the religious experience that suggests that complaint is antithetical to faith. In my research (Beck, 2007), I have called this a "bipolar model," with faith and complaint working against each other along a single continuum; each is pitted against the other. I show this model schematically in Figure 4.

What we see in this bipolar model is a reciprocal relationship between faith and complaint. As complaint increases faith, is expected to attenuate and weaken. Conversely, as faith strengthens complaint should disappear. This is the psychological model behind Brueggemann's claim that "we have thought that acknowledgement of negativity was somehow an act of unfaith." It is the same model that creates the sense that James's sick soul or the experience of Mother Teresa is paradoxical. In the bipolar model, faith and complaint exist at the expense of the other. They cannot occupy the same experiential space.

However, as we have seen in the psalms and in the empirical psychological literature regarding relationship with God, it appears that high complaint can coexist with faith. In the psalms we see this in the

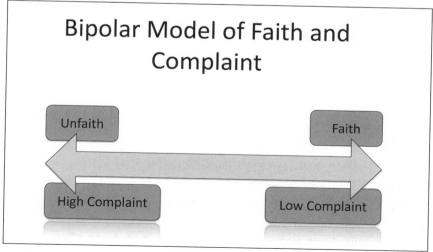

Figure 4. Bipolar model of faith and complaint.

plea to praise movement. And in the God-attachment research, we find that relationship with God can be infused with feelings of distress, conflict, ambivalence, abandonment, and abuse.

For example, in a study of mine (Beck, 2006a), I factor analyzed popular measures of God-attachment used in the psychological literature such as the *Spiritual Assessment Inventory* (SAI; Hall & Edwards, 1996, 2002) and the *Attachment to God Inventory* (AGI; Beck & McDonald, 2004). As discussed, both these measures assess the positive and negative, more ambivalent, aspects of the God-relationship. For example, tapping the positive aspects of the God-relationship the AGI and SAI include items such as "I am totally dependent upon God for everything in my life" (AGI), "My experiences with God are very intimate and emotional" (AGI), "God's presence feels very real to me" (SAI), and "I am aware of God's presence in times of need" (SAI). However, both the SAI and AGI, in their efforts to capture the more ambivalent aspects of relationality with God, include items that capture concerns about God's reliability and trustworthiness ("I feel that God has let me down" (SAI), "I often feel angry with God for not responding to me when I want"(AGI); skepticism about God's love and affection ("I wonder sometimes if God genuinely cares for my welfare" (SAI), "Sometimes I feel that God loves others more than me" (AGI); experiences of separation or abandonment "God seems far away from me" (SAI), "I am jealous when others feel God's presence when I cannot" (AGI); negative emotions "I struggle with anger toward God" (SAI), "I often feel angry with God for not responding to me when I want: (AGI); and theodicy concerns "I sometimes think, 'Why does God allow bad things to happen to me?'" (SAI), "I get upset when I feel God helps others, but forgets about me" (AGI).

When I factor analyzed these measures (a factor analysis is a statistical technique used to identify how various measures hang or cluster together, generally due to their overlapping and shared content), what I observed was that a two-dimensional model, rather than a single bipolar model, best captured the experience of being in relationship with

God as assessed by these relational measures. The positive and negative aspects of the God experience did not fall on opposite ends of a single continuum as assumed by the bipolar model discussed above. Rather two dimensions emerged, dimensions I labeled "communion" and "complaint." This two-dimensional structure shown in Figure 5 suggested that communion (engagement with God) could exist alongside complaint, mapping the same experiential topography seen in the psalms and in the sick soul experience.

When compared to the bipolar model, the richness of the two-dimensional communion and complaint model is evident. Specifically, the experience of complaint is no longer seen as antithetical to engagement or communion with God. The two experiences can coexist in the high communion-high complaint quadrant. To help with speaking about these quadrants, and to compare and contrast the experiences captured in each, in Beck (2007) I borrowed a seasonal metaphor from Martin Marty's (1997) book *A Cry of Absence: Reflections for the*

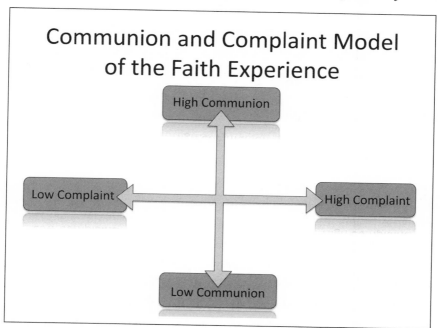

Figure 5. Communion and complaint model of the faith experience.

Winter of the Heart where he describes two distinct faith experiences: a "summery spirituality" that is characterized by positivity and optimism and a "wintry" believer who experiences a "Siberia of the heart" (p. 7). See Figure 6. The "summer experience" of faith is captured by the high communion-low complaint quadrant where the relationship with God is intimate, engaged, and generally free of negativity, disappointment, complaint, or lament. Believers in this quadrant—I have referred to them as "summer Christians" (Beck, 2002)—correspond to William James's description of the healthy-minded religious experience. By contrast, the "winter experience" of faith—or Mother Teresa's "saints of darkness"—is captured in the high communion-high complaint quadrant. These are William James's sick souls, believers who are engaged with God but who experience doubt, negativity, and god-forsakenness. Connecting to the biblical experience, psalms of orientation and moral symmetry are to be found in the summer experience quadrant and psalms of disorientation are located in the winter experience quadrant. To fill out the quadrants, I have labeled (Beck, 2007) the high complaint-low communion quadrant as "spiritual critic": complaint, skepticism, or doubt about God is offered outside of any real or passionate engagement with God. The low communion-low complaint quadrant I have labeled "disengaged." This is the location of a person who might endorse believing in God on a poll or survey but for whom the relationship with God does not occupy much, if any, of his psychological experience—a nominal, in name only believer.

8.

The importance of all this biblical and psychological analysis is that it supports the description of the religious experience by William James in *The Varieties of Religious Experience*. It also helps us translate the healthy-minded and sick soul typology into the Christian experience, our particular case study going forward in assessing the rival theories—illusion or varieties?—of Sigmund Freud and William James. Summarizing, at the end of the last chapter we wondered if James's description of the

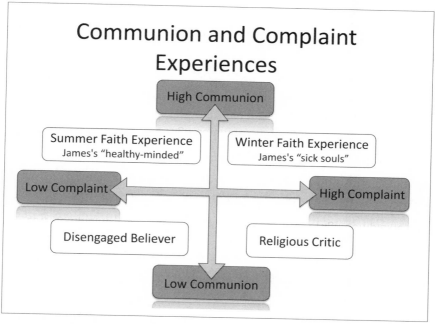

Figure 6. Communion and complaint experiences.

sick soul was coherent, psychologically and theologically. In positing the sick soul, James argued that there are religious believers who appear more existentially open, believers who are either unable or unwilling to use religious belief as a means of existential consolation.

We also noted that this existential openness comes with an emotional price tag. By maximizing evil, by focusing on the ambiguity, pain, and god-forsakenness of life, these believers must tolerate emotional unrest. Within the Christian experience, as we have seen, this emotional distress in the face of evil—the moral asymmetry caused by God's experienced abandonment of the world—is expressed as doubt, complaint, lament, or protest toward God. This is the speech and experience found in the psalms of disorientation and within the letters of Mother Teresa. And while the assumption might be, for those working with the bipolar model of the relationship between faith and complaint, that these experiences are symptoms of a loss or failure of faith, we have discovered that negativity and faith are not antithetical.

In both the biblical witness and in the psychological research relationship with God is found to be much more complex than what the bipolar model suggests.

Going forward then, it seems that the theory of William James positing the existence of religious varieties has passed a preliminary test. Based upon empirical psychological research and the biblical narrative, we can readily identify the sick soul and healthy-minded types within the Christian experience, or what I have called summer and winter Christians or believers. If this is the case, it suggests that some Christian believers can and often do refuse to allow their beliefs to hide or repress the uglier and more existentially ambiguous aspects of life. Existentially speaking, these believers are willing to suffer psychically in order to be more honest about the moral asymmetry, evil, suffering, and apparent absurdity of life. To be sure, this honesty places an intense strain upon faith. But as we have seen, these experiences are not antithetical to faith. As paradoxical as it seemed initially, the experiences of faith and negativity do intermingle and mix in the same phenomenological space: the high communion-high complaint quadrant of the winter faith experience.

And in light of all this, it begins to seem that Freud's model of religious belief might indeed be too narrow and simplistic to capture the richness witnessed in the lives of saints like Mother Teresa, the emotional landscape of the psalms, or the communion-complaint faith experience of ordinary Christians. To be sure, as Brueggemann (1984) described earlier in this chapter, and as we concluded in Part 1, we must agree with Freud that the Christian faith *can* be used as a "cover-up . . . a frightened, numb denial and deception that does not want to acknowledge or experience the disorientation of life." In fact, we might even expect this to be the norm; that, generally speaking, Christian believers (and believers from other faiths) use faith to repress, hide, avoid, or deny the existential realities of human existence. But now, in light of what we have learned in this chapter by following the lead of William James, we wonder if religious belief is *necessarily* involved in achieving existential consolation. Freud's model of religion as illusion appears unable to capture the full and rich diversity and complexity of the religious experience.

Chapter 7

DEFENSIVE AND EXISTENTIAL BELIEVERS

1.

HERE IN PART 2 WE HAVE BEEN WRESTLING WITH THE RELIgious experience William James labeled the sick soul. In the last chapter, we attempted to describe and ground the sick soul experience within the Christian tradition. Such a grounding is necessary if we are to move forward in assessing the rival formulations of William James and Sigmund Freud. We need a particular test case and ours will be the Christian experience. Consequently, we need to continue to wrestle with how the religious experiences that Freud and James describe manifest themselves within this particular religious community. Again, Freud's argument is that Christian belief, as an example of religious belief generally, is being deployed to achieve existential consolation and solace. And as we have observed, there is empirical laboratory support from the TMT literature that appears to support Freud's claim (e.g., Greenberg et al., 1990). It appears that Christian believers do deploy their beliefs to cope with death anxiety.

But does this mean that *all* Christian believers deploy their beliefs in this existentially defensive manner? Again, Freud's account of religious experience is totalizing and reductionistic, allowing no room for religious varieties. William James, in his description of the healthy-minded experience, agrees with Freud that there are religious persons who deploy religious belief as a means to minimize evil and maximize the existential comfort they can experience. However, in contrast to Freud, James does not attempt to stuff the entirety of religious experience into the healthy-minded box. James posits religious varieties, suggesting that there appear to be some religious believers who eschew existential consolation, refusing to deploy their beliefs to minimize or attenuate the existential distress life can create. The point in all this, as I have argued across the last two chapters, is that if the sick soul experience is legitimate then religious belief is not necessarily involved in existential repression. Of course, religious belief *can* be involved in existential repression, and often is, but in the face of religious varieties we have to conclude that existential repression is not the sole origin or motivation behind religious belief. The diagnosis of belief as existential consolation cannot be generalized to the entire religious population and must, rather, be considered on a case by case basis. How is belief functioning, existentially speaking, for this particular believer or within this particular faith community?

2.

In the last chapter, we reviewed the evidence that suggests religious varieties can indeed be found within the Christian experience. This in itself makes us wonder if Freud's reductionistic approach is able to capture the full range and complexity of the religious experience, both generally and for the Christian faith experience in particular.

The evidence in the last chapter was largely experiential and phenomenological in nature, focusing upon the lived experience of faith, of both the healthy-minded and the sick soul. This approach mirrors the method of James in *The Varieties of Religious Experience* in which James eschewed a consideration of religious beliefs, creeds, doctrine, dogma, and theology to focus intensively upon religious experience as experience. Much of this experience, we observed, is affective in nature: the emotional aspects of religious belief. The healthy-minded experience is thus defined as one of peace, comfort, well-being, and tranquility. The sick soul, by contrast (and the label "sick" hints at this), is an experience of angst, distress, complaint, lament, and even despair.

As discussed in the last chapter, we find both sorts of experiences within the Christian experience. Christian populations appear to have both summer and winter believers, the healthy-minded and the sick souls. The Christian faith experience is not homogeneous; it appears to contain varieties. Still, this experiential focus is incomplete as it fails to consider and describe how beliefs as beliefs are being deployed and shifted to achieve (or eschew) existential consolation. So in this chapter we want to move beyond the affective aspects of the faith experience—the summer and winter experiences of faith—to describe how actual beliefs—theological propositions—are adopted, deployed, and managed to achieve (or eschew) consolation and solace in the face of an existentially disconcerting reality. We are shifting here in this chapter from experience to belief. The two, of course, are related. And that is the point of this analysis, to connect the dots between beliefs about God to the experience of God. How, exactly, does the healthy-minded, summer believers deploy their beliefs about God to minimize the evil in life experiences? By contrast, how exactly does the sick soul, winter believers deploy beliefs to maximize evil? In light of the communion-complaint model of the Christian experience described in the last chapter, we know the summer and winter believers can be identified by the degree of complaint they each experience. We can assume that this complaint is driven by distinctive cognitive attributions related to life experience. In the midst of the ambiguities of life, the summer believer believes that God is present and in control. By contrast, in the face of the chaos of life, the winter believer believes God to be absent, indifferent, or antagonistic. Same world, two different sets of theological attributions, with each set leading to distinct religious experiences—healthy-minded versus the sick soul.

So our goal in this chapter will be to work backwards from the religious experience to specify the kinds of beliefs and theological attributions that create the sick soul or healthy-minded experience. By connecting the dots between belief and experience we will gain a more holistic and complete picture of the religious mind. This will be important for one additional reason. One of the benefits in specifying the experiential and theological features of the sick soul and healthy-minded experience within the Christian tradition is that it will allow us to measure, assess, and identify these types in social scientific research. With precise descriptions in hand we can create assessment tools, akin to personality tests, that can help us identify the religious varieties within Christian samples. And, having identified the religious types, we can go on to create experimental tests to see if, in fact, the types behave differently, particularly when existential defensiveness is being examined. Such tests would provide preliminary data to assess the rival models of Freud and James.

Let me make clear how this might happen. Consider again the terror management study conducted by Greenberg et al. (1990) in which Christian participants denigrated a Jewish person in reaction to a death-awareness prime. Recall, Christian participants displayed worldview defense when existentially unsettled. Religious belief appeared to be involved in providing a buffer against death anxiety and thus needed to be defended against the existential threat of the Other. This finding seems to support Freud's contention that religious belief is inherently a mechanism used to provide existential consolation.

But, if William James is correct, we cannot treat Christian samples, as was done in Greenberg et al. (1990), as a homogeneous group. If we follow James we should assume that there were sick souls *and* healthy-minded believers in the Christian sample of Greenberg et al. And, if this was the case, we might wonder if the sick souls and the healthy-minded participants were behaving in a similar way. Did *both* religious types display worldview defense in the mortality-salience condition? Or did *only* the healthy-minded? Because if James is correct that sick souls do not repress their awareness of death, we can hypothesize that sick souls would be relatively unaffected by a mortality-salience manipulation. If you think about death a lot, as do sick souls according to James, a death-awareness prime is not going to be particularly novel or upsetting. By contrast, if religious belief is being used to repress death anxiety, as James felt it was doing in the healthy-minded experience, then we can assume that the death-awareness prime in Greenberg et al. would have been an uncomfortable experience for the healthy-minded participants.

In short, we see here a way to empirically test the rival models of William James and Sigmund Freud. If James was right that there are religious varieties and some religious believers are not deploying their beliefs to achieve existential consolation, then we can expect the religious varieties to behave differently when they engage with existential issues or stimuli. For example, one group—the healthy-minded—might display worldview defense where the other group—the sick souls—would not. But if Freud is correct, if *all* religious belief—no matter what your Jamesian type—is engaged in existential consolation, then we should see no difference between the religious types in studies like Greenberg et al. (1990). According to Freud, *all* participants—sick soul or healthy-minded—should behave in roughly the same way: deploying religious belief to maximize existential comfort. Such a finding would suggest that James was wrong, that there are no religious varieties which vary in their degree of existential repression or awareness.

In summary, if we could measure and classify the religious types we see here a way to put the rival hypotheses of James and Freud to the test. We could identify the sick souled and the healthy-minded within Christian populations and then observe how they handle existential material. If they respond differently, and in the predicted manner, we have support for James's varieties as described in *The Varieties of Religious Experience*. If, by contrast, we observe no differences between the types, our conclusions lean toward Freud's formulation in *The Future of an Illusion*, the notion that all religious belief reduces to illusion and the need for existential consolation.

Part 3 of this book, you should be pleased to know, is devoted to just these sorts of empirical tests, four empirical case studies in total.

In fact, a replication of the Greenberg et al. (1990) study as described above is the subject of Chapter 8. Before we can turn to these empirical case studies we need to return to the issue of measurement. How should we assess the differences between the sick soul and healthy-minded experiences?

3.

It is surprising that, in the 100 years since the publication of *The Varieties of Religious Experience,* no one had tried to create assessment tools to identify James's religious types. When I first turned to this literature many years ago, I fully expected there to be a robust empirical literature about the correlates associated with the sick soul versus the healthy-minded types. The whole notion of there even being religious types in *The Varieties* seemed perfectly suited to psychological research keen on assessing individual differences as is routinely done in personality research. For example, most individuals label themselves as either extrovert or introvert, and there are plenty of psychological tests that can help you assess this facet of your personality. I fully expected something similar, but less well-known, to exist in the psychology of religion literature: a sampling of assessment tools that were routinely used by researchers to assess and study James's types.

And yet, I found nothing. When I began my investigations into the role of existential repression in religious experience, I could find no assessment tools explicitly developed to help assess and identify James's types. The closest fit I was able to find in the empirical literature was Daniel Batson's (Batson, Schoenrade, & Ventis, 1993) construct of "religion as quest." But as quest was not developed to assess James's types, I wanted to have in hand a tool that was explicitly developed to distinguish the healthy-minded from the sick soul. Failing to find such an instrument I set out to create one, ultimately developing the *Defensive Theology Scale* (DTS; Beck, 2004, 2006b).

In setting out to assess James's types as described in *Varieties,* I decided to eschew James's experiential approach to focus tightly upon religious belief. I was less interested in assessing the Christian experience of lament and complaint than I was in identifying those beliefs—or, more accurately, the suite of beliefs—that were implicated in producing the healthy-minded versus the sick soul experience. In this I was following Freud's focus in *The Future of an Illusion*, a focus that often reappears in Freudian-inspired arguments like those heard from the New Atheists. Specifically, it is claimed that existential solace is achieved by believing outlandish (from the atheistic perspective) things about reality. Take, as a simple example, the belief about a life after death. It is argued that the Christian belief in heaven exists and persists because it is existentially comforting. So Freud's argument goes. The role of belief in existential repression is clearly illustrated in this example. A very particular proposition is endorsed ("I believe when I die I'll go to heaven") and that proposition, that belief, produces existential comfort, presumably by attenuating death anxiety. In light of this relationship between belief and consolation, it seemed to me that one approach in distinguishing the healthy-minded from the sick soul would be to identify a set of Christian beliefs that seemed particularly implicated in producing existential comfort and solace.

One problem I immediately faced with this approach was that I had to wrestle with the role of Christian orthodoxy. Specifically, the simple belief in God, it could be argued, is existentially comforting. In fact, that is precisely what Freud argued. The trouble is that the creedally orthodox, whether sick souls or healthy-minded, would endorse a belief in God. While it may be true that a belief in God is a belief adopted and used for existential consolation, we cannot use that belief to discriminate between the sick souls and the healthy-minded. In light of this, I needed to identify beliefs within the Christian experience that were involved in existential repression but that would be differentially endorsed by James's types, if these types indeed existed.

For guidance I turned back to the existential psychologists we discussed in Part 1. Again, as Ernest Becker has taught us, existential repression is a universal condition. We are all, even Freud, trying to secure meaning, self-esteem, and significance in the face of death. The religious believer is not alone in this situation. So one way forward in creating the assessment tool I needed was to identify common forms of existential repression and defensiveness and then to locate their religious analogues. If we follow the existential psychologists, we can assume that everyone is deploying their worldview as a buffer to handle existential anxiety. And if this is so, all we need to do is identify the religious version of these anxiety buffers.

According to Yalom's (1980) influential analysis, existential defensiveness—religious or nonreligious—tends to manifest in two different ways. The first form of defensiveness Yalom describes as "specialness." Specialness is, at root, a form of denial, the belief that the laws of physical, mortal existence do not in the end apply to us. Yalom describes:

> We all know that in the basic boundaries of existence we are no different from others. No one on a conscious level denies that. Yet deep, deep down each of us believes . . . that the rule of mortality applies to others but certainly not to ourselves. (p. 118)

We are generally aware that this belief is irrational. As Yalom goes on to note, "Occasionally one is caught off guard when this belief pops into consciousness, and is surprised by one's own irrationality" (p. 118). And yet this belief appears to be, for most of us, our default mode of operation. This is not too worrisome as this fundamental denial about our situation helps us maintain a daily existential equanimity. To be flooded or preoccupied with existential anxiety on a moment to moment basis would be intolerable. So in its mild and workaday manifestations, the defense mechanism of specialness, the working assumption that we will be around forever, can be very adaptive. But the belief in one's existential specialness can become extreme and pathological.

A second form of existential defensiveness Yalom calls "the ultimate rescuer," the belief "in the existence of a personal omnipotent intercessor: a force or being that eternally observes, loves and protects us" (1980, p. 129). Yalom here is very close to Freud's analysis in *The*

Future of an Illusion, the notion that in the face of a hostile universe the religious believer posits the existence of an ultimate rescuer who will protect him. However, Yalom does not only focus upon religion. Following Ernest Becker, Yalom notes that "some individuals discover their rescuer not in a supernatural being but in their earthly surroundings, either in a leader or in some higher cause" (p. 129). The key here is that someone (or something) out there—a god, a cause, a company, a loved one, a bank account, or even modern medicine—will save me, inserting itself between myself and the hostile universe. With the rescuer buffering us from misfortune and death, feeling protected, we grow calmer and able to carry on with daily existence.

These two forms of existential defense—specialness and the ultimate rescuer—although distinct, tend to function in unison, mutually reinforcing each other. Yalom summarizes:

> Most individuals defend against death anxiety through both a delusional belief in their own inviolability *and* a belief in the existence of an ultimate rescuer. . . . These two defenses . . . are closely interdependent. *Because* we have an observing, omnipotent being or force continually concerned with out welfare, we are unique and immortal and have the courage to emerge from embeddedness. *Because* we are unique and special beings, special forces in the universe are concerned with us. Though our ultimate rescuer is omnipotent, he is at the same time, our eternal servant. (1980, p. 141)

If we follow Yalom's analysis regarding the two fundamental defense mechanisms against death anxiety, we can sketch out, theologically and psychologically, how they might work within the Christian faith experience to produce the healthy-minded experience. Recall, as described in the last chapter the healthy-minded experience, or what I have labeled the summer believer experience within the Christian faith, is characterized by intimate communion with God. More, this intimacy is free of negativity and complaint. The world feels morally symmetrical; the goodness of the believer is reliably rewarded. This is an experience that, in the language of William James (1902/1987), "looks on all things and sees that they are good."

Of course, when life is going well—full of love, health, and fulfilling work—we all taste of the healthy-minded experience. Life is good in these moments. But our concern here has less to do with these moments than with a fear-based denial, insisting that life is good because we are hiding from harsh realities. We are talking here about Walter Brueggemann's (1984) assessment in the last chapter that some Christians engage in "a cover-up" driven by a "frightened, numb denial and deception that does not want to acknowledge or experience the disorientation of life." This is healthy-mindedness as a form of existential defensiveness: the kind Freud described in *The Future of an Illusion*. And following Yalom we can see how this defensiveness might work. We expect the notion of specialness and the notion that God is an eternal servant to feature prominently. Specifically, the believer will be special in relation to others in the protection, knowledge, direction, attention, and solicitousness she receives from God. All things are good, even events most would consider to be objectively bad, because the eternal servant is always present to provide protection or confer ready-made meaning. In seeking to describe the various aspects of such a healthy-minded theology within the Christian experience, a theological system that would maximize existential comfort, I have (in a preliminary and exploratory way) identified five themes (Beck, 2006b):

1. **Special Protection**: In the face of a hostile universe, the belief that God will especially protect the believer (and loved ones) from misfortune, illness, or death. The universe is existentially tamed.
2. **Special Insight**: In the face of difficult life decisions, the belief that God will provide clear guidance and direction. God's guidance reduces the existential burden of choice.

3. **Special Destiny**: In the face of a life where meaning is fragile, the belief that God has created a special purpose for one's life, a destiny that makes life intrinsically meaningful.

4. **Divine Solicitousness**: The belief that the omnipotent God is constantly available and interested in aiding the believer, even with the mundane and trivial. God is an eternal servant, our cosmic butler.

5. **Denial of Randomness**: In a life full of random, tragic, and seemingly meaningless events, the belief that God's purpose and plan is at work. No event, however horrific or tragic, is existentially confusing or disconcerting. All is going according to plan.

Taken as a whole and to the extreme this theological configuration would seem to be implicated in existential defensiveness. At a variety of locations where life seems existentially threatening, difficult, or complex, these beliefs step in and reduce the anxiety. What was once a source of anxiety is now tamed, existentially speaking. So we seem to have in hand, in a preliminary way, the beliefs described by Freud (1927/1989) in *The Future of an Illusion*:

> And thus a store of ideas is created, born from man's need to make his helplessness tolerable. . . . Here is the gist of the matter. Life in this world serves a higher purpose. . . . Everything that happens in this world is an expression of the intentions of an intelligence superior to us, which in the end, though its ways and byways are difficult to follow, orders everything for the best that is, to make it enjoyable for us. Over each one of us there watches a benevolent Providence which is only seemingly stern and which will not suffer us to become a plaything of the overmighty and pitiless forces of nature. Death itself is not extinction, is not a return to inorganic lifelessness, but the beginning of a new kind of existence which lies on the path of

development to something higher. . . . In the end all good is rewarded and all evil punished, if not actually in this form of life then in the later existences that begin after death. In this way all the terrors, the sufferings and the hardships of life are destined to be obliterated. (pp. 23–24)

In light of this, in my research I have called this suite of beliefs "defensive theology" (Beck, 2004, 2006b) and have used these beliefs to create an assessment tool, the *Defensive Theology Scale* (DTS; Beck, 2006b), to help identify the healthy-minded from the sick souls in Christian populations. In the language of the DTS, those displaying the beliefs above to an extreme degree are called "defensive believers." Those eschewing the beliefs are called "existential believers."

4.

Before describing the DTS in more detail, it might be helpful to connect the defensive theology described above with the healthy-minded experience. Again, in the last chapter we examined the experiences of the healthy-minded and the sick soul. Here our considerations are more theological in nature: how beliefs are adopted and deployed to create or eschew existential consolation. So we should try, before moving on, to tighten up the connections between belief and experience. How, exactly, is the defensive theology described above implicated in existential consolation and the summer Christian experience of healthy-mindedness?

The first three features listed above in the defensive theology profile —special protection, insight, and destiny—are attempting to capture Yalom's notion of specialness. The common thread here is that life is existentially difficult in numerous ways and that the believers, due to their relationship with God, are especially buffered from these common sources of existential anxiety. Most directly, life can be physically threatening—illnesses, accidents, and death are constant threats. More subtly, the meaning of life is fragile—life can seem absurd, superficial, pointless, and devoid of meaning. In a related way, we face the burden of constructing meaning: making choices in an attempt to create a life deemed significant by ourselves and others. But these choices, due to the existential load they carry, are hard to make. We worry that we might make the wrong choice—picking the wrong career, choosing the wrong spouse—and cause catastrophic damage to our life projects. There is an old German proverb that says, "He who has choice has torment." In light of all this, God can step in to solve each existential crisis. God can protect the believer from misfortune. God can directly help the believer in making difficult life decisions. And, finally, God can provide the believer with a ready-made path to significance and meaning.

A background assumption in each of these cases of specialness is the one Yalom pointed to above, the notion that God, while transcendent and omnipotent, is at our beck and call, an eternal servant. I have labeled this belief "divine solicitousness." At times ,this belief can border on the notion that God is a genie in a bottle, available on a moment to moment basis to grant our every wish. In extreme cases God is called upon to help us deal with daily hassles and irritants, such as helping us find our lost car keys or turning red lights to green when we are running late. In the words of Freud (1927/1989), a belief in divine solicitousness suggests that God "orders everything for the best . . . to make [life] enjoyable for us." Obviously, the belief in such an eternal servant is existentially reassuring.

Finally, life presents us with a host of epistemological challenges. How are we to make meaning in a world that is disordered, random, and chaotic? What is the meaning of the tsunami, the cancer diagnosis, or the tragic car accident? Left naked and uninterpreted such events create existential anxiety, the feeling that we are the playthings of fate. To attenuate this anxiety we might deny the appearance of randomness and insist that, despite appearances, God has a plan and is in control of these events. As Freud (1927/1989) noted, this is the belief that

Everything that happens in this world is an expression of the intentions of an intelligence superior to us, which in the end, though its ways and byways are difficult to follow. . . . [God] will not suffer us to become a plaything of the overmighty and pitiless forces of nature. (p. 23)

No doubt religious believers of all stripes believe that God is providentially in control of the universe. But again, what we are describing here is what Brueggemann (1984) called a "frightened, numb denial and deception that does not want to acknowledge or experience the disorientation of life." What we are elucidating is the too-quick fix, the too-easy interpretation of suffering, pain, trauma, and tragedy. And when we witness the healthy-minded rush to minimize evil in the face of horrific suffering, what we are likely observing is less an act of faith than an unwillingness to engage honestly with a broken and fractured reality, a disinclination to move into the sick soul experience of complaint, lament, and spiritual despair. And in these instances we suspect that the faith claim "God is in control," while perhaps theologically true, has more to do with emotional coping: the deployment of a belief to deny, avoid, or repress existential anxiety.

In sum, look back over the five features of defensive theology—special protection, special insight, special destiny, divine solicitousness, and denial of randomness—and imagine a believer endorsing every theme and extreme versions of each. As I hope is obvious, such a theological configuration appears, following Yalom and Freud, to maximize existential consolation. Life is less threatening. Choices are easier because God tells us what to do. God's plan and will for us makes life inherently meaningful. God is at our beck and call, willing to help us out in any circumstance large or small. And, finally, God is in control of everything; even apparent random suffering is a part of a master plan, so no worries. Across the board, as we can see, the defensive theological profile leaves very few, if any, existential loose ends. Religious belief in this configuration seems ideally suited to manage and repress every source of existential tension.

Having described, in a preliminary way, the theology behind the healthy-minded faith experience (at least within the Christian tradition) we now might ask: How widespread are these beliefs? Does every Christian believer believe such things?

Freud, it appears, believed so. In describing the defensive theological configuration in *The Future of an Illusion* it seems Freud felt that he had exhausted the religious experience. Religious belief, according to Freud (1927/1989), simply consisted of the adoption of supernatural beliefs to attenuate and assuage existential anxiety. Religious belief once adopted would allow for "all the terrors, the sufferings and the hardships of life to be obliterated."

But if James was correct, there are religious persons—sick souls— who eschew defensive theological beliefs. These are our saints of darkness who experience a keen sense of god-forsakenness. Consequently, in the face of God's absence or silence these believers will tend to deny special protection, special insight, special destiny, divine solicitousness, and a denial of randomness. Life for these sick souls is more disorienting and existentially ambiguous. There are no quick or easy religious fixes to the human predicament. Consequently, existential anxiety is expressed via lament, protest, and complaint.

And it might be objected, once again, that such a faith stance is not recognizable as faith, that the refusal to allow God to function as an existential fix or band aid is tantamount to unbelief. However, the evidence presented in the last chapter suggests that faith and complaint are not bipolar opposites. Faith does not necessarily imply a defensive theology. Faith oftentimes expresses the exact opposite, the admission that life is disordered and that the believer is adrift in a hostile cosmos. This is the faith experience of lament, the cry of the winter believer, the sick soul. Faith exists but it is *not* being used to repress existential anxiety. Faith and existential disorientation, as seen in the communion-complaint model discussed in the last chapter, can exist alongside each other.

More will be said about the sick soul faith experience in the final chapter of this book. For now, however, we simply need to describe aspects of a defensive faith configuration to allow for tests of the rival models of religious experience described by William James and Sigmund Freud. Having here described a defensive theological configuration we can go on to assess Christian persons to see if Christians do vary in the degree to which they endorse and deploy these beliefs. Assuming some diversity within the Christian population, as strongly suggested in the last two chapters, we can now proceed to examine how these defensive versus existential believers react in the face of existential stimuli. Should we find differences between these believers—between the defensive-healthy-minded and the existential-sick soul—we would have preliminary evidence that the Christian faith experience is diverse, and that while many believers may deploy faith to achieve existential consolation, there are others who appear to deploy belief in a nondefensive manner.

5.

In three of the four case empirical studies in Part 3, defensive theology is assessed and examined. Again, the measure I developed to assess this faith configuration is called the *Defensive Theology Scale* (DTS), and it will prove helpful to describe the DTS content and, for social scientists, highlight its psychometric properties. This overview will allow me to refer to the DTS in Part 3 without having to review or repeat what the DTS is measuring and why. In addition, an inspection of the DTS items will provide us with some additional and very specific examples of the beliefs I've been labeling defensive.

Before reviewing the content of the DTS, let me offer some guidance for religious readers. My encouragement, having talked about the DTS a great deal with religious people, is not to fixate overmuch any one particular item. No one belief marks a faith stance defensive. Further, our interest here is not to determine if any given belief is true or not true, theologically speaking. Readers of the DTS items might want to quibble that a given belief is labeled defensive. These objections tend to run toward the personal with the general frame: "I believe X to be true, and you label that belief 'defensive.' Are you saying I'm being defensive?"

In response, I would like to borrow an old Freudian quip: "Sometimes a cigar is just a cigar." That is, sometimes a belief is just a belief. Again, readers should not fixate too strongly on any one belief. And even if they did, we need to step back and remember the frame for this entire analysis. We are not in the frame of classical apologetics, a discussion about the warrants (biblical or theological) that might justify a belief being true. We are, rather, engaged in a new sort of apologetics, an analysis of the function of religious belief. We are less interested in if a given belief in the DTS is *true* than to ask what it feels like, existentially speaking, to hold such a belief. Our level of analysis here is psychological rather than theological.

So my recommendation is this. To understand the DTS simply look at the beliefs as a whole and imagine someone strongly endorsing the set. Then ask yourself, what would be the emotional and existential experience produced by that faith configuration? In light of the discussions earlier in this chapter, I suggest that a clear and strong endorsement across the DTS item set would produce the healthy-minded experience as described by both Freud and James. That is not meant to be a value judgment, psychologically or theologically. It is simply the recognition that beliefs such as special protection, special insight, special destiny, divine solicitousness, and a denial of randomness are more existentially comforting than the disavowal of these beliefs. It is more comforting, existentially speaking, to believe that God is nearby and helping you than that God is absent or antagonistic toward you. This seemingly commonsensical observation is driving the logic of the DTS.

The DTS (Beck, 2006b)—found in Table 1—is a 22-item self-report scale developed to be a research instrument to assess the defensive theological configuration described above. As a research instrument, the DTS is not normed and is not intended to be used to create a score for individuals. The DTS is not intended to diagnosis or label an individual's religious experience and should not be used in that manner. Rather, the DTS was developed to test hypotheses regarding the role and nature of existential defensiveness in Christian populations. When administered in laboratory settings, the DTS allows a researcher to compare and contrast those scoring high on the DTS with those scoring low on the measure. Although scores can vary continuously on the DTS, it will be convenient to call those scoring high on the DTS "defensive believers" and those scoring low as "existential believers." These labels correspond, respectively, to James's healthy-minded and sick soul types, or my labels of summer versus winter believers. Summarizing, high scores on the DTS should produce the existential consolation associated with the healthy-minded, summer faith experience. Low scores on the DTS should be associated with the sick soul, winter faith experience.

Table 1: The Defensive Theology Scale (Beck, 2006b)						
DEFENSIVE THEOLOGY SCALE						
Directions: Below each item lists various beliefs about God and his relationship with you and the world around you. Please read each statement carefully and indicated the degree to which you agree with the statement using the scale below:						
1 Strongly disagree	**2**	**3**	**4** Neutral/ Mixed	**5**	**6**	**7** Strongly agree
1. I believe God protects me from illness and misfortune.						
2. When making a choice or tough decision, God gives me clear answers and directions.						
3. God answers even my smallest requests in prayer (e.g., like helping me get to a meeting when I am late).						
4. Despite being a child of God, I will have just as many traumatic things happen to me during my life as anyone else.						
5. God controls every event around us, down to the smallest details.						
6. God has a very specific plan for my life that I must search for and find.						
7. I believe that fewer bad things will happen to me in this life because God is protecting me from harm.						
8. I don't think God intervenes much in the small details of my life, even if I do care about them.						
9. God gives me clear and obvious signs to communicate His will to me.						
10. If you have deep faith and pure motives, God will grant even your smallest requests.						
11. A lot of evil in the world is just due to random events with no Divine goal or purpose .						
12. God's Hand is directing all the daily events of my life.						
13. God has a destiny for me to find and fulfill.						
14. My life will be happier because God will keep evil things from happening to me.						
15. Most of the events around us are random and don't reveal much about God's intentions						
16. God clearly guides me along the path He wants me to take.						

17. Nothing is too small, like finding my lost keys, to pray to God about.
18. Every event around us is a sign of God's larger plans and purposes.
19. Before I was even born, God had a detailed plan for the course of my life.
20. God doesn't give me clear directions as to what I should do with the big decisions in my life.
21. Although prayer is very important to me, I don't think prayer really affects the events of the world that much.
22. God gives me special insights about the events taking place around me or involving other people.
Note. DTS Scoring instructions: Items 4, 8, 11, 15, 20, and 21 are reverse scored. Sum of all items creates DTS score.

As can be seen by examining Table 1, the DTS items can be grouped under the five themes discussed above, themes that seem implicated in a defensive theological configuration. To make this more clear, Table 2 presents the DTS items grouped under the five themes:

Table 2: The Defensive Theology Scale Items Grouped by Theme
Special Protection:
1. I believe God protects me from illness and misfortune.
4. Despite being a child of God, I will have just as many traumatic things happen to me during my life as anyone else. (R)
7. I believe that fewer bad things will happen to me in this life because God is protecting me from harm.
14. My life will be happier because God will keep evil things from happening to me.
Special Insight:
2. When making a choice or tough decision, God gives me clear answers and directions.
9. God gives me clear and obvious signs to communicate His will to me.
16. God clearly guides me along the path He wants me to take.
20. God doesn't give me clear directions as to what I should do with the big decisions in my life. (R)
22. God gives me special insights about the events taking place around me or involving other people.
Special Destiny:
6. God has a very specific plan for my life that I must search for and find.
13. God has a destiny for me to find and fulfill.
19. Before I was even born, God had a detailed plan for the course of my life.
Divine Solicitousness:
3. God answers even my smallest requests in prayer (e.g., like helping me get to a meeting when I am late).
8. I don't think God intervenes much in the small details of my life, even if I do care about them. (R)
10. If you have deep faith and pure motives, God will grant even your smallest requests.

17. Nothing is too small, like finding my lost keys, to pray to God about.
21. Although prayer is very important to me, I don't think prayer really affects the events of the world that much. (R)
Denial of Randomness:
5. God controls every event around us, down to the smallest details.
11. A lot of evil in the world is just due to random events with no Divine goal or purpose.
12. God's Hand is directing all the daily events of my life.
15. Most of the events around us are random and don't reveal much about God's intentions. (R)
18. Every event around us is a sign of God's larger plans and purposes.
Note. R = reverse-scored item

Again, it is recommended that you simulate the faith experience that would be produced by consistently high scores across the 22 DTS items. Contrast that simulated faith experience, existentially speaking, with the simulated experience of someone eschewing these beliefs, someone displaying low scores on the DTS. For interested social scientists, a brief overview of the psychometric properties of the DTS are discussed in the footnote.[1]

6.

We have now reached the end of Part 2. To recap, at the end of Part 1 we reviewed the theoretical and empirical evidence supportive of Freud's contention that the function of religious belief is existential consolation. The conclusion we drew was that Freud has to be taken seriously; there are good reasons, as TMT studies have shown, to believe that religious individuals adopt and deploy their faith as a means of attenuating existential anxiety. Supporting Freud, as we discovered here

1   Bassett et al. (2009) used the DTS in four different samples, assessing college students and faculty/staff at a Christian liberal arts college. Across these samples the Cronbach alpha estimates of internal consistency among the DTS items ranged from .89 to .92. Overall, in Bassett et al., the DTS displayed positive correlation with a measure of intrinsic religiosity (Gorsuch & McPherson, 1989) with r^2's of .20, .00, .30, and .28. The DTS was also observed to be negatively correlated with Batson's measure of Quest (Batson & Schonerade, 1991) across the four samples with r^2's of .02, .26, .14, and .07. In my own research (Beck, 2006b, 2009a, 2009b) Cronbach alphas for the DTS have been consistently high, ranging from .89 to .91. In results similar to Bassett et al., in Beck (2006b, 2009a) DTS ratings had, respectively, r^2's of .14 and .15 with Batson's measure of Quest. In Beck (2009a, 2009b) DTS scores had r^2's of .27 and .23 with a measure of Christian orthodoxy (Fullerton & Hunsberger, 1982).

in Part 2, is William James's description of the healthy-minded religious experience. Specifically, in James's description of the healthy-minded type we have a description very close to Freud's: a religious experience aimed at psychically avoiding difficult existential confrontations. However, most of Part 2 has been preoccupied with how James goes beyond Freud, moving on to describe a second type of religious experience, what James called the sick soul. This religious type, according to James, appears to be a religious experience that eschews existential consolation. This is a religious experience Freud failed to investigate in *The Future of an Illusion*, feeling that it held "little human interest."

In short, what we find in Freud and James are two rival hypotheses regarding the role of existential consolation in religious belief. Both thinkers recognize the function of existential consolation in religious belief. However, where Freud reduced religious belief to illusion James posits religious *varieties*, suggesting that religious belief is not necessarily involved in existential repression and defensiveness.

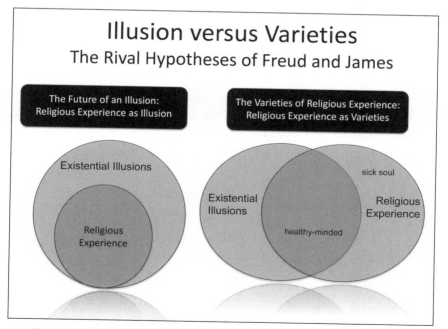

Figure 7. Illusion versus varieties.

At the end of Chapter 5 we contrasted the two models—illusion versus varieties—shown here again in Figure 7. In Figure 7 we recall how, in Freud's model, the entirety of religious experience is captured by existential illusion (which is a larger set because, as Ernest Becker noted, existential illusions can be nonreligious as well as religious in nature). By contrast, while James admits overlap between religious experience and existential illusion—in the type he called healthy-minded—James posits a second type, the sick soul, a religious experience free of the existential repression described by Freud in *The Future of an Illusion*. The contrast between these models suggests that, should a sick soul religious experience exist, we would have in hand empirical evidence that Freud's theory should be treated as less than comprehensive and exhaustive. Freud might be describing a *part* of the religious experience in *The Future of an Illusion*, perhaps even the largest part, but he would not be describing religious experience in its complex and heterogeneous totality.

So a great deal, theoretically and empirically speaking, appears to hinge on the existence of the sick soul experience. The sick soul is a test case that probes the comprehensiveness of Freud's theory in *The Future of an Illusion*. And so we asked, is the sick soul experience coherent, theologically and psychologically? Does it exist?

In the last two chapters, we have wrestled with the paradoxical nature of the sick soul experience. At the heart of the paradox, we have discovered, is a simplistic model of the faith experience that places faith and complaint on opposite ends of a continuum. A model of religious belief that suggests that faith and complaint—the Christian experience of god-forsakenness—are antithetical and contradictory. But if we replace this bipolar model with the two-dimensional communion-complaint model, a model supported by both empirical research and the Christian faith experience, we come to see that faith is not antithetical to the existential anxieties expressed in Christian lament.

Finally, here in this chapter, having established a prima facie case for the legitimacy of the sick soul experience, we took up an analysis of the theological contents of a defensive faith stance, an attempt to map belief onto experience. This more theological focus is important because existential repression is believed to occur at this level of analysis, with the adoption and deployment of beliefs to manage our existential emotions. A comforting religious worldview—a particular faith configuration—is adopted to hide, manage, or repress existential content and anxiety. If we can describe this faith configuration with some specificity within a specific religious population, as we have tried to do in this chapter, we would be well positioned to assess and then compare religious individuals who adopt or eschew these defensive beliefs. Do these individuals behave *differently* in how they manage existential anxiety? If they do, we have preliminary evidence for James's religious varieties. If not, if all religious believers appear to behave uniformly in the face of existential stimuli despite their scores on measures like the DTS, then we side with Freud's simpler and more parsimonious model of religious belief, that all religious belief reduces to illusion.

In light of all this, we are now positioned to move on to Part 3 in which four empirical case studies are presented, each exploring some facet of the rival hypotheses of Sigmund Freud and William James: four explorations into the varieties and illusions of religious experience.

Part 3

VARIETIES AND ILLUSIONS: FOUR CASE STUDIES

Chapter 8

WORLDVIEW DEFENSE REVISITED

WHY DO PEOPLE BELIEVE IN GOD? THAT IS A COMPLEX QUESTION with no simple or easy answer. Prior to the work of the masters of suspicion such as Darwin, Marx, and Freud, religious and nonreligious alike have tended to approach this question as an issue of evidence and reason: Was religious belief justifiable on rational grounds? Many found the evidence to be sufficient, while others have demurred. Still, the rules of the game seemed clear and transparent. Anyone could play.

But with works such as Freud's *The Future of an Illusion* radically new sorts of answers to the question entered the debate. And these answers had less to do with evidence and classical proofs for the existence of God than with psychological motivation, desire, and wish. Perhaps people believe in God because it makes life easier. Less scary. Or less tragic and absurd.

Suddenly, the ground had shifted. The contents of belief—theology, creeds, doctrine, apologetics—were brushed aside so that the motivations of the believer could become the object of analysis, the focus of the conversation. A cloud of suspicion now hovered over these motives. The wellspring of faith was rendered cryptic. And in the face of these doubts, a concern began to grow: Is it even possible that the religious believer could be trusted to peer into the murky depths of his desires and return with an answer to—"Why do *you* believe in God?"— that would be honest, authentic, and uncontaminated by unconscious desires?

1.

It might seem odd that here in Part 3 we have to turn to empirical psychological research to begin to reapproach the question: Why do people believe in God? But as noted in the Prelude, we are here engaged in a new apologetics. With the rise of suspicious accounts regarding religious motivation we are forced to play a game in which theology and classical apologetics are less relevant and persuasive. The debate, having shifted to issues related to unconscious motivations, has moved into the realm of psychology, which admittedly is an odd place to find ourselves. Who could have expected that these questions would have to be adjudicated in psychological laboratories?

There are two reasons we need to pursue these laboratory studies. First, as noted, central questions are now hovering about the issue of human motivation. What are the psychological motivations behind religious belief? Are they pure, a simple desire to seek the truth? Or are they contaminated by our fears and hopes? If we want to dig into these questions, we need to take up the tools of psychological research. And this relates to the second reason regarding the importance of psychological research in getting answers to our questions. Suspicious accounts of religious faith have not only caused a shift in content—from the theological to the psychological—but they have also altered what is considered to be a legitimate methodology. Specifically, if there is some suspicion regarding the believer's motives, if these motives are being called into question, the believer is effectively marginalized as a witness. The testimony of the believer, her account of her own inner workings and psychological motivations, is dismissed as unreliable. The introspection of believers is to be treated with the greatest suspicion as just so much self-justification, if not outright delusion. In the wake of thinkers such as Sigmund Freud, we have become keenly aware of how our self-descriptions—our self-talk about who we are and why we are the way we are—can become radically decoupled from reality. If Freud taught us anything, it is that we are masters of self-deception.

The point here goes to methodology. We find ourselves needing to investigate the motivations behind religious belief. We want to ask religious believers, "Why do you believe in God?" And yet the data we might obtain in this effort, the testimony of believers, is deemed to be unreliable, biased, and untrustworthy. So how are we to proceed?

It seems that we are stymied. And, looking at the cultural debate regarding the motivations behind religious belief, the attacks and counterattacks between religious believers and people like the New Atheists, it seems that the entire debate has degenerated into mere mudslinging with no visible progress being made. Skeptics of religion, following Freud, question the authenticity of religious belief by pointing to contaminated motivations. Religious believers, when they examine their motivations, see something quite different and object to these characterizations. Back and forth it goes, with neither group well-positioned to make the final judgment. Skeptics of religion do not have access to the motivations of religious believers. And religious believers, while having access, cannot be trusted to be reliable reporters. So there seems little hope of making progress.

Yet if we turn to psychological research, we might find a way to inch forward. True, it is very unlikely we will find definitive answers to these questions. However, we might make some progress, or at least open up new areas of discussion in what has become a tiresome and weary debate. The hope for progress is due to the fact that psychological research is equipped with the tools relevant to the topic at hand: the analysis of human motivation. More, psychological research gets around the methodological limitations of personal testimonial. By examining the behaviors of samples, using both experimental and statistical controls, psychological research is able to collect data less affected by the introspective biases of an individual believer.

2.

And so we turn, here in Part 3, to a collection of empirical studies I have conducted (along with some wonderful colleagues) that might prove helpful in illuminating the rival models of religious experience proposed by Sigmund Freud and William James. In each case study our question will be the same: Does the religious sample under consideration (our focus will be on Christian populations) behave in a uniform and homogeneous manner when dealing with difficult existential material or stimuli? Do religious believers act the same? And if the behavior is homogeneous, does it tend toward maximizing existential consolation and attenuating existential anxiety? Again, if Freud's model of religious experience is comprehensive we should see the Christian samples studied here in Part 3 behaving in a uniform fashion. More, this behavior should be aimed at providing existential comfort and solace. Again, according to Freud religious faith has one essential function: the provision of existential consolation. Thus, religious believers should consistently and uniformly (a prediction of homogeneity) adopt and deploy their beliefs for this purpose (a prediction of unidirectionality). In the face of such findings, existential consolation would be found to be the function, the purpose, and *the motive* behind religious belief. Existential consolation would be the answer to the question, "Why do people believe in God?"

However, according to William James the motivations behind religious faith are not homogeneous or unidirectional. The title of James's seminal work—*The Varieties of Religious Experience*—highlights this view. At a minimum, James posits two religious types, each with distinct motivational configurations. The healthy-minded type, the mirror of Freud's descriptions, will seek to deploy faith to avoid existential anxiety. By contrast, the sick soul is motivated to seek out the existential confrontation no matter how painful, in the belief that, as James (1902/1987) wrote, these experiences are "the best key to life's significance, and possibly the only openers of our eyes to the deepest levels of truth." Here, then, with James's notion of religious varieties we have a hypothesis of *heter* ogeneity and *multi*-directionality when it comes to the motivations behind religious belief.

Our way forward, then, is to evaluate the evidence for the rival models of Freud versus James: illusion or varieties. Evidence of homogeneity and uni-directionality in the studies discussed here in Part 3 would be supportive of Freud's simple one size fits all model in *The Future of an Illusion*, consistent with the view that religious belief is motivated, across the board, as a need for existential consolation. By contrast, should evidence of hetero-geneity and multi-directionality be observed, we will move towards James's notion of religious varieties. This conclusion would suggest that while many religious believers may (and likely often do) deploy faith to produce existential solace, faith would not be necessarily involved in this function given the diversity of religious varieties. In the face of religious varieties, we would have to assess religious motivation on a case by case basis and would not be able to generalize a single motivation across the diverse terrain of the religious experience.

3.

In light of all this, let's in this chapter return to an important study described in Part 1 that provided empirical support for Freud's notion that religious belief is motivated by a need for existential consolation. Recall, this research emerged from the work on what is known as Terror Management Theory (TMT). This research takes its cue from Ernest Becker's existential reformulation of some of Freud's psychodynamic insights. Specifically Becker, along with the existential psychologists, agrees with Freud that our waking life is largely dominated by defense mechanisms deployed to avoid, repress, or channel unconscious neurotic anxieties. However, where Freud believed that the source of this anxiety was oedipal in nature (sexual and rivalrous feelings about mothers and fathers), the existential psychologists posited that our unconscious fears are the result of existential confrontations, primarily the prospect of our eventual death. The fear of death threatens to intrude into consciousness, disrupting our emotional equilibrium and calling into question the ultimate significance of our life projects. To regain and maintain a degree of functional equanimity in the face of death, we deploy psychic defenses to help repress our fear of death. According to Ernest Becker, the most significant of these defenses is the construction of cultural worldviews, collectively agreed upon paths that confer significance and meaning to one's life. We gain self-esteem by pursuing these paths and reap the reward of feeling that, despite the specter of death, my life meant something.

On a day-to-day basis, then, life within the cultural matrix works as a denial of death by keeping us busy or distracted with culturally approved life projects. We might struggle for years to get promoted at work, but rarely in the middle of those long hours at the office do we stop and ask what is the point—the issue of ultimate significance—of this quest to make more money. And when we do pause to ask these sorts of questions, we often come up empty-handed. In short, while cultural worldviews generally work, they are also very brittle. By adhering to these worldviews, we leave ourselves vulnerable to an existential analysis that can leave us feeling that life is nothing but a rat race, that life is just as Macbeth depicted it:

> Life's but a walking shadow, a poor player
> That struts and frets his hour upon the stage
> And then is heard no more: it is a tale
> Told by an idiot, full of sound and fury,
> Signifying nothing. (Shakespeare, 1623/2009, 5.5.25–27)

Few of us can sit very long with such sentiments, not without some serious mental health consequences. Moments of existential worry or despair, for most of us, tend to be fleeting. The crush, pace, and demands of life typically pull us out of these morbid reveries and back into our to-do lists. The cultural worldview eventually snaps back into place, reasserting itself if only tenuously. The anxiety about death and the absurdity of life fades back out of consciousness. And the day moves on.

Perhaps nowhere is the cultural worldview more vulnerable than in the encounter of the ideological Other, the engagement with a person who subscribes to a completely different religious, political, or value system. Imagine a Christian engaging for the first time with a Muslim. As Ernest Becker noted, for worldviews to work, existentially speaking, they need to be true. If worldviews are going to confer meaning and significance in the face of death they need to be anchored in eternity, in locations of timeless truths far beyond the flux of daily existence. This is why worldviews, even secular atheistic worldviews, are considered to be religious. Worldviews are the values, the locations of ultimate concern, that anchor our collective way of life. The pinch comes then when we encounter Others who order their collective existence around a different set of values, truths, and gods. The mere existence of these Others, as representatives of alternative worldviews, is an implicit (and at times explicit) critique that we are the ones in sole possession of the truth. That our god is the true God. That our way of life is eternal, transcendent, and thus superior. In short, the encounter with the ideological Other is an existential crisis, a moment when all we hold most dear and sacred is implicitly or explicitly called into question. In the face of the Other, a crack forms in the wall of our existential shield and, behind those cracks, a raging existential flood of despair and anxiety threatens to engulf us.

According to TMT and Ernest Becker, rather than face that existential flood in the encounter of the Other we engage in worldview defense. Rather than face the anxiety of questioning the absoluteness of our worldview, we simply denigrate or demonize the Other. We double down on our worldview, convincing ourselves that our values and faith are locations of absolute truth and that the Other must be wrong. In mild cases this can be accomplished through simple disagreement with the Other, but in severe cases the Other is viewed as a threat and thus becomes an object of violence. This is, according to Ernest Becker, the great tragedy of human existence. The very things that give our life meaning—our worldviews—are the very sources of human evil. We kill to protect our existential comfort.

Again, these worldviews are not to be solely identified with religious belief, although for many, for obvious reasons, there is a tight association. In our discussions in Part 1 and 2, we have noted that religious belief is best seen as a subset within a larger set of cultural worldviews aimed at handling existential anxiety. And as we have also noted, Freud himself treated psychoanalysis as his own private faith, his own route to making his life significant and meaningful. Still, the fact that religious belief functions as a cultural worldview, a route toward significance, meaning, and even immortality in the face of death, makes it natural and appropriate for TMT researchers to examine the existential dynamics involved in religious faith. Thus the question can be asked: Do religious persons engage in worldview defense in the encounter with an ideological Other, particularly in the face of death?

The study along these lines that caught our attention in Chapter 4 was one conducted by Greenberg et al. (1990). It will be recalled that Greenberg et al. had Christian participants rate the personalities of two individuals, one Jewish, the other Christian. Prior to rating these people half the Christian participants were exposed to a mortality-salience manipulation, a death-awareness prime that involved writing a brief essay about the experience of dying. The other Christian participants were in a control condition.

Overall, Greenberg et al. (1990) observed that the Christian participants who underwent the death awareness priming rated the Christian target (the in-group member) more favorably relative to the Jewish target (the ideological Other), seeing their fellow Christian as more honest, trustworthy, intelligent, and kind. More, the Christian participants in the death-awareness condition were more likely to attribute stereotypically anti-Semitic traits to the Jewish target, rating the Jewish person as more stingy, manipulative, arrogant, snobbish, and obnoxious relative to the Christian. These trends were not observed with the Christians in the control condition. Overall, this pattern of results suggests that the Christian participants were engaging in worldview defense, denigrating an ideological Other to bolster their worldview in the face of death. Feeling unsettled by the death prime the Christian participants denigrated a Jewish person. This is the sort of behavior we would expect if the religious worldview was being adopted and deployed as an existential buffer and defense mechanism. In sum, the behavior of the Christians in Greenberg et al. is consistent with Freud's assessment of religious faith in *The Future of an Illusion*. The Christian participants were using faith to avoid an existential confrontation along with its accompanying existential anxiety. Rather than moving into the space of existential uncertainty created by the Other, the Christian participants doubled down on their worldview by denigrating the out-group member. They engaged in worldview defense.

4.

While the results of Greenberg et al. (1990) are broadly supportive of Freud's view in *The Future of an Illusion,* our encounter with William James in Part 2 leads us to ask some questions. Specifically, as noted above, the issue between Freud and James applies to homogeneity. We wonder, in light of religious varieties, if all of the Christian participants in Greenberg et al. were behaving in a uniform manner. To be sure, the group averages showed evidence of worldview defense, but we wonder if there was a minority—the sick souls in particular—who might have behaved differently in the face of the death-awareness prime. Again, according to James, sick souls live with death as a present and constant psychic companion. And if that is the case, is it reasonable to expect that the sick souls in Greenberg et al. would have been troubled, surprised, or disturbed by a death awareness prime?

We cannot answer that question based upon the results of Greenberg et al. (1990) because they did not assess religious varieties within their Christian sample. That is to be expected as Greenberg et al. was simply using the Christian faith as one among many worldviews that could help assess the larger, more general question about the role of worldviews as existential anxiety buffers. Greenberg et al. were not attempting a fine-grained assessment of religious experience and were not trying to compare and contrast the existential motivations within the Christian population. Greenberg et al. were not aiming to assess the rival models of religious experience presented in *The Future of an Illusion* and *The Varieties of Religious Experience*.

But that is very much the question that interests us here. We wonder if we could assess James's religious varieties—the healthy-minded and the sick souls—to see if they behave differently when an ideological Other is encountered in the face of a death-awareness prime. And should we find evidence that these types do behave differently, we would have to nuance the overall conclusion of Greenberg et al. (1990). Specifically, while it may be true that many religious believers do engage in worldview defense—denigrating Others, particularly when existentially unsettled—there are other religious believers who refuse (consciously or unconsciously) to denigrate out-group members, even in the face of death. Such a finding would suggest that religious belief, for these individuals, is not being deployed to manage existential anxiety.

5.

In 2006 I published a study in the *Journal of Psychology and Theology*— "Defensive versus Existential Religion: Is Religious Defensiveness Predictive of Worldview Defense?"—to start, in a preliminary way, an investigation into these questions (Beck, 2006b). The overall structure of the study followed Greenberg et al. (1990) with some minor and one major difference. First, in my study the ideological Other was Buddhist rather than Jewish. This choice was mainly an attempt to get closer to the lived experience of the Abilene Christian University students who were participating in my study. Abilene Christian University hosts very few Jewish students, but we have many students who come from Asian cultures. Thus, the existential encounter with the Other most likely happens on our campus is Christian-Buddhist rather than Christian-Jewish. A second reason for the switch was to extend the results of Greenberg et al. If the participants in my study displayed worldview defense toward a Buddhist target, I would have shown that the results of Greenberg et al. were not due to the troubled history of Christian-Jewish relations but were, in fact, evidence of a more general defensiveness toward Others.

But the most important change I introduced to the procedure of Greenberg et al. (1990) was the administration of the DTS to every Christian participant prior to the study. It will be recalled from Chapter 7 that the DTS was developed to assess a theological configuration (special protection, special insight, special destiny, divine solicitousness, denial of randomness) that is implicated in providing existential consolation. To review, high scorers on the DTS would be more healthy-minded relative to those scoring lower on the DTS, those eschewing beliefs like special protection. By administering the DTS, my hope was to identify something akin to James's types in the Christian participants involved in the study. By doing so the goal was to determine if these two groups behaved similarly toward the ideological Other, particularly in the death prime condition. If no differences were observed between the groups I would have essentially replicated the findings of Greenberg et al. with a different ideological target (Buddhist rather than Jewish), a finding important in its own right. However, if the high versus low DTS scorers behaved differently we would have evidence for James's varieties, particularly if the low DTS scores (those corresponding to James's sick soul) did not denigrate the ideological Other. Such an outcome would provide evidence for heterogeneity and multidirectionality when examining the existential motivations within the sample. Not every Christian participant in the study would have been deploying their faith—their worldview—to fend off existential anxiety.

To give a brief overview of the study, the first step was to have the 207 Christian undergraduate volunteers fill out the DTS. A median-split was performed on these DTS scores, with half of the participants designated as high on the DTS and the other half as low on the DTS. These groups were intended, as described in Chapter 7, to sort the sick souls from the healthy-minded participants in the sample.

After completing the DTS, the participants were randomly assigned to the mortality salience or control condition. In the mortality-salience condition a death-awareness prime was used. This prime was the same one used in Greenberg et al. (1990) and involved the participants writing short essays answering two prompts intended to make mortality salient: "Describe below the feelings that the thought of your own death arouses within you" and "Describe below what you think will happen to you physically when you die and once you are dead." In the control condition, participants wrote short essays concerning their opinions regarding TV programming: "Describe below your opinion as to whether television has a positive or negative impact upon society" and "If you were the CEO of a major TV network, what changes would you make to improve the quality of TV?" After the mortality-salience and control-manipulations, participants were then given a cover story informing them of a "second" study unrelated to the essays they had just written.

As a part of the "second study" participants were told that they would be reading two student essays that were being considered for potential publication in the freshmen-seminar textbook for a chapter devoted to religious diversity. One essay was written by a Christian (in-group member) and the other was written by a Buddhist (out-group member). In the pro-Christian essay the Christian author tells of being raised in Buddhist culture by American missionary parents. The author goes on in the essay to express a desire to become a missionary and to return to the land of the author's youth youth to work evangelistically among the Buddhist population. A quote from the pro-Christian essay:

> Although I am sympathetic to Buddhist belief and practice, I really do believe that Buddhism is mistaken and that belief in Jesus is the only true path to God. This belief has motivated me to become a missions major at ACU with plans to return and follow in the footsteps of my parents.

The second essay was ostensibly written by a non-American Buddhist student who has come to the United States to study at Abilene Christian

University. At Abilene Christian University, the student tells of an encounter with Christianity and expresses a desire to share, evangelistically, the Buddhist faith with fellow Christian classmates. A selection from the pro-Buddhism essay:

> In the United States I was surprised by the amount of ignorance regarding the Buddhist religion. As I listened to Christians in Bible classes at Abilene Christian University, I felt that I have something beneficial to share with others. I believe there are some things that Christianity can learn from Buddhism.... The Christian belief system appears to be more judgmental than Buddhism. Christians see things as either right or wrong, black or white. To a Buddhist, the lines between black and white allow for areas of gray.... Christianity can also learn from Buddhism because Buddhism allows for the adoption of useful teachings from other world religions. As a Buddhist I can find wisdom in the book of Ecclesiastes, but Christian's [sic] don't often supplement their reading of the Bible with teachings from the Koran or the writings of Confucius.... I hope I can spend more time teaching my Christian friends about Buddhism.

The goal in the construction of these essays was to place the in-group and out-group target in different positions as teacher versus student. In the pro-Christian essay, Christianity is in the teacher role and Buddhism is the student requiring education. In the pro-Buddhist essay, these roles are reversed with Buddhism being cast as the teacher seeking to guide Christianity as the misguided student.

To assess worldview defense after reading the two essays the participants gave their impressions of each author using the adjectives used in Greenberg et al. (1990), rating the applicability of adjectives such as honest, arrogant, intelligent, insensitive, obnoxious, tolerant, and likable. The adjective ratings were scored in such a way so that higher scores indicated a more favorable rating of the author (more honest, intelligent, tolerant and likable and less arrogant or obnoxious) and then summed to create an overall score. Finally, the overall favorability ratings of the pro-Buddhist essay author was subtracted from the overall rating for the pro-Christian essay author. Thus, a total score of 0.0 would indicate no difference between author impressions (Buddhist favorability ratings would equal Christian favorability ratings). Positive scores would indicate that the Christian author was rated more favorably relative to the Buddhist author. By contrast, negative scores would indicate that the Buddhist author was rated more favorably relative to the Christian author.

In light of Greenberg et al. (1990), one expected outcome for this study was that the Christian participants, uniformly, would display worldview defense in the mortality-salience condition. That is, those participants who were existentially unsettled by the death-awareness prime would display in-group favoritism and out-group denigration by rating the Christian more favorably relative to the Buddhist. This pattern of results would suggest that the Christian participants were deploying their faith as an anxiety buffer, as a means to attenuate existential anxiety.

However, as noted above, Greenberg et al. (1990) treated their Christian participants as a homogenous sample. Greenberg et al. did not assess anything equivalent to William James's types, discriminating between Christians who may be more or less reactive to existential stimuli. However, in my 2006b study the religious types were assessed using the DTS. Consequently, my study was better positioned to illuminate the models of religious experience posited by James and Freud. Specifically, did the sick souls, those scoring low on the DTS, display worldview defense in the study? Conversely, did the healthy-minded, those scoring high on the DTS, display worldview defense?

6.

Overall, the pattern of results observed in my 2006b study supported the thesis of William James. Those high versus low on the DTS measure—our proxy for identifying the healthy-minded and sick soul religious varieties—behaved differently when engaging the ideological Other. More, the two groups behaved in the manner we predicted: those scoring high on the DTS (the healthy-minded) displayed worldview defense while those scoring low on the DTS (the sick souls) did not.

One interesting and unexpected finding was also observed in the study. Following the TMT research, it was predicted that worldview defense (denigrating the out-group target relative to the in-group target) would be observed only in the mortality-salience condition. All things being equal, the healthy-minded were not expected to display world-view defense in any consistent manner. It is only when existentially troubled or anxious that we expect to see the worldview deployed to repress anxiety. The mortality salience condition, with its death aware-ness prime, is trying to create this anxiety and thus activate world-view defense. However, in my study those scoring high on the DTS (the healthy-minded) displayed worldview defense across conditions. Across *both* the control and death awareness groups those scoring high on the DTS displayed the in-group bias symptomatic of worldview defense.[2]

In summary: across conditions, the high scoring DTS group, those displaying an existentially defensive theological profile, rated the Christian author significantly more favorable relative to the Buddhist author. Again, this means that the Christian participants who James would classify as healthy-minded were significantly more likely to rate the Christian author as more honest, likable, tolerant, and intelligent when compared to a Buddhist. More, the Buddhist author was rated as more arrogant, insensitive, and obnoxious. This finding is similar to the pattern of results observed in the original Greenberg et al. (1990) study. These results appear to point to a latent aggression or hostility within the psyche of the healthy-minded toward those who hold different

---

2 The outcome of the 2 x 2 factorial ANOVA indicated that there was no main effect for mortality salience ($F1,197 = .31, p = .577$). However, there was a main effect for the high versus low DTS groups ($F1,197 = 6.29, p = .013$; High DTS group mean = 11.41, Low DTS group mean = 3.33). Finally, there was no significant mortality salience x DTS score interaction ($F1,197 = .02, p = .877$).

religious worldviews. We can assume that this is due to the implicit existential threat posed by ideological Others, the suggestion that our worldview might be fallible and thus unable to provide the existential consolation we so desperately need. To defend against this anxiety the ideological Other is viewed as less intelligent, honest, or trustworthy. Such attitudes allow us to dismiss the existential threat of the Other as the Other is seen as mistaken, uneducated, or immoral.

This pattern of results is worrisome. However, as suggested by William James, the Christian participants in the study did not behave as an undifferentiated, homogeneous group. Specifically, those scoring lower on the DTS, those who eschewed existentially consoling beliefs, did not engage in worldview defense. The sick souls in the study saw no difference between the Christian and Buddhist authors. Across both the control and mortality-salience conditions, those scoring low on the DTS rated the Christian and Buddhist as equally honest, arrogant, intelligent, insensitive, obnoxious, tolerant, and likable. The ideological position of the author—in-group or out-group—appeared to make no difference to those scoring low on the DTS. Sick souls did not display worldview defense. They saw the Other as equal to their fellow Christian.

7.

This pattern of results, that scores on the DTS were associated with the presence or absence of worldview defense, appears to support the Jamesian notion of religious varieties. As James might have predicted, the healthy-minded in the study appeared to display worldview defense, showing a latent distrust and hostility toward the ideological Other. The healthy-minded in the study appeared to be in a defensive posture, predisposed to protect, via a denigration of the Other, their worldview from critique and scrutiny. While such defense is understandable, the ethical worry behind this defensive crouch, this predisposition to distrust and denigrate Others, is that this latent hostility can scale up during times of communal distress and outrage leading to ostracism, violence, and even genocide. This was the worry expressed by Ernest Becker in *Escape from Evil.* The very things that give life meaning and significance, when held defensively, are also the engines of violence, hate, and human evil.

And yet the sick souls in the study did not display worldview defense, suggesting that some of the Christian participants were not deploying their faith in a way to manage or reduce existential anxiety. The sick souls did not denigrate the Other and seemed capable of seeing the Other on equal terms. This is a hopeful pattern of results and it suggests that faith, at least for some of the Christian participants, was not being used to hide from the implicit existential critique posed by the Other. No doubt exposing oneself to this critique is existential unsettling, but the price seems worth it if the result is meeting the Other on equal footing. Existential anxiety is endured to find better ethical footing.

8.

Before going on, it might be helpful to pause and note just how odd, strange, and unexpected is this pattern of results. If you have read to this point in the book, the findings of my 2006b study seem perfectly expected and reasonable. But, as you have no doubt noticed, we have made a quite a theoretical journey to get to this point. So let me suggest that we step back for a moment and consider the results of the 2006b study with fresh eyes. By doing so, we should feel a bit puzzled about

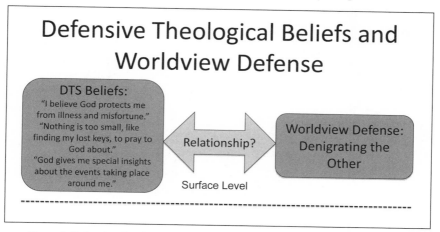

Figure 8. Defensive theological beliefs and worldview defense.

why DTS scores had anything at all to do with Christian attitudes about a Buddhist.

Think about it. Why would believing that, say, God will protect you from misfortune (a DTS belief-item) have anything to do with perceptions of a Buddhist? There is seemingly no connection between the two. Why would the beliefs associated with the DTS be associated with worldview defense, the denigration of ideological Others? On the surface, as in Figure 8, there seems to be no relationship between the two.

However, based upon the work of Freud, Ernest Becker, and the TMT research, we are positioned to see that the connection is due to underlying psychodynamics, the deployment of faith as an existential defense mechanism as in Figure 9.

This existential defensiveness, driven by a need for existential consolation, explains both why DTS beliefs are adopted (they are existentially comforting) and why the Christian participants denigrated an ideological Other (to protect the worldview from existential critique). All this supports the formulation offered by Freud in *The Future of an Illusion*.

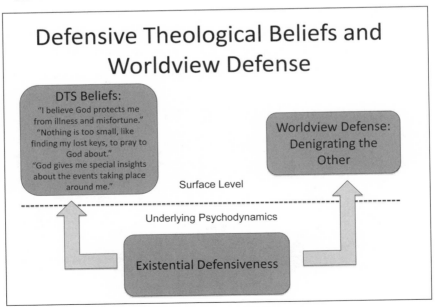

Figure 9. Defensive theological beliefs and worldview defense (expanded).

And yet, in light of the findings from my 2006b study, not every Christian participant fits the dynamics just described. Those participants eschewing the existentially consoling DTS beliefs also displayed a reticence to denigrate an ideological Other to bolster and defend the Christian worldview from the implicit critique of the out-group member. This pattern of behavior, seen in Figure 10, in contrast to those scoring high on the DTS, points to a *reduced* need for existential consolation:

9.

The overarching subject of this book is to ask and answer the question: Why do people believe in God? Again, while there are many answers to that question, perhaps the most provocative answer has come from thinkers like Sigmund Freud: people believe in God because that belief helps assuage existential anxiety. As noted at the start of this chapter, the provocative nature of this answer has proven to be almost as great as our inability to get any traction concerning the evidence for or against

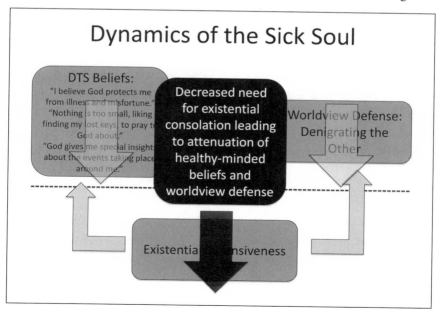

Figure 10. Dynamics of the sick soul.

it. By positing unconscious feelings and motivations—a deep seated existential terror that is repressed—we struggle to get a handle on the phenomenon. Biblical study and theology are of no help here, nor is the testimony of religious believers. Due to the defense mechanisms believed to be at work, religious believers are considered to be biased and unreliable witnesses. So how are we to address the issue?

If the relevant issues revolve around human motivation we must, it seems, turn toward scientific disciplines, like psychology, that have the tools and know-how to tease apart human motivations, even unconscious motivations. If we want to determine if Freud's view of religious belief was accurate, then we need to get into the laboratory to see if indeed that is the case. No other method seems able to move the debate forward.

But if we are to test Freud's formulation, and others like it, we need to articulate the alternative hypothesis and describe it with enough precision so that that we can sort through rival interpretations of the data. Specifically, what would religious belief look like if it were *not* fundamentally motivated by existential consolation? As we have seen, the work of William James has proven to be very helpful in answering this question. We have taken up James's descriptions of the healthy-minded and sick soul experiences with a particular focus on how these types display differential needs for existential consolation. And our review of the Christian faith experience, biblically and experientially, suggested that James's types might indeed describe real differences in religious populations.

And so the question comes to this: Do James's types behave similarly when handing existential material? More specifically, do those holding consoling beliefs display existential defensiveness (e.g., engage in worldview defense) while those eschewing those beliefs do not (e.g., not engage in worldview defense)? Will the participants in TMT-like studies follow Freud's prediction and behave in a homogenous fashion, or will they behave differently as religious varieties and show evidence for heterogeneity?

The results of my 2006b study appear to support William James. While some Christian participants displayed worldview defense, others did not. More, those participants who displayed worldview defense were those espousing existentially consoling beliefs (i.e., high DTS scores). Conversely, those eschewing existentially consoling beliefs (i.e., low DTS scores) did not engage in worldview defense. These differences point to heterogeneity in the existential motivations behind Christian belief. While it seems clear that existential consolation is implicated in Christian belief it, also seems clear that Christian believers can be motivated by other factors. Contra Freud, we have preliminary evidence that Christian belief is not necessarily involved in existential consolation.

10.

It is difficult to overstate the importance of this finding. For almost one hundred years it has been almost impossible to make progress regarding Freud's critique of religious belief in *The Future of an Illusion*. For most of this time skeptics and believers have largely engaged in a fruitless flame-throwing war producing more heat than light. This is largely due to the fact that the battle has been waged on the wrong turf. Again, the issues here are not philosophical or theological. In *The Future of an Illusion,* Freud is making an empirical claim about human psychology. So until the issue was taken up in psychological laboratories, there was legitimately no way to make progress. Few, if any, seemed to notice that problem. With the rise of functional accounts of religious belief the topic had changed, dramatically so. And not many noticed.

But progress may indeed be on the horizon. My 2006b study was the first empirical study to formally set out and test Freud's thesis in *The Future of an Illusion*. And while it is a bit disconcerting to find my own research in such direct conversation with someone of Freud's stature and influence, the results of that study, while tentative and preliminary, suggest that Freud's theory should be treated as less than comprehensive. What was observed among the participants in my laboratory was something more akin to what William James describes in *The Varieties of Religious Experience.* The Christian participants showed differences in how they handled existential stimuli, suggesting that needs for existential consolation varied among the participants. And while tentative, these results represent no small movement forward in the debate concerning, as Abraham Heschel (1955) described it, the "authenticity of faith."

Chapter 9

FEELING QUEASY ABOUT THE INCARNATION

HERE IN PART 3 WE ARE EXAMINING VARIOUS EMPIRICAL CASE studies aimed at investigating the rival hypotheses of Freud and James regarding religious experience. Specifically, we are looking for evidence that Christian believers handle existential material in different ways. Following Freud's and James's descriptions of the healthy-minded religious type, we expect some Christian believers to deploy their faith to minimize existential discomfort. In contrast, following James's description of the sick soul, it is expected that some Christian believers resist deploying their beliefs as a means to assuage existential anxiety.

In the last chapter we examined the case of worldview defense: how Christians respond to the existential challenges of an ideological Other. And, consistent with James's notion of religious varieties, we saw a diversity of responses among Christian participants. As predicted, those who appeared more healthy-minded (higher scores on the DTS) were more likely to engage in worldview defense, while those participants displaying a sick soul faith configuration (lower scores on the DTS) did not engage in worldview defense. This pattern of results appears to support James's thesis that there are religious varieties, a finding that puts pressure on Freud's contention that religious belief is necessarily involved in creating an existentially comforting illusion.

In this chapter we take up another case study examining how Christian participants deal with a different source of existential anxiety: the human body. Again following the lead of Ernest Becker, recent TMT research has shown our inhabiting of a body to be an existential, anxiety-inducing predicament. In light of that, we will examine in this chapter how this existential ambivalence about the body may be implicated in theological disputes within the Christian tradition regarding the doctrine of the Incarnation, the notion that God fully participated in the human bodily condition. If existential anxieties are involved in these theological disputes about the physical body of Jesus, we have another case where existential defensiveness may be assessed. Along these lines, this chapter will review the findings of a study where DTS scores—our proxy measure of healthy-mindedness and the sick soul— were used to predict what I have called "incarnational ambivalence": discomfort in imagining a fully human Jesus. The goal, once again, is to see if the healthy-minded and the sick souls (as assessed by the DTS) handle existential stimuli differently; in this case, to see how they handle the existentially unsettling vision of a fully human Jesus.

1.

Throughout Christian history, at different times and places, believers have expressed ambivalence regarding the doctrine of the Incarnation, the belief that God in the person of Jesus fully participated in the human condition. There has always been something scandalous and shocking about God taking a fully human form. In the early centuries of the church this incarnational ambivalence—discomfort in imagining a fully human Jesus—was observed in the Gnostic and Docetic heresies. Yet incarnational ambivalence has been observed in every era up to our own, particularly in Protestantism (see Hall & Thoennes, 2006; Lee, 1987).

What is the source of this discomfort? Why do many Christians feel queasy about the Incarnation? Recent work in TMT may provide one answer. Specifically, across a variety of studies it has been shown that people feel ambivalent toward their bodies and bodily functions (e.g., sex) because the body is a mortality or death reminder. If this analysis is correct, it might explain why many Christians, from the earliest days of the church, have resisted the notion of the Incarnation. Perhaps a fully human Jesus is theologically and psychologically worrisome because Jesus becomes too vulnerable to the forces of decay, the very forces that cause us such deep existential dread. Phrased another way, a superhuman Jesus, not affected by bodily functions, pain, or vulnerability, might seem a better prospect, psychologically speaking, to rescue us from our existential anxieties.

But if this is so, we wonder, given our concerns in this book, if all Christians flee the body of Jesus out of existential anxiety? That is, we would expect those who deploy their faith in an existentially defensive manner to be the ones most affected by incarnational ambivalence, to be the believers most disturbed by the physical body of Jesus. Conversely, we would expect less existentially defensive Christian believers to display less incarnational ambivalence, a greater willingness to welcome the existential ambiguities inherent in imagining God inhabiting a physical body, a body vulnerable to illness, sexual urges, and the daily rituals of urination and defecation. In sum, is there evidence for religious varieties in how Christians approach the existential anxieties inherent in this core doctrine of their faith?

2.

As noted, ambivalence concerning the body and the Incarnation has a long history in Christian thought starting with the Gnostic heresies. Although an in-depth account of Gnosticism is beyond the scope of this chapter, a theological overview of the Gnostic influence upon Christian thought might be helpful, particularly as body and incarnational ambivalence is still encountered in various sectors of Christianity.

For our purposes, we need only focus on two features of Gnostic theology. First, the Gnostics had a very low view of the material universe, deeming it to be created by a malevolent deity who could not be the true God of goodness and love. This view manifested itself in an extreme matter and spirit dualism: the material universe was depraved, broken, and evil while the spirit existed in a realm of beauty, health, and perfection. Salvation, then, in the Gnostic view, was the liberation of the spirit from the evil encasement of the body and the material cosmos. As Bart Ehrman (2003) has summarized Gnostic belief:

> There must be a greater God above this world, one who did not create this world. In this understanding, the material world itself—material existence in all its forms—is inferior at best or evil at worst, and so is the God, then, who created it. There must be a nonmaterial God unconnected with this world, above the creator God of the Old Testament, a God who neither created this world nor brought suffering to it, who wants to relieve his people from their suffering—not by redeeming this world but by delivering them from it, liberating them from their entrapment in this material existence. (p. 119)

The second feature of Gnostic theology is related to the first. Specifically, the value-laden matter and spirit dualism of the Gnostics affected their view of the body. If matter is evil then the body, as a material object, must also be evil. Given that the body was a source of evil and depravity many of the Gnostics advocated mortification (Ehrman, 2003):

> Gnostics were ascetic, advocating the strict regulation and harsh treatment of the body. Their logic was that since the body is evil, it should be punished, since attachment to the body is the *problem* of human existence, and since it is so easy to become attached to the body through pleasure, the body should be denied all pleasure. (p. 126)

Obviously, this view of the body had implications for how the Gnostic Christians viewed the body of Jesus in the Incarnation. Specifically, if the body is evil was it possible for Jesus, the Son of God, to have an actual, physical, fully human body? As Erhman (2003) notes, this was "one of the puzzles the Gnostics had to solve, and different Gnostic thinkers did so in different ways" (p. 124). It is not necessary here to review these theological systems except to note that they are expressions of incarnational ambivalence, an anxiety at the notion that Jesus did indeed exist in a fully human body.

This historical survey of Gnostic views of the body would be of little interest if it were not for the fact that these Gnostic ideas have lingered and continue to be a part of the Christianity tradition, both past and present. As Philip Lee (1987) has noted in his historical survey of Gnostic influences upon Christianity, "From Simeon Stylites to St. Francis of Assisi to certain aspects of Calvinism, the aversion to this world with a desire to escape it has been one of the most prominent strands in the fabric of Christianity" (p. 49). Further, Lee argues that this aversion has "led to some unfortunate attitudes toward the flesh, human nature, and sexuality" (p. 53) within Christianity.

Lee's historical survey provides ample and interesting examples of pervasive and continuing body ambivalence within the Christian faith. Take, as an example of the rejection of the physical, this assessment of Jonathan Edwards, a father of American evangelicalism (cited in Lee, 1987):

> The world is all over dirty. Everywhere it is covered with that which tends to defile the feet of the traveler. Our streets are dirty and muddy, intimating that the world is full of that which tends to defile the soul, that worldly objects and worldly concerns and worldly company tend to pollute us. (p. 87)

A similar example, this one more focused on body ambivalence, comes from the Puritan leader Cotton Mather. Mather's lament about the depravity of the body is triggered by his encounter with a dog while urinating (cited in Lee, 1987):

> I was once emptying the Cistern of Nature, and making Water at the Wall. At the same Time, there came a Dog, who did so

too, before me. Thought I: "What mean and vile Things are the Children of Men, in this mortal State! How much do our natural Necessities abase us and place us in some regard, on the Level with the very Dogs!" (p. 131)

Perhaps nowhere is body ambivalence more acutely felt within Christianity than in the area of sexuality, in which, at various times and places, mere participation in sexual intercourse, even within the marital bond, was considered by Christians to be disgusting and depraved.

These views of the body, seemingly driven by a disgust surrounding bodily functions such as urination or sex, have also affected Christian views regarding the Incarnation. Sharing the concerns of the Gnostics, Christians from all eras have wondered if Jesus fully participated in the human condition, physically speaking. Given the pervasive body ambivalence throughout Christian history the temptation has always been to resist a fully embodied Jesus. As noted above, the Gnostic impulse across the centuries has pushed many Christians to adopt a disembodied or superhuman vision of Jesus: "Gnostics of all eras have maintained a most profound mistrust of the body . . . [and] their disdain for the physical led them to a docetic, disembodied view of Christ" (Lee, 1987, p. 130).

We still observe this incarnational ambivalence in many Christian communities where candid discussion concerning topics such as the sexuality of Jesus is considered inappropriate and illicit. Many will remember the outrage within the Christian community regarding the portrayal of Jesus's sexuality in *The Last Temptation of Christ*, the novel by Nikos Kazantzakis and the Martin Scorsese film. Such reactions point to a lingering incarnational ambivalence within many sectors of Christianity.

3.

Given the pervasiveness of this body ambivalence within Christianity, it seems reasonable to ask if any psychological factors are at work. Once again, the literature of TMT will prove helpful.

To this point we have mainly focused on the TMT literature regarding worldview defense. But beyond worldview defense, TMT research has also examined how various facets of everyday existence can become existentially problematic, particularly when they function as death reminders. We are unsettled upon being reminded of our death and thus tend to repress or avoid aspects of life that make death salient. Again taking a cue from Ernest Becker and his book *The Denial of Death*, a great deal of this TMT research has focused on how the body functions as a mortality reminder. Specifically, the vulnerability of our bodies highlights the existential predicament that we will one day decay and die. Further, the gritty physicality of the body (e.g., blood, sweat, odors, waste) highlights our animal nature, which also functions as an existential affront to our aspirations of being immortal spiritual creatures. Cotton Mather's encounter with the dog springs to mind. As Becker (1973) has described:

> The essence of man is really its paradoxical nature, the fact that he is half animal and half symbolic. . . . This is the paradox: he is out of nature and hopelessly in it; he is dual, up in the stars and yet housed in a heart-pumping, breath-gasping body. . . . His body is a material and fleshy casing that is alien to him in many ways—the strangest and most repugnant way being that it aches and bleeds and will decay and die. . . . It is a terrifying dilemma to be in and have to live with. (pp. 30–34)

Based upon these insights, an impressive body of empirical work has strongly linked body ambivalence to death concerns. For example, mortality and death concerns have been linked to sexual ambivalence (Goldenberg, Cox, Pyszczynski, Greenberg, & Solomon, 2002; Goldenberg, Pyszczynski, McCoy, Greenburg, & Solomon, 1999; Landau et al., 2006), avoidance of physical sensation (Goldenberg et al., 2004), concerns over physical appearance (Goldenberg, McCoy, Pyszczynski, Greenberg, & Solomon, 2000), and resistance to human and animal comparisons (Goldenberg et al., 2001). Much of this research is summarized by Goldenberg, Pyszczynski, Greenberg, and Solomon (2000, p. 203) who conclude: "The body is a problem because it makes evident our similarity to other animals; this similarity is a threat because it reminds us that we are eventually going to die."

4.

Given the link between mortality concerns and body ambivalence, it seems reasonable to posit that a fear of death might be driving, or at least implicated in, incarnational ambivalence. If our physical bodies—with their sexual cravings, waste products, and vulnerabilities—activate death concerns, there might exist some psychological resistance to allowing Jesus, the Divine Son of God, to fully participate in human existence. The body is felt, at some level, to be too degrading for Jesus. This drives an existential queasiness in imagining Jesus being physically weak, vulnerable, experiencing bodily urges (e.g., sexual arousal) or participating in bodily functions (e.g., defecation).

If this is so, if existential anxiety is implicated in incarnational ambivalence, we have here a second case where the rival hypotheses of Freud and James might be examined. Specifically, if the notion of Jesus Christ fully participating in the human condition is existentially worrisome, we would expect the healthy-minded, who deploy faith as a buffer against existential anxiety, to be the most resistant and upset with incarnational imagery. Conversely, sick souls, who are more willing to embrace existential anxiety, should be more willing to entertain robust incarnational depictions of the life of Jesus. This case study is also of interest as it moves away from how Christian believers engage with those outside of the faith—worldview defense—toward how Christians manage their own doctrinal beliefs, particularly when those beliefs create existential tension or anxiety. This is another, but less obvious, example about what was discussed in prior chapters about the construction of the DTS: how religious beliefs are adopted, shifted, deployed, and managed to repress or reduce existential anxiety. This case also hints at the intriguing possibility that doctrinal disputes among Christians, historically and in our present day, might have less to do with theology than with psychology. Christians may be coming into conflict because they possess different tolerance levels when they engage with the existentially difficult aspects of their faith.

5.

In order to test these hypotheses regarding how the Jamesian types might handle existentially troubling incarnational images, I conducted a study that was subsequently published in the *Journal of Psychology and Theology* in 2009a.

The first challenge of the study was to create a measure of incarnational ambivalence as this construct had never been assessed or examined in the psychological literature. The procedure I used was to create of list of various hypothetical body scenarios concerning Jesus's life on earth. These scenarios were selected because each had been found to activate death and mortality concerns (Goldenberg et al., 2001). Subsequently, four broad body scenarios were identified and used: body fluids, body flaws, hygiene, and physical vulnerability. Respondents were asked to read a specific body scenario and imagine Jesus experiencing (or being affected by) the physical condition: "Although Christians believe Jesus was human as well as divine, people differ in how they imagine this. Below are various statements concerning Jesus and his human body. Read each item and then give your response using the rating scales below." Under the category of body fluids there were three scenarios: diarrhea, nocturnal emissions, and vomit. Under the body flaws category there were four scenarios: scarring, tooth decay, near-sightedness, and malformation. Under the hygiene category there were three scenarios: bad breath, body odor, and dandruff. Finally, under the physical vulnerability category there were two scenarios: chronic back pain and chronic headaches.

After reading each scenario, the respondents were asked to imagine each body scenario applying to Jesus and then rate each hypothetical along four scales, rated from 1 = *strongly disagree* to 7 = *strongly agree*.

The four rating scale prompts were as follows: "This image makes me uncomfortable"; "This image is demeaning to Jesus"; "This image is unrealistic; and "This image is unbiblical." The first two prompts were drafted to capture an emotional response to each scenario (i.e., discomfort, offense) while the final two prompts were drafted to capture a more intellectual, perhaps theological, response. When analyzed after data collection, it was observed that the four rating scales were highly intercorrelated. Participants who expressed discomfort with the incarnational scenarios also reported that the scenarios were demeaning to Jesus, unrealistic, and unbiblical (and vice versa). Consequently, the ratings were summed across the various images to create a total score assessing incarnational ambivalence (with higher scores indicating greater ambivalence).

Beyond this measure of incarnational ambivalence, the 228 Christian participants also completed measures of death anxiety and Christian orthodoxy (a measure of belief in the core doctrinal and creedal commitments of the Christian faith) along with the DTS.

6.

Overall, the pattern of results was consistent with the findings we observed in the last chapter regarding worldview defense, the notion that the Jamesian types handle existential stimuli differently. First, it was observed that creedal orthodoxy ratings were uncorrelated with the measure of incarnational ambivalence ($r = .01$). Feeling uncomfortable with the incarnational images appeared to have nothing to do with accepting or rejecting Christian doctrine generally. However, DTS scores were observed to be significantly associated with incarnational ambivalence ratings ($r = .30$, $p < .001$). This trend was consistent with expectations. Those scoring high on the DTS (the healthy-minded profile in which existentially consoling beliefs are endorsed) were the participants who expressed the most discomfort in imagining Jesus affected by or participating in the various incarnational scenarios. By contrast, those scoring low on the DTS (the sick souls) reported greater comfort—theologically and emotionally—with the body images. Confirming the existential frame of this trend, death anxiety was also observed to be significantly associated with incarnational ambivalence ($r = .13, p < .05$), with greater death anxiety predicting greater discomfort with imagining a fully human Jesus.

Overall, these findings point to additional support for the notion of religious varieties. Once again, as observed in the last chapter, we find evidence for a set of Christian participants who appear to be using their beliefs to manage or reduce existential anxiety. In the prior chapter, we saw this effort manifested in worldview defense, the denigration of an ideological Other. In this chapter we see this existential management manifested theologically, where doctrinal implications of the faith are pushed away when they create anxiety. Again, given that the human body is a source of existential anxiety, it stands to reason that many Christian believers will attempt to deny the fully implications of the Incarnation to manage their own existential insecurities. In this way existential fears would be driving a Gnostic flight from the body, both Jesus's and our own.

7.

In light of this additional evidence, let's conclude this chapter to note, once again, just how unexpected and peculiar these results are. As we saw in the last chapter, equipped with the background theory it seems obvious that DTS scores and death anxiety would be predictive of incarnational ambivalence. But if we step back for a moment, the association is far from obvious. Why, for example, is believing in something like God's helping you find lost car keys (as an example of divine solicitousness) associated with discomfort at the notion that Jesus might have experienced diarrhea? See Figure 11.

What's the connection here? As we saw with worldview defense, there appears to be no surface-level connection between these two variables. However, in light of all our investigations into the existential dynamics of faith, we are now able to see the subterranean connection:

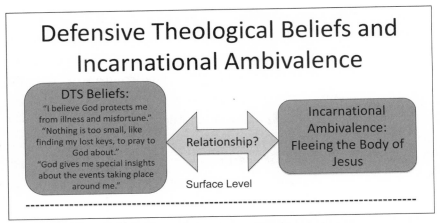

Figure 11. Defensive theological beliefs and incarnational ambivalence.

how a need for existential consolation is driving *both* DTS belief adoption and the discomfort in imagining a fully human Jesus. See Figure 12.

Again, these dynamics, as with the dynamics observed with worldview defense, are supportive of Freud's description of religious belief in *The Future of an Illusion*. Religious beliefs—about either divine solicitousness or about the metabolic life of Jesus—are being pushed and pulled by an underlying need for existential consolation. Particular beliefs are adopted (or resisted) because of the existential comfort they provide.

But while Freud insisted that all religious belief functions in this manner, here in this second case study we continue to find diversity among the Christian participants. In the incarnational ambivalence study, there was a subset of Christian believers who eschewed the suite of DTS beliefs and, as predicted, these were the same participants who reported greater comfort with the full, albeit existentially troubling, implications of the Incarnation. Imagining Jesus affected by illness, sexual urges, and metabolic functions did not appear to bother the sick souls, despite these experiences being implicated in the empirical literature as death reminders. The existential equanimity of the sick souls in the face of these images appears to be due to their reticence to adjust their theology to maximize existential comfort.

In conclusion, we have here one additional piece of evidence for religious varieties. Christian believers—the healthy-minded and the sick souls, respectively—appear to display different patterns of motivations in handling existential material. Some, as described by Freud, appear motivated to use faith to repress or reduce existential anxiety. By contrast, as described in James's account of the sick soul, other Christian believers appear willing to engage with difficult and unsettling existential material. And, building upon the findings of the last chapter, these differences appear to manifest themselves not only in how religious believers engage ideological Others but also in how faith communities debate the core doctrinal commitments of their faith, particularly when those doctrines prove to be existentially worrisome.

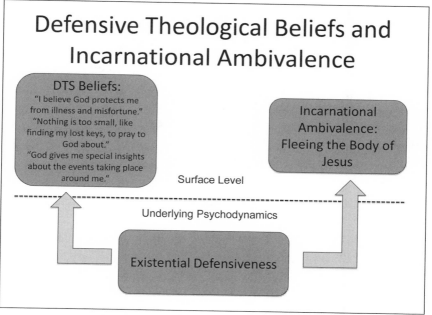

Figure 12. Defensive theological beliefs and incarnational ambivalence (expanded).

Chapter 10

THE THOMAS KINKADE EFFECT

1.

IN THE LAST TWO CHAPTERS WE HAVE BEEN EXAMINING HOW Christian believers react to stimuli or situations that prompt existential anxiety. In Chapter 8, the existential anxiety was associated with an encounter with an ideological Other, a person who subscribes to an alternative worldview and thus presents us with an implicit challenge about the truth of our worldview. In Chapter 9, the existential predicament was associated with the human body, the anxiety we experience when we contemplate how vulnerable we are to illness, injury, and death. In each case we observed how some religious believers try to shield themselves from the existential anxiety associated with these stimuli (Otherness or the body). In Chapter 8, we noted how Christian participants engaged in worldview defense by denigrating an out-group member. In Chapter 9, we saw how participants resisted images that too closely identified Jesus with the human body. These observations are consistent with Freud's claim that the function of religious belief is the management of existential anxiety, that the purpose of faith is to create a state of existential ease, comfort, solace, and consolation.

Yet in the two studies described in Chapters 8 and 9, we also observed that there was a set of Christian participants, those whom William James described as sick souls, who did not engage in worldview defense in the face of Otherness and who seemed comfortable with the gritty existential implications associated with the Incarnation. All in all these findings suggest that, while needs for existential consolation appear to be present within Christian populations, Christians show some diversity in the degree to which they use faith to manage, reduce, or repress existential anxiety. So far we have better evidence for religious varieties than for the notion that religious belief reduces to illusions of consolation.

In this chapter we examine a different source of existential solace or anxiety: the world of art and aesthetics. Art—whether visual, musical, theatrical, or literary—has always been a means by which cultures have either confronted our existential predicament or been comforted in the face of a hostile and cold universe. Art can be either escapist—an avoidance of reality—or a forceful way to encounter the darkest aspects of life. There is a world of difference, existentially speaking, between Picasso's *Guernica* and Thomas Kinkade or between Kafka's *Metamorphosis* and Harlequin romances. And importantly for our purposes, TMT researchers have begun to study the existential issues involved in art, particularly modern and abstract art.

In light of the diverse existential usages of art and the recent TMT research into the existential anxieties that modern art can produce, here in Chapter 10 we will consider our third case study: an examination of the use of art within Christian populations to determine if needs for existential consolation are involved in Christian aesthetic judgments and preferences. And beyond an additional test comparing the theories of James and Freud regarding the nature of religious experience, this issue is also of interest given a great deal of recent concern among Christian artists about a perceived decline in the quality of Christian art, from music to movies to the visual arts. Many Christian artists are asking, why is Christian art so often bad and of poor quality?

Perhaps, as we examine the varieties of religious aesthetics, our existential analysis might shed some light on that question.

2.

Visual art has a long and rich tradition within the Christian faith. From the first Christian art in the Roman catacombs to da Vinci's *The Last Supper* to Michelangelo's Sistine Chapel frescoes to the work of contemporary practicing Christian artists, art has profoundly affected Christian worship, personal devotion, and the larger Christian culture. And yet with the rise of Christian retail, many Christian artists are lamenting the quality of the Christian art bought and sold in Christian bookstores and retail outlets, artwork that is often used for devotional purposes or to adorn worship spaces. Specifically, many Christian artists see a general decline in Christian aesthetic judgments, as poor or superficial artwork appears to be dominating the Christian visual culture. Take, as an example, the assessment of the poet Steve Turner (2001) in his book *Imagine: A Vision for Christians in the Arts*:

> [Aspiring Christian artists] are usually frustrated that there is so little distinctive Christian content in the contemporary arts, but on the other hand, they are embarrassed at the low standards of much of what is promoted as "Christian art." (p. 10)

This evaluation of Christian artists' frustration jives with Turner's own judgment:

> This perspective confirmed what I had instinctively felt for some time—that a lot of art created by Christians was bad and a lot of art created by non-Christians was good. . . . Because the work that bore the name Christian was often poor in quality and naïve in understanding, Christianity by implication seemed insipid and uninspiring. (p. 12)

And Turner is not alone in this assessment. Take, as another example, the analysis of Philip Graham Ryken (2006) in his book *Art for God's Sake*:

The question becomes, therefore, whether as Christians we will aspire to high aesthetic standards. All too often we settle for something that is functional, but not beautiful. We gravitate toward what is familiar, popular, or commercial, with little regard for the enduring values of artistic excellence. Sometimes what we produce can be described only as *kitsch*—tacky artwork of poor quality that appeals to low tastes. The average Christian bookstore is full of the stuff, as real artists will tell us, if we will only listen. (p. 14)

If we accept these judgments, we might ask: Why is Christian art often so bad? Many think a root cause is theological. Specifically, when Christian artists depict the world they must wrestle with how they portray the more troubling existential aspects of human existence, aspects of life that may seem to threaten or challenge faith. Should a Christian artist depict the ugliness, the brokenness, and the god-forsakenness found in the world? Consider for instance the work of one of the most recognizable Christian artists, Thomas Kinkade. Kinkade has said that his idyllic paintings are portrayals of the world "without the Fall" (Balmer, 2000). In his avoidance of the ugly and more painful facets of existence, believed in the Christian faith to be due to the Fall in the Garden of Eden, it seems that the guiding aesthetic of Kinkade's work is quintessentially healthy-minded: art that, to quote William James (1902/1987), "deliberately excludes evil from its field of vision."

But many artists, Christian and non-Christian, wonder if this impulse can be truthful to human experience. Again, using James's description of healthy-mindedness, the question is if art of this sort is not exhibiting a "blindness and insensibility to opposing facts" and is being used as a "weapon for self-protection against disturbance." As the graphic artist Ned Bustard (2006) observes in *It Was Good: Making Art for the Glory of God*:

Inevitably it seems that most attempts to picture good tend to offer the viewer disingenuous, sugary sweet propaganda.

Ignoring the implications of the Fall, these artists paint the worlds as a shiny, happy place. The quintessential example of this in our day is found in Thomas Kinkade's general philosophy. Kinkade professes to be a Christian but has said, "I like to portray a world without the Fall." (p. 18)

The concern here is that good art should be truthful to the human experience and predicament; the alternative becomes a sort of naïve propaganda. Supporting this view, Bustard cites the opinion of Edward Knippers, one of the most influential Christian artists working today:

> Speaking to the issue of the portrayal of goodness in art, Knippers [insists] "Goodness needs to be attached to the real world because if you separate it from reality what you are left with is Disney World." The believer's art should be rooted in the rich soil of believing that humanity is far worse off than we think and God's grace extends far beyond what we can imagine. It is in this understanding and not the two-dimensional, sweet, niceness of Snow White that we can produce good fruit that is rich in the fullness of our humanity. (p. 24)

According to this view, true beauty is not achieved by willfully removing the signs of death, suffering, or brokenness. True beauty aims to find God's grace in unlikely and painful places. Take, as an example, Tim Lowly's *Carry Me*. In *Carry Me*, seen in Figure 13, Lowly draws his severely mentally and physically handicapped daughter Temma being lifted upward by six young women. Temma's eyes are closed. She appears peaceful and restful. The eyes of the six women look upward, toward us or God. *Carry Me* is not, to quote Bustard again, a work of "sugary sweet propaganda" which ignores the existentially difficult aspects of life by painting the world as "a shiny, happy place." *Carry Me* actually creates an existential moment by confronting us with the broken body of Temma. Yet beauty is found in *Carry Me* by allowing love and trust to be manifested in the midst of the brokenness. Adrienne Chaplin (2006) writes of

Figure 13. Carry Me.

Carry Me: "By allowing the broken body of Temma to stand for the brokenness of us all, we are encouraged to reflect on our shared humanity" (p. 49). What we find in *Carry Me* is very different from the healthy-minded aesthetic of a Thomas Kinkade, where we find "a method," according to William James (1902/1987), "of averting one's attention from evil." By contrast, what we see in *Carry Me* might be described as the aesthetics of the sick soul: the belief, quoting James again, that the difficult facets of life, such as the body of Temma, "are a genuine portion of reality; and that [these parts of life] may after all be the best key to life's significance, and possibly the only openers of our eyes to the deepest levels of truth."

3.

To summarize, perhaps one explanation for certain Christian aesthetic trends stems from a reluctance to confront the more difficult existential aspects of a broken and fractured existence. Perhaps some Christian art is not trying to depict reality but is rather attempting to help us cope with or avoid reality. By this point in the book this question should be very familiar. Is religious faith able to be truthful about reality or is it simply a means to *avoid* reality? It appears that the use and function of art, particularly among religious believers, may be another way to empirically approach these questions. But is there any evidence that suggests that aesthetic judgments are indeed affected by existential anxieties? Interestingly, there is.

A recent study by Landau, Greenberg, Solomon, Pyszczynski and Martens (2006) examined reactions to abstract art from the perspective of TMT. Landau et al. (2006) speculated that one of the reasons people object to abstract art is that it is existentially unsettling. Being formless, chaotic, and resistant to interpretation, abstract art can create (intentionally or unintentionally) an experience of fracture and befuddlement, perhaps because it is a reflection of the existential predicament of modern existence. In this, modern art can create a crisis of meaning. Quoting Landau et al.: "Modern art, which appears to many as irregular mosaics of pointless shapes and meaningless splatters, may be disliked because of an existential concern with maintaining meaning" (p. 881).

To test this thesis, Landau et al. (2006) conducted a variety of studies in which participants were exposed to both representational and abstract art after undergoing the now familiar death-awareness manipulation (i.e., being asked to write an essay about the experience of dying). If existential concerns are implicated in rejecting abstract art, then the expectation was that a death-prime manipulation would exacerbate this effect. That is, those in the death-prime condition would be more dismissive of abstract art relative to control participants. Overall, across a series of studies, that is the effect Landau et al. observed. Death awareness prompted greater rejection of abstract art. It appeared that art was being used to help create existential meaning and it was frustrating to participants when the abstract artwork frustrated those attempts. Landau et al. conclude:

> In sum, art has the potential to contribute critically to beliefs in the significance of ordinary experience and the existence of extraordinary worlds, helping imbue reality with an overall sense of order, beauty, and purpose, thereby helping people to maintain psychological equanimity in the face of death. (p. 890)

The research of Landau et al. (2006) has important implications for our investigation of Christian aesthetics. As noted above, some worry that Christian art often fails to confront the more difficult aspects of reality. The resulting product is often sweet or Disney-like. In light of Landau et al.'s research, we have in hand one possible explanation for this trend. Christian art may be being produced and purchased because

THE AUTHENTICITY OF FAITH

it helps "imbue reality with an overall sense of order, beauty, and purpose, thereby helping people to maintain psychological equanimity in the face of death." Christian art is often sweet because it functions, on some level, as a form of existential comfort and consolation. If this is so, Christian art might not be as challenging, existentially speaking, as it could be because many Christians are preferring art for the emotional comfort it can provide.

4.

A recent study of mine published in 2010, conducted with my colleagues Dan McGregor, Brooke Woodrow, Andrea Haugen, and Kyna Killion, set out to examine this exact question. Are existential anxieties implicated in Christian aesthetic judgments and preferences?

In our study we had Christian participants randomly assigned to either a control or mortality-salience condition using the procedure of Landau et al. (2006). Participants were then presented with two pieces of artwork, one neutral and the other overtly Christian. The Christian artwork was selected to be representative of the kind sold in Christian retail stores and Christian bookstores. The piece used was the painting *Never Alone* by the popular Christian artist Ron DiCianni, which depicts a student being watched by a guardian angel. The neutral artwork was selected to be representative of master-level art but not iconic or readily recognizable (i.e., we were not going to show them a Monet or the *Mona Lisa*). The piece used was *Stone City, Iowa* by Grant Wood (most famous for his iconic *American Gothic* painting) which, at the time of this writing, is on permanent exhibit at Omaha's Joslyn Art Museum. The goal in selecting these two pieces was to create a quality differential, having participants compare commercial Christian art to a piece of art deemed masterful by the artistic community (artists and critics).

After the standard TMT experimental manipulations (control versus mortality salience), the participants in each condition were given a copy of each piece of artwork (8.5 x 11 inch color copies) and asked to record their preferences and aesthetic judgments for each. The rating items were the same used by Landau et al. (2006): "How much do you like this art-work?"; "How much does this particular artwork appeal to you at a gut level?"; and "Relative to other art you've seen, how interested would you be in checking out more art like this?" Each question was rated on a 1–9 Likert scale (1 = *Not at all*) to (9 = *Very much*), and then summed to create a total impression score for each piece of artwork.

Overall, the results were consistent with the notion that existential anxieties are implicated in Christian aesthetic judgments. Two trends were of particular note. First, across the board the Christian partici-pants in the study preferred the Christian art to the neutral art. In itself this preference is interesting as a case could be made that this is empiri-cal evidence pointing to a decline in Christian aesthetic standards. This is not meant to be a criticism of Mr. DiCianni's work, but it is startling that *Stone City, Iowa*, currently hanging in an art museum, received sig-nificantly *lower* ratings by our Christian participants. It appeared that the Christian participants were making their aesthetic choices based upon the overt Christian content of *Never Alone*, gravitating toward the art that bolstered and supported their belief system. If that is the case, it is perhaps not surprising that the theme of *Never Alone*—a guardian angel looking over a student—would be particularly comforting to our college student participants.

Importantly for our purposes, this trend was intensified in the mor-tality-salience condition. After exposure to the death-awareness prime, preferences for the Christian artwork increased while preferences for the neutral artwork decreased.[3] Having taken a moment to consider the eventuality of their own death, the Christian participants were much more attracted to the Christian artwork and more dismissive of the art that did not bolster their worldview in the face of death. These trends mirror the worldview defense trends we have observed in earlier chap-ters. But here, rather than denigrating ideological Others, Christian

---

3   The results of the Mixed 2 (Priming Condition: Death vs. Dental) x 2 (Artwork: Christian vs. Neutral Art) ANOVA showed no main effect for Priming (p = .512), a main effect for Artwork (p < .001), and a significant Priming x Artwork interaction (p = .004).

artwork is being used to support and bolster the worldview in the face of death. In this, Christian art is functioning as a form of *propaganda*: art less interested in challenging its audience than supporting, confirming, and strengthening the audience's values, belief system, and worldview. From the conclusion of Beck et al. (2010):

> It appeared that Christian participants were inherently biased to prefer artwork that symbolized their worldview and belief system, regardless of artistic merit. Further, this trend was intensified in the death prime condition. After a death prime, preferences for the Christian art increased while decreasing for the neutral art. Such an effect is consistent with the notion that artwork is being preferred by some Christians for its existential function (e.g., as a means to address death anxiety). (p. 307)

5.

In light of Beck et al. (2010), we might call this attraction to existentially comforting art within Christian populations "The Thomas Kinkade effect." This is meant as no disrespect to Kinkade, who is an artist of considerable talent. It is only a comment on his stated objective in producing his artwork, the portrayal of the world without the Fall, and why that portrayal may be attractive to Christian believers, existentially speaking.

However, we should note that Beck et al. (2010) didn't address the differences between what we might call high art and the artwork we use to adorn our homes. We may be very willing and interested to go to a museum for an existential engagement with modern art but reluctant to use such art to decorate our living rooms. We like our homes to be comforting shelters from the storms and anxieties of life. Consequently, we—the religious and non-religious alike—choose to hang on our walls images that soothe us.

Still, this observation only converges upon a point made by Ernest Becker that we discussed in Part 1: the fact that everyone, whether religious or nonreligious, engages in worldview defense. Everyone, regardless of faith stance, has some interest in creating a home that functions as an existential womb, a place of peace and tranquility, a location of rest in the middle of a chaotic world. And, given this impulse, it is reasonable to see aesthetic choices being made to maximize the comfort we feel in these places. The Thomas Kinkade effect is a ubiquitous phenomenon.

But even if the Thomas Kinkade effect affects believers and nonbelievers alike, the presence of the phenomenon does not help us assess William James's thesis regarding religious varieties. We wonder how the aesthetic choices of the healthy-minded and the sick souls might vary. Keeping with what we've already observed in Chapters 8 and 9, we might expect the sick souls to be less interested in Kinkadian art and display a greater interest in engaging art that strips away the sweet veneer to life. We would expect sick souls to resist the Thomas Kinkade effect. By contrast, we might expect the healthy-minded to be more attracted to Kinkadian art given its objective in presenting us with an uncomplicated, Disney-like world without the Fall.

6.

This comparison between the aesthetic impulses of the religious varieties was not conducted in our 2010 study, which was narrowly focused on determining if existential issues were implicated in Christian aesthetic judgments. Religious varieties weren't examined in Beck et al. However, the participants in our 2010 study did complete a variety of pretest measures that were not examined in the original study. One of these scales was the DTS. And while the DTS was not a focus of analysis in Beck et al., the fact that the participants completed the DTS allowed me to return to that data set for the purposes of this chapter. The goal of this analysis was straightforward: given the evidence of the Thomas Kinkade effect in Beck et al., what do we find when we examine the role of religious varieties in that sample?

What I found when I ran these additional analyses was that the effect of death-awareness priming upon the artwork ratings was removed when I controlled for DTS scores.[4] In addition, in this analysis the DTS scores were observed to be predictive of the Thomas Kinkade effect. Those scoring higher on the DTS—those fitting the healthy-minded type—displayed a greater preference for the Christian artwork over Grant Wood's *Stone City, Iowa*. By contrast, sick souls—those scoring low on the DTS—showed the exact opposite trend.[5]

This finding closely mirrors the pattern of results observed in Chapter 8 regarding worldview defense. Specifically, any existential defensiveness on display (denigrating an out-group target, be that target artwork or an Other) is better explained by an appeal to religious varieties than to the mortality-salience priming. It appears that the religious varieties—the healthy-minded and the sick soul—simply approach existential situations in different ways. The former tend toward existential comfort; the latter move in the opposite direction. In the world of art, the healthy-minded seem to display the Thomas Kinkade effect while the sick souls seem more resistant to that impulse. The healthy-minded seem motivated to avoid an existential engagement with Others or artwork that might challenge their worldview (or at least fail to provide overt support for their worldview) while sick souls seem interested in engaging Others or artwork that challenges their faith.

In sum, our analysis in this chapter of how Christian participants interact with artwork supports the observations from the case studies in the prior two chapters. We find once again evidence for religious varieties; Christian participants are displaying diversity in how they engage with existential stimuli. When it comes to the use and function of art,

---

4   An ANCOVA was run. The dependent variable was the overall rating difference between the Christian artwork and the Neutral artwork (Christian – Neutral) where higher scores indicate that the Christian artwork was preferred over the Neutral artwork. The independent variable was Priming condition (Death-awareness prime versus Control). The covariate was DTS ratings. Overall, when controlling for DTS scores, Priming condition had no with relationship upon artwork ratings ($p = .102$). DTS scores, by contrast, did have a significant impact upon artwork ratings ($p < .001$), with higher DTS scores (a more healthy-minded profile) associated with a greater preference for the Christian art relative to the neutral art. When not controlling for DTS scores, priming condition was significantly associated with artwork ratings ($p < .05$).
5   The correlation between DTS scores and overall rating difference (Christian – Neutral) was $r = .23, p < .001$.

some Christians, the healthy-minded in particular, appear to use art to avoid or sugarcoat reality. The healthy-minded appear to display the Thomas Kinkade effect, a preference for art that avoids the existential ambiguities of the Fall. By contrast, sick souls seem less inclined to display this impulse and thus appear more willing to engage with art that moves them more directly into an existential confrontation with reality.

Finally, not only do these observations help us assess the rival models of William James and Sigmund Freud, but they may also go a fair distance in helping us understand some of the recent aesthetic trends within the Christian population. Art is not always valued for art's sake. Many times, we seek out art for existential comfort and consolation, and these needs affect our aesthetic judgments and preferences. Sometimes, particularly in the existential womb of our living rooms, we like to see Thomas Kinkade hanging on the wall.

Chapter 11

THE GOD WHO CRACKED

OVER THE LAST THREE CHAPTERS WE HAVE OBSERVED HOW Christian believers engage with existential material, stimuli, or situations, from how they encounter ideological Others to the human body to artwork. In each case we have noted that Christian believers do not appear to behave in a uniform and homogeneous manner. While it is true, as Freud described, that many religious believers do appear to deploy their beliefs as a means to maximize existential consolation, there also seems to be a set of believers who seek out, or are at least willing to endure, existential tension (tensions found in engaging Others, theology, or the world of art). Stepping back and taking in the last three chapters, this observation lends support for William James's notion of religious varieties, suggesting that James's contrast between how the healthy-minded and sick soul types handle existential anxiety is describing real differences within religious populations. This is not to say Freud's analysis in *The Future of an Illusion* is wrong, as in each of the last three chapters, we have also observed ample evidence for the defensive faith-as-narcotic dynamic Freud described. However, we are increasingly suspicious that Freud's theory of religious belief is as comprehensive as he claimed it to be.

The last three chapters have reviewed research in which the DTS was used to assess James's healthy-minded and sick soul types. In each case we noted how those scoring high on the DTS (persons endorsing existentially consoling beliefs) differed from those scoring low on the DTS (persons eschewing existentially consoling beliefs). And while this procedure appears effective in getting at some of the diversity within the Christian population it is not the only way we might try to examine religious varieties. In this chapter, we will examine a final case study in which the DTS was not used, but where we continue to find evidence for the healthy-minded and sick soul experiences as described by James in *The Varieties of Religious Experience*.

1.

For much of this book, we have been examining how religious belief might be shifted around, at a surface level, to meet a deeper—perhaps unconscious—need for existential comfort. We have argued that many religious believers subscribe to views such as divine solicitousness and special protection because it is comforting to believe that the cosmos is fundamentally benevolent and willing to help us. We want to feel safe and cared for. And while it is true that a fundamental confession of the Christian faith is that God is loving and desirous of our well-being, we also know, from within the biblical witness itself, that God is often experienced as absent or silent. And, in extreme cases, God can also be experienced as antagonistic, the source of our pain and affliction. These experiences, as we discussed in Chapter 6, define the territory of the sick soul, the landscape of lament. Existential comfort is more difficult to locate in these experiences, like looking for water in a dry land. In the face of a suffering and broken world, belief in divine solicitousness and special protection are hard to come by for sick souls. In fact, just the opposite seems to be the case: God is decidedly *un*helpful and, rather than providing protection, is allowing suffering to continue, often in ways that leave us trembling in sadness, shock, despair, and horror.

These experiences are difficult to face. They infuse life with a sense of existential despair. Even though it might be easier, simply as a matter of coping, to hide our eyes from life (as many do), the sick souls refuse to look away. They refuse the too easy retreat into existentially consoling beliefs. And the price they pay for this is allowing a painful tension to sit at the center of their faith experience, a belief in a God who is often not present and who often fails to rescue. While such an experience seems paradoxical, our discussions (Chapter 6 in particular) have suggested that these experiences are not diseased or episodic. As we saw with Mother Teresa's forty-year experience of spiritual darkness, the condition of lament can be the major chord of the faith journey.

These observations suggest that the quest for existential consolation might not only affect beliefs about what God *does* (does God protect me or help me find lost car keys?) but also about who God *is*. That is, if God is not helping or protecting me, if God has gone missing, we begin to wonder in the midst of our suffering if God truly cares. Beliefs about the actions (or inactions) of God begin to affect beliefs about the nature of God. It becomes hard, theologically and emotionally, to reconcile the experience of suffering with the belief that God cares for us.

This, as many know, is the experience of theodicy within the Christian faith, the struggle to reconcile the experience of suffering with the claim that God is both omnipotent and loving. Psychologically speaking, there is a cognitive dissonance here, a tension that is uncomfortable to maintain. And importantly for the purposes of this chapter, this tension—the experience of suffering and the belief in a loving, all-powerful God—is particularly acute in monotheistic faith traditions. In polytheistic systems discordant life events can be quickly attributed to malevolent deities. But when there is a single, omnipotent God the positive and negative experiences of life get laid at the one God's feet. Consider passages like Isaiah 45:6–7 (KJV): "I am the LORD and there is none else. I form light, and create darkness: I make peace, and create evil: I the LORD do all these things."

Here Isaiah 45 presents us with a very strong and startling monotheistic formulation: Everything—good and bad, weal and woe, peace and evil—comes from God.

However, the problem with Isaiah 45, psychologically speaking, is that when prosperity and disaster are both attributed to God, the believer's relationship with God can become emotionally and theologically complicated, resulting in the experience of lament. Theodicy is no mere theological puzzle; in monotheistic faiths such as Christianity it is experienced as an acute experiential burden. In my research I call this "the emotional burden of monotheism."

2.

How do religious believers handle this burden? How do Christians, in particular, reconcile their experience of suffering with their claims about a benevolent and omnipotent Deity?

As the psychologist Leon Festinger pointed out in his seminal work *When Prophesy Fails*, we find the experience of cognitive dissonance uncomfortable. In the face of this discomfort we rearrange beliefs to achieve harmony between beliefs and experience. Theodicy, as we have described it, is an experience of cognitive dissonance, particularly in monotheistic faiths. So how is this dissonance resolved in the lives of religious believers? Interestingly, in *Varieties* William James describes one thing that might happen. James argues that while monotheism works well as a creedal assertion in practice it is difficult to attribute both good and evil to the one God without the relationship to God becoming anxious, confused, and ambivalent. So, to resolve these tensions in daily life, believers will "crack" God into two parts to create a dualism in which the positive aspects of life are attributed to God and the painful aspects of life are attributed to a malevolent force, a force either equal to God (in a strict dualism) or a rebellious renegade agent that God allows some scope of influence (e.g., Satan in the Christian tradition). Here is James (1902/1987) describing this cracking of mono-theism to cope with the cognitive dissonance caused by life suffering:

> If we admit that evil is an essential part of our being and the key to the interpretation of our life, we load ourselves down with a difficulty that has always proved burdensome in philosophies of religion. Theism, whenever it has erected itself into a systematic philosophy of the universe, has shown a reluctance to let God be anything less that All-in-All. In other words, philosophic theism has always shown a tendency to become pantheistic and monistic, and to consider the world as one unit as absolute fact; and this has been at variance with popular or practical theism, which latter has ever been more or less frankly pluralistic, not to say polytheistic, and shown itself perfectly well satisfied with a universe composed of many original principles, provided we be only allowed to believe that the divine principle remains supreme, and that the others are subordinate. In this latter case God is not necessarily responsible for the existence of evil; he would only be responsible if it were not finally overcome. But on the monistic or pantheistic view, evil, like everything else, must have its foundation in God, and the difficulty is to see how this can possibly be the case if God is absolutely good. . . . The only *obvious* escape from this paradox here is to cut loose from the monistic assumption altogether, and to allow the world to have existed from its origin in pluralistic form, as an aggregate or collection of higher and lower things and principles, rather than an absolute unitary fact. . . . Now the gospel of healthy-mindedness, as we have described it, casts its vote distinctly for this pluralistic view. (p. 124–125)

James here is mainly discussing "philosophical theism," thus his discussion of monism and pantheism. But the dynamics he is describing can be readily applied to monotheistic faiths. As noted above, the strict monotheism of Isaiah 45—God as the source of good and evil—is difficult to maintain, not just theologically but also experientially. How does the believer relate to such an unpredictable Deity? As James notes, when God is "All-in-All" the experience of evil creates a "difficulty" in knowing "if God is absolutely good." In light of this difficulty, within the believer's lived experience (what James calls the "popular or practical theism") there is a shift toward a "polytheism," in which there are believed to be lesser "subordinate" forces in the world that are "responsible for the existence of evil." The positive outcome of this polytheistic move is that the believer no longer has to understand or experience God as the origin and source of evil. This effectively resolves the cognitive dissonance. Weal and woe are not attributed to God as found in Isaiah 45. Rather, only goodness flows from God. Evil, pain, and suffering come from some other cosmic agent, from God's rival, enemy, or opposing force. Suddenly, the believer's relationship with God becomes significantly less complicated. The emotional burden of monotheism has been lifted. God is experienced as wholly and consistently good.

Importantly for our purposes, James suggests in his discussion that the healthy-minded would gravitate toward the polytheistic solution in resolving the dissonances in explaining their experiences of evil. Although James is not clear about why he makes this assertion, we can see the logic at work, particularly in light of our discussions over previous chapters. If healthy-minded believers are driven by a need to keep their religious experience with God uncomplicated and positive, then the problem of evil poses a challenge, particularly if the believers come from a monotheistic faith tradition in which they have to wrestle with the dissonances inherent in Isaiah 45. This will prove difficult, creating emotional tensions that will infuse the God-relationship with negativity and ambivalence. But being motivated by healthy-minded impulses (i.e., wanting the faith experience to be a source of comfort rather than struggle) the believers will crack their faith experience, creating a dualistic or polytheistic model where, practically if not creedally, the good in life is attributed to God and the evil in life is attributed *elsewhere*. This cracking effectively resolves the dilemma and allows the experience of

God to become uncomplicated and uncontaminated by negative affect, doubt, or lament.

By contrast, we can expect monotheistic sick souls to be more resistant to this cracking. Less motivated by needs for comfort or solace, sick souls should be more willing to tolerate the existentially difficult implications of their faith. Sick souls should be more, rather than less, willing to attribute suffering *to* God, to follow Isaiah 45 and hold God responsible for the whole of life. The result is the experience of monotheistic lament we find in the psalms of complaint. Again, this is the experiential space described in Chapter 6—high complaint and high communion—that captures the experience of the sick soul. As noted then, this is an experience filled with theological tension and cognitive dissonance. Consequently, there is emotional and psychological discomfort. The healthy-minded, according to James, will seek to exit this space as quickly as possible, usually by cracking the faith experience. However, sick souls, being less motivated by a need for comfort, are more likely to linger in this space, perhaps spending their entire lives within this experience. Sick souls would accomplish this by remaining rugged monotheists, refusing to crack God. Sick souls will try to shoulder the full emotional burden of monotheism.

What we see in all this is another way to test the rival theories of Freud and James. At the very least, we can explore here the theological and psychological dynamics that James predicted would be associated with the healthy-minded and sick soul types. According to James, it seems that some monotheistic religious believers are more or less willing to shoulder the emotional burden inherent in their religious worldview (i.e., the monotheistic implications of Isaiah 45). Healthy-minded believers seeking to minimize psychic discomfort should, according to James, shy away from the emotional and theological tensions found within the experience of evil. They would do this by cracking the faith experience, systematically refusing to attribute evil to God and assigning the blame elsewhere. Monotheistic sick souls, by contrast, being less motivated by a need for psychic comfort should be more willing to live with the tensions found with the experience of evil, being, as monotheists, more willing to lay the blame for suffering at God's feet. By doing this the sick soul moves into an experience filled with doubt, anxiety, ambivalence, and even anger—the experience of monotheistic lament as found within the lament psalms. Consequently, by looking for these dynamics in a Christian population we have another means to test James's thesis regarding religious varieties. We can examine how religious believers make theological shifts to resolve the sources of cognitive dissonance within their faith experience.

3.

Our case study remains with the Christian faith. Christianity is a monotheistic faith but the figure of Satan in the New Testament, as the enemy of the people of God, infuses a dualism into the faith that should allow us to assess the cracking dynamics described by William James. As the writer and theologian Gregory Boyd (2001) has noted, the monotheistic position (where God is controlling all events, good and bad)

> makes it exceedingly difficult to reconcile the evil in our world with the omnipotence and perfect goodness of God. It is not easy to believe—and for some of us, not possible to believe—that there is a specific providential purpose being served by certain horrifying experiences. (pp. 13–14)

To get around this "exceedingly difficult" problem, Christians can attribute "horrifying experiences" to Satan rather than God's "providential purpose."

Historically, given the role of Satan in Christian belief, Christianity has always been tempted by dualistic polytheism. From the great heresies of Gnosticism and Marcionism in the first and second centuries to Manichaeanism in the third and fourth centuries and Catharism in the thirteenth century, many Christians have tried to resolve the emotional burden of monotheism by positing two gods, one good and the other evil. Although these movements were declared to be heretical, each was a powerful force in its day. And the reason is easy to see. As described above, the psychological appeal of ditheism is that it provides a resolution to the ambivalences inherent in monotheism. The good god, the god of Jesus Christ, becomes a relatively uncomplicated character, full of unmitigated goodness and love. The pain, suffering, and evils of life can be systematically shifted to the second, malevolent god.

While Christianity has decisively rejected the ditheistic heresies, dualistic notions continue to linger within Christianity via the character of Satan. In the oldest books of the Tanakh (Old Testament) Satan appears as a minor actor. But in postexilic Judaism and early Christianity, the Satan construct intensified. Rather than simply being a Heavenly Prosecutor, Satan becomes the enemy of God and the personification of evil. As articulated in I Peter 5:8: "Be self-controlled and alert. Your enemy the devil prowls around like a roaring lion looking for someone to devour." Although not strictly a ditheism, this intensification of the Satan construct produces a weak polytheistic dualism where the blessings of life can be attributed to God and the sufferings of life can be blamed, to some degree, upon the activity of the Devil.

Why did Satan become a more significant figure during postexilic Judaism? The intensification of the Satan character may have been motivated by the same theodicy concerns we have been describing. In the face of suffering, a stronger Satan may have helped to resolve some of the emotional burden inherent in monotheism among postexilic Judaism. For example, Jack Miles (2001) has suggested that postexilic Israel faced its supreme crisis of theodicy (the destruction of the nation) at the very time they were exposed to Persian Zoroastrianism (the dominant faith of the host nation). Although Persian Zoroastrianism had a pantheon of gods, its central vision was dualistic with two deities—one Good and the other Evil—dominating the metaphysical scene. Miles argues that this exposure to Zoroastrian dualism, in the face of Israel's national and theological nightmare, led to an elaboration of the Old Testament Satan character along with an enhanced angelology and demonology. Consequently, Israel's theodicy questions came to be answered with a dualistic warfare model, where the spiritual forces of goodness were arrayed against the spiritual forces of darkness. This warfare model is best illustrated in the postexilic book of Daniel (cf. Daniel 10:20–21). Miles (2001) summarizes this entire line of argument:

> My translation reflects my belief that the linked angelology and demonology of Hellenistic Judaism and early Christianity are ultimately Persian in origin. . . . [First,] Yahweh began to function as exclusively a principle of good rather than as, simultaneously, a principle of good and of evil. The consequences are obvious: As God became both a consistently good god and the only real god, the question How could a good god permit . . . ? suddenly became unavoidable and indeed is faced for the first time. . . .
>
> Just at this point in its history, as it happened, Israel was massively exposed to a persuasive answer to the new question. The empire that succeeded the Babylonian in Israel was the Persian, and Persian Zoroastrianism recognized two competing deities: Ahura Mazdah, the personification of good, and Angra Mainyu, the personification of evil. These two were not the only supernatural beings in existence, but all others were organized around them. The process by which Persian religious thought penetrated Israelite thought is impossible to reconstruct, for the record of their interaction during the two centuries when Persia ruled Israel is extremely slender. It is undeniable, however, that after this period the long Israelite entanglement with Semitic polytheism seems to be over, while a dramatic growth in the importance of Satan, or the Devil, is easy to document, not to mention a concomitant growth in the number and importance of angels serving God and of devils serving the "new" Satan. . . . One sees this change most easily in the extracanonical Jewish literature of the last pre-Christian centuries. (pp. 300–302)

Although Miles's historical reconstruction is speculative, many other theologians have made similar observations. The theologian S. M. Heim (2001) summarizes how, throughout Christian history, the devil has been used to create a functional dualistic faith to alleviate the theodicy burden upon God:

> The devil [has] offered a backdoor escape from the theodicy dilemma, by providing an informal vehicle for a manichaean or gnostic alternative to it. So the devil was sometimes tugged toward a manichaean status (a power equal and opposite to God, responsible for evil) or toward the gnostic status of a quasi-creator (a lower divinity responsible for the deficient character of material creation). (p. 87)

This brief historical review suggests that the dynamic described by William James may be observed within Christian populations. The Christian belief in Satan allows for a functional dualism to emerge within the Christian experience where some of the evil of life can be blamed on the devil rather than God. And while this shift may not completely answer the questions of theodicy, it does ease, if only a bit, the emotional burden of monotheism.

Relationship with God can be complicated. In the midst of pain and suffering we wonder if God truly cares about us. This feeling is exacerbated if God is believed to be the actual cause of our pain. But what if God is not the cause? What if a second malevolent force—Satan—is the cause of my suffering? Some, if not all, of the woe of life could be attributed to Satan's actions. If so, then at least some portion of the pain and suffering of my life isn't attributed directly to God. In the end, this allows my relationship with God to be slightly *less* conflicted and ambivalent.

4.

But is there any evidence for this formulation? In the face of suffering, do Christian believers use Satan to reduce the emotional burden of monotheism? In 2008, Sara Taylor and I published a study that tried to get at these dynamics. The goal of the study was fairly straightforward. Our argument was that Christian believers with strong Satan constructs (i.e., believers who have a very robust notion of Satan's activity, power, and scope in the world) are attributionally close to a dualistic religious formulation. That is, for these believers much of the pain and suffering in life is being systematically shifted away from God and onto Satan. By contrast, Christian believers with weaker Satan concepts (i.e., believers who may believe in Satan but see him as a minor player in their lives) were assumed to be attributionally closer to a monotheistic position, where the good *and* the bad in life are laid at the feet of God. For these believers, their relationship with God should be more ambivalent and thus should be rated in less glowing terms when compared with their counterparts.' More, we also expected to see strong Satan concepts functioning as a theodicy, where believers with stronger Satan concepts would direct less blame toward God for the evils and sufferings of the human condition. By contrast, believers with weaker notions of Satan were expected to blame God more for pain and suffering.

Our first goal was to create a measure that would assess the strength of a Christian believer's Satan concept. How active, powerful, and aggressive do particular people believe Satan to be in their day-to-day life? To assess beliefs along these lines we drafted eight items to create the Strength of the Satan Concept (SSC) measure. The SSC items (rated on a 1–6 Likert scale, (1 = *Strongly disagree*) to (6 = *Strongly agree*), with items 3 and 6 reverse scored):

1. Satan can cause misfortune, accidents, or illness to fall upon good people.
2. In my spiritual life, I feel I am involved in an ongoing battle against Satan.
3. I don't think Satan can do much to interfere in people's lives.
4. Satan is a present and active force in human affairs.

5. Satan roams the earth actively seeking to defeat the people of God.
6. I don't believe Satan attacks, harms, and/or interferes with people.
7. I believe that Satan (or his agents) can influence people to act in evil or destructive ways.
8. Failing to respect the power of Satan in the world leaves you ignorant and vulnerable to his attacks.

Higher scores on the SSC items indicate a very strong Satan construct in which Satan is believed to be actively engaged with and affecting daily life experiences. In this, higher SSC scores paint a picture of a functional dualism within the religious experience. I use the word "functional" to suggest that while the person does not necessarily believe, creedally speaking, that Satan is a power equal to God, daily life is experienced and explained in a dualistic fashion. The dualism here is functional and experiential rather than creedal or theological. By contrast, lower scores point toward a weaker Satan construct and a more monotheistic experience.

After creating a measure for the experience of Satan, we turned to create a measure that could assess how much a believer blames God for the sufferings of life. We called the seven items we drafted for this purpose the Theodic Complaint Scale (each TCS item was rated on a 1–6 Likert scale, *"Strongly disagree"* to *"Strongly agree"*):

1. The amount of suffering and pain in the world makes me doubt that God cares about the world.
2. I blame God for the amount of pain and suffering in the world.
3. I think God has let the world get out of control.
4. God is responsible for allowing all the pain and suffering in the world.
5. It troubles me that God does not prevent pain and suffering in the world.

6. I am disappointed in God for creating a world full of pain and suffering.
7. It is largely God's fault for allowing so much pain and suffering in the world.

High scores on the TCS items point to a believer who is holding God directly responsible for the pain and suffering in the world with the associated feelings of disappointment in God. In addition to the TCS items, we also used two other measures to assess the quality of the God relationship: the Attachment to God Inventory (Beck & McDonald, 2004) and the Spiritual Well-Being Scale (Ellison, 1983; Ellison & Smith, 1991).

When we correlated these measures, the trends supported the notion that beliefs in Satan were being used to ease the emotional burden of monotheism. For example, persons reporting more robust notions of Satan also reported more satisfying relationships with God as assessed by the God-relationship measures.[6] The greater the experience of Satan, the more positive the experience with God.

Most importantly for our purposes was the correlation between beliefs in Satan's activity in the world and theodicy complaint. Overall, a significant negative correlation was observed between SSC and TCS ratings.[7] Participants with robust notions of Satan, a dualistic experience, tended to blame God less for the suffering in human existence. Conversely, participants with weaker, more attenuated Satan constructs, more of a monotheistic experience, tended to blame God more for pain and suffering. All told, this was the pattern of results described by William James in *Varieties*. A healthy-minded faith experience with God, in which positivity dominates, was associated with a dualistic formulation where the evil of life was shifted away from God and onto Satan. By contrast, a sick soul experience of God, in which negativity is present in the faith experience, was associated with a more monothe-

---

6   SSC and SWS-Religious $r = .41, p < .001$; SSC and AGI-Avoidance $r = -.25, p < .001$
7   SSC and TCS $r = -.24, p < .001$

istic stance where blame for life suffering was not attributed to Satan but to God directly.

5.

Because of the correlational nature of our 2008 study, we need to careful in interpreting its findings. While we observed statistical associations between beliefs in Satan and the God relationship we cannot determine if beliefs in Satan were, consciously or unconsciously, adopted or deployed to handle the emotional burden the experience of suffering places upon monotheistic believers. Still, the results of our research are supportive of such a conclusion. And while there was not an explicit attempt in our 2008 study to identify and sort the healthy-minded from the sick souls, the dynamics observed in that study do provide one more bit of data that can be used in adjudicating between the theories of James and Freud.

Specifically, what we observed in this research is something very similar to what we have observed across Chapters 8–10: some religious believers deploy particular beliefs to achieve emotional or existential comfort. William James (1902/1987) argued that evil is a "genuine portion of reality" and that it may be "the best key to life's significance, and possibly the only openers of our eyes to the deepest levels of truth." And yet for monotheists evil presents a snarly problem, both theologically and experientially. Is God, as Isaiah 45 claims, the origin of good *and* evil? The answer here dramatically affects my experience of God. How can God be experienced as loving and trustworthy if God is the cause of the suffering in my life? The tensions here are enormous. The cognitive dissonance is uncomfortable and distressing. Seeking relief, many monotheists may crack the God experience to shift blame away from God. In the Christian faith, some of this blame can be shifted onto the figure of Satan. Historically, many Christians have made heretical leaps in this direction, trading in a monotheistic (but emotionally complicated) orthodoxy for a cleaner (emotionally speaking) dualistic formulation. And even though most Christians avoid these heresies, the results of my research suggest that, functionally speaking, Christians can operate as dualists on a day to day basis. They do this by positing a very active Satan in the world who is responsible (rather than God) for much of the suffering and chaos they find around them. The happy result is that the relationship with God becomes less complicated and ambivalent. God is experienced as wholly good and benevolent. Isaiah 45 recedes.

Of course, shifting blame onto Satan doesn't actually resolve the hard questions of theodicy. Why, for example, does a good and omnipotent God allow Satan such power over humans? Why doesn't God protect us from Satan's attack? Satan or not, in a monotheistic faith doesn't the ultimate responsibility for suffering fall upon God? These are important and interesting theological questions, but a bit beside the point psychologically speaking. The use of Satan as a functional theodicy, as way of explaining the suffering of life without blaming God overmuch, is not really an exercise in theology. It is rather a means of coping, a way to reduce the cognitive dissonance created by monotheistic belief in a world full of pain and suffering.

According to Freud, this coping is the function of religious belief, the adoption and deployment of a belief system to minimize psychic pain and maximize consolation. Consequently, we see in our 2008 study additional evidence that Freud is describing a legitimate dynamic within the religious experience.

However, we are struck again by the prescience of William James's notion of religious varieties. Like Freud, James recognized that the healthy-minded religious experience will gravitate toward a dualism in the face of life pain. This is indeed what we observed in my laboratory. However, consistent with the notion of religious varieties, we also observed religious believers whose experience with God was more ambivalent and filled with disappointment due to the fact that these believers appear to refuse to let God off the hook. Shouldering the emotional burden of monotheism, these believers appear to move into the paradoxical high communion-high complaint space described within the Christian tradition by the psalms of lament.

6.

In conclusion, here in our fourth and final empirical case study we find additional evidence for religious varieties. And while we have noted evidence that faith is often used as a means of existential coping, we have repeatedly observed here in Part 3 how the model of faith formulated by Freud in *The Future of an Illusion* fails to describe the whole of the religious experience. Faith appears to encompass more than illusion and existential coping.

Across the four empirical case studies presented in Part 3, we have been seeking to adjudicate between the rival models of Sigmund Freud and William James regarding the nature of religious experience. The verdict? In light of the empirical evidence, we tentatively cast our vote for William James.

It is *varieties* over illusion.

Conclusion

THE AUTHENTICITY OF FAITH

1.

WHY DO PEOPLE BELIEVE IN GOD?

Obviously, there is no single answer to that question. If we stand within the great tradition of Christian apologetics, we get one sort of answer. Belief in God is justifiable on epistemological grounds. Reason and evidence are marshaled to create and maintain belief.

But with the rise of biological, psychological, and sociological accounts from the masters of suspicion, thinkers such as Darwin, Freud, and Marx, new answers about the origins of religious belief have been proposed. These answers have little to do with the bread and butter of classical apologetics. Rather, these accounts dig deep to question the subterranean motivations of faith. I have called these theories functional accounts because they share an interest in specifying the value of faith—the goal, purpose, and function of belief. Generally speaking, these functions have little to do with the overt contents or professed motivations for faith. On the surface the faithful claim that their faith results from a dispassionate and reasonable assessment of the evidence.

But functional accounts treat these surface level commentaries with skepticism. The contention is that believers do not have access to their true motivations. And even if they did, they would be unwilling or unable to admit to them.

This is why Freud's opening salvo in *The Future of an Illusion* introduced a radical change in how believers and nonbelievers would come to discuss the origins of religious belief. Freud (1927/1989) had asked, "In what does the particular value of religious ideas lie?" That focus on value was a profound changing of the subject. No longer would the historical, theological, creedal, and doctrinal contents of faith be the sole object of discussion and debate. A focus had shifted to the value of faith, the way religious belief functioned in the life of the believer. It was a shift from theology to coping. How does religious belief help us *cope* with life and existence?

Freud assumed as many do that here, at the level of psychological coping, we had finally arrived at the truth, the real reason people believed in God. Belief in God helps us cope with our fears, both real and existential. As Freud argued in *The Future of an Illusion*, while modern humans have done much to tame nature, we are still vulnerable. We are still shaken, emotionally and physically, by tsunamis, earthquakes, hurricanes, tornados, and disease. Further, death remains the unanswered challenge. As Freud summarized:

> No one is under the illusion that nature has already been vanquished. . . . There are the elements, which seem to mock at all human control: the earth, which quakes and is torn apart and buries all human life and its works; water, which deluges and drowns everything in a turmoil; storms, which blow everything before them; there are diseases . . . and finally there is the painful riddle of death, against which no medicine has yet been found, nor probably will be. With these forces nature rises up against us, majestic, cruel and inexorable; she brings to our mind once more our weakness and helplessness. (p. 19)

How are we to cope in the face of such hostile and indifferent forces? How are we to avoid the existential terror of death? As Freud argued, "Man's self-regard, seriously menaced, calls for consolation" (p. 20).

This is where, according to Freud, religious belief steps in. In the face of our terror and existential despair "a store of ideas is created, born from man's need to make his helplessness tolerable" (1927/1989, p. 23). What are these ideas? Freud goes on to list many of them: "Life in this world serves a higher purpose," "Over each one of us there watches a benevolent Providence," "Death itself is not extinction . . . but the beginning of a new kind of existence," and "In the end all good is rewarded and all evil punished" (pp. 23–24). By adopting these and similar beliefs "all the terrors, the sufferings and the hardships of life are destined to be obliterated."

For Freud, then, fear is what motivates belief in God. Fear of nature. Fear of death. Fear of meaninglessness. And while these fears may be understandable and reasonable, Freud pushes further, suggesting that a retreat into comforting religious illusions is no mature or healthy way to deal with our anxieties and uncertainties. As Freud argued, this "infantilism" should "be surmounted. Men cannot remain children forever; they must in the end go out into 'hostile life'" (1927/1989, p. 62–63). We must, Freud claimed, grow up and get an "education to reality."

2.

Most people are aware of Freud's basic attack on religious belief. Crudely put, religious belief is a cop-out. Religious belief is for those who lack the courage to face life and death honestly and stoically. The atheist, by contrast, thus appears to us to be a person of courage and integrity, the individual with the emotional strength to face the facts. According to Freud, nonbelievers are adults who have grown out of childhood fantasies. Believers, however, remain stuck in fear, clinging to superstitious but sweetly consoling illusions.

Not surprisingly, religious believers are quick to object to these simplistic and crude comparisons between believers and nonbelievers.

As well they should. Still, if we are honest, there is cogency in Freud's analysis. For as he noted in *The Future of an Illusion* it is more than a little suspicious that the beliefs we adopt so closely mirror our deepest fears. It seems more than a little suspicious that, in the face of death, religious believers posit a life after death. And in the face of a chaotic and dangerous world, that there is a powerful and benevolent Deity who is on our side and willing to help. If we are honest, we see Freud's point. The whole thing looks a bit fishy. A bit too neat and tidy.

Still, this proves nothing. Our *wishes* imply nothing about *ontology*. Just because I wish X to be the case doesn't have any bearing upon the existence of X. Just because a person wishes God to exist says nothing about if God does, indeed, exist. Logically, this makes sense. But it's hard to shake the powerful circumstantial evidence of Freud's observation that wish mirrors belief so closely.

In fact, the evidence is a bit more than circumstantial. As we noted in Part 1, recent work in TMT has suggested that religious believers do deploy their beliefs as a buffer against existential anxiety. In light of this empirical laboratory evidence, Freud cannot be shaken off so easily. Leaving the distinction between wish and ontology aside, it seems that religious believers do deploy faith in much the manner described by Freud in *The Future of an Illusion*. And while it is true that these psychological observations can be logically quarantined from questions of ontology (e.g., Does God exist?), they are powerfully supportive of Freud's analysis of faith in *The Future of an Illusion*, making it that much harder to brush Freud aside. Freud needs to be taken seriously.

And this is as it should be. For at the end of the day, even religious believers know that faith is often a form of wishful thinking. We get why Marx called faith the opiate of the masses. We understand why there are no atheists in foxholes. We can see why there are deathbed conversions. We have to admit it: faith *is* consoling. Faith makes life less bitter and sad. Faith makes death less meaningless.

3.

So where does that leave us? For religious believers, in a somewhat uncomfortable position. Freud's criticism seems reasonable. Freud, despite his militant atheism, is not just criticizing religion. He is describing a real phenomenon, one backed by laboratory research and easily recognized by both believers and nonbelievers. And while these psychologically based criticisms of faith do not have any logical purchase upon the ultimate claim regarding God's existence, they do alter the debate and place believers on the defensive. For if Freud is correct, if believers are using their faith as a means for existential consolation, why should we trust their appeals to reason and evidence when it is clear that they cannot be objective and fair conversation partners? In the end, the atheist will argue that you cannot dispassionately discuss hard questions when your conversation partner is *afraid*. As Freud noted, "The believer will not let his belief be torn from him, either by arguments or by prohibitions. And even if this did succeed with some it would be cruelty" (1927/1989, p. 62).

So we are left, then, in the wake of *The Future of an Illusion* (along with other works of suspicion) with the analysis of Abraham Joshua Heschel (1955) from the quote that started this book:

> It has long been known that need and desire play a part in the shaping of beliefs. But is it true, as modern psychology often claims, that our religious beliefs are nothing but attempts to satisfy subconscious wishes? That the conception of God is merely a projection of self-seeking emotions, an objectification of subjective needs, the self in disguise? Indeed, the tendency to question the genuineness of man's concerns about God is a challenge no less serious than the tendency to question the existence of God. We are in greater need of a proof for the authenticity of faith than of a proof for the existence of God. (pp. 35–36)

This is the terrain for a new sort of apologetics. No longer are we seeking a proof for the existence of God. We are, rather, now sifting through psychological "need and desire" to determine how they "play a part in the shaping of beliefs." For in light of the work of the masters of suspicion, there is now a "tendency to question the genuineness of man's concerns about God." Thus we face a "greater need of a proof for the authenticity of faith than a proof for the existence of God."

But is such a proof even possible? And what might it mean to say that faith is authentic and genuine?

The first thing to say about such a proof is that it is not going to be a proof like those we might find in mathematics or logic. Any proof is going to have to take up Freud's analysis where he left it, in the realm of psychology. At the end of the day, Freud is making an empirical claim about how faith works in the minds of religious believers. More, the evidence we have seen that is supportive of Freud is emerging, as expected, from psychological laboratories. Thus, the proof Heschel is looking for is not going to be found in seminaries or in the theological literature. Those are the places where proofs for the existence of God might be found, the location of classical apologetics. But we are looking for something quite difference: evidence for the authenticity of faith which will of necessity involve examining and sorting through psychological needs and motivations and how these relate to faith. No doubt it is strange to see issues of faith sorted out in psychological laboratories. But as Heschel notes, Freud has pushed us into a strange new world.

4.

What might it mean to say that faith is authentic? There are, I expect, a variety of answers to this question. In this book we have tried to frame authenticity in light of Freud's criticism of faith. For Freud, faith is inauthentic, a form of illusion, because it is not educated to reality. Faith is inauthentic because, at root, it is a form of obfuscation, a dishonesty about the terrors, pain, and absurdities of life. The key psychological symptom of this dishonesty and inauthenticity is existential consolation.

This is why both Freud and Marx compare faith to a narcotic. Faith is a kind of existential drug that has both analgesic and anxiolytic effects. Faith reduces the psychic suffering and anxiety associated with human existence. For Freud then, authenticity is about being willing to endure the sufferings and anxieties of life.

So the question becomes, is it possible to have a faith that refuses to allow faith to become a means of existential consolation? Is it possible to have a faith that is less interested in positing a life after death or a hovering protective Deity than in confronting the terrors of life? Is it possible to have a faith where, due to existential honesty, psychic pain and anxiety are regular features of the faith experience? Is it, in short, possible to have a *non*narcotic faith?

And what might such a faith look like?

In seeking an answer to that question, our journey took us to William James and *The Varieties of Religious Experience*. Unlike Freud's reductionistic one size fits all analysis, in *Varieties* James suggests that the motivations behind religious belief are varied and multifaceted. Of particular interest for our purposes is James's analysis regarding how needs for existential consolation might vary within religious populations. James is very quick to agree with Freud that many religious believers, whom James (1902/1987) labeled healthy-minded, seem to be motivated by a desire to "deliberately exclude evil from its field of vision" and to "look on all things and see that they are good." Like Freud, James describes this need for consolation as a sort of blindness to the facts of life where faith is used as an "instinctive weapon for self-protection" against the anxieties of life. James even converges upon Freud and Marx's faith as narcotic metaphor suggesting that healthy-mindedness is a form of "congenital anesthesia."

But where James parts ways with Freud is in his positing of what he calls the sick soul. According to James, here is a religious experience that does not avoid but embraces the existential ambiguities of life. This is a faith experience that wants to confront and maximize evil. Here, faith is not functioning as a means of existential consolation. Rather, faith draws one deeper and deeper into the existential predicament.

Does this sort of religious experience make any sense? Consider the analysis of the theologian Jürgen Moltmann as he describes how faith relates to the problem of suffering in the world. As Moltmann (1993) describes it:

> It is in suffering that the whole human question about God arises; for incomprehensible suffering calls the God of men and women in question. The suffering of a single innocent child is an irrefutable rebuttal of the notion of the almighty and kindly God in heaven. For a God who lets the innocent suffer and who permits senseless death is not worthy to be called God at all. . . . The theism of the almighty and kindly God comes to an end on the rock of suffering. (p. 47)

For Moltmann, in the face of this conflict—belief in God in the face of innocent children suffering—faith isn't the effort to avoid the resultant doubt and anxiety. Rather, faith draws the believer toward a deeper participation with the suffering:

> The question of theodicy is not a speculative question. . . . It is *the open wound of life in this world*. It is the real task of faith and theology to make it possible for us to survive, to go on living, with this open wound. The person who believes will not rest content with any slickly explanatory answer to the theodicy question. And he will also resist any attempts to soften the question down. The more a person believes, the more deeply he experiences pain over the suffering in the world. (p. 49)

Faith in this view is not leading us away from pain, anxiety, doubt, and suffering, toward the psychological narcotic of existential consolation. Rather, faith is leading us deeper into suffering, doubt, and despair. Faith makes the experience of suffering *more* acute rather than *less*.

This is a religious experience very different from anything Freud envisioned in *The Future of an Illusion*. According to Freud (1927/1989), once the role of existential consolation is removed from faith, religious belief should "lose all human interest." One wonders, then, what Freud would make of Moltmann's description of faith.

Not that we should criticize Freud overmuch. The sick soul experience does seem paradoxical, strange, and counterintuitive. It is not a wonder Freud missed it. And yet our survey of the Christian experience points to both the existence and vibrancy of this mode of faith. As we discussed in Chapter 6, a part of the paradox stems from the assumption that communion and engagement with God is antithetical to lament, complaint, and doubt. Freud, along with many religious believers, appeared to be working with this bipolar model of the faith experience, where, as faith increases, complaint (the experience of what Moltmann (1993) describes as "the open wound of life") necessarily decreases. No doubt this is often the case with healthy-minded believers who deploy faith as a buffer against the harshness of life. But as my research concerning the structure of religious experience has suggested (Beck, 2006a), communion and complaint are not two poles along a single continuum. Rather, as illustrated in Chapter 6, a two-dimensional model, where communion and complaint exist at right angles, best captures the structure of the religious experience. Given this landscape, we see how communion and complaint can coexist, mingling together in the sick soul or winter Christian experience. And again, this experience is amply attested to within the Christian experience as observed in the lament psalms of the Old Testament and within the biographies of saints of darkness like Mother Teresa.

5.

In short, what I have argued for in these pages is that the existence of the sick soul may provide one way to answer Heschel's request for a proof regarding the authenticity of faith. Specifically, if Freud argued that religious belief is inauthentic because it is used as a means of existential consolation, then we might explore religious experiences where existential consolation is systematically rejected. And should we find evidence for such faith experiences, we would have in hand data suggesting that faith can be authentic, if not across the board than at least for some individuals. We would have in this instance evidence (though no proof) that faith does not *necessarily* involve existential illusion, that faith can be educated to reality.

The research described in Parts 2 and 3 sets out the evidence that such a faith experience does indeed exist. Across the four empirical case studies reviewed in Part 3, it appeared that a subset within the Christian samples studies, those conforming to the sick soul type, engaged with existential stimuli in ways distinct from their healthy-minded counterparts. And in each case we saw the sick souls behaving as William James predicted they would: these sick souls avoided comfortable existential options to engage with material that would create *greater* existential anxiety or distress.

The sick souls were more open to engage with ideological Others, despite the fact that ideological Others create questions regarding the legitimacy of one's religious worldview. Still, sick souls refused to denigrate the Other, even in the face of a death-awareness prime. More, the sick souls appeared more comfortable with the existential anxieties associated with the human body. This allowed them to embrace doctrines that have historically caused a great deal of anxiety within the Christian tradition. Further, sick souls appeared less drawn to existential propaganda such as artwork that bolstered their worldview and hid the Fall from their eyes and consciousness. Lastly, sick souls seemed more willing to hold their God accountable for the pain and suffering of life. This caused their communion with God to become ambivalent, doubt filled, and full of lament, creating the winter faith experience (high communion-high complaint) described in Chapter 6.

Throughout this book, then, we have monitored a debate between the towering figures of Sigmund Freud and William James as they posited two rival hypotheses regarding the nature of religious experience. Is religious experience best described by existential *varieties* or as an *illusion*? The outcome of this debate would allow us to determine if an authentic faith was possible. And, all told, we have found the evidence to tip toward James rather than Freud. Time and again we have found evidence for religious varieties, which suggests that Freud's analysis, while legitimate, is not comprehensive. And while this evidence by no means proves the authenticity of faith, it does suggest that religious belief cannot be so quickly reduced to existential illusion.

And so, for now at least, we cast our vote with *The Varieties of Religious Experience* over *The Future of an Illusion*.

6.

While this outcome may seem to be a victory for people of faith we might need to offer some clarification lest this conclusion be misunderstood.

Let me state the issue clearly: Freud was right. Maybe not totally, 100% right, but right nonetheless. That is going to be a hard message for many religious believers to internalize. And yet religious believers should listen to Freud because he was able to place his finger upon a legitimate dynamic within the religious experience, one with important ethical consequences.

What might be the value, religiously speaking, of taking Freud seriously? Let me offer one reason. At root, Freud's argument is that religious belief is often based upon fear. Fear of life. Fear of death. Fear of outsiders. More, as described by Ernest Becker in *Escape from Evil*, this fear often prompts acts of exclusion and violence. We noted this dynamic in our discussions about Christian participants displaying worldview defense (e.g., denigrating Others) in the TMT literature. It is thus ethically important for religious populations to confront the role of fear in belief adoption and deployment. Fear-based religious communities will be bastions of reactive intolerance and violence. In all of this, we find Freud offering a prophetic critique of religion—a vital and ethically important critique.

This criticism is particularly important given the ideological pluralism we experience in the modern world. For most of human history, people lived and died in isolated ideological pockets. In the West prior to the Protestant Reformation, people rarely encountered ideological

Others. Neighbors and nations shared the same values, religion, and worldview. But in this age of globalization and the Internet, we routinely come into contact with a diversity of worldviews. Our neighbors and coworkers may be Catholic, Jewish, Buddhist, Muslim, Wiccan, or atheist. In the face of these Others we fear a relativization of our worldview. My religious faith, the foundation of ultimate value and meaning for my life, is implicitly called into question by these ideological neighbors. How can I be sure that the God I worship is the correct God? Or if there even is a God? In our pluralistic world, where contact with ideological Others is routine, questions such as these are everyday fare. And life becomes filled with existential anxiety.

In the face of this anxiety we often find people engaging in worldview defense, especially in the denigrating of out-group members. This leads to a somewhat paradoxical social outcome. Rather than pluralism making us more tolerant and accepting of difference, we find an increase in intolerance and suspicion. As we all know, although it seems counterintuitive, the rise of extreme fundamentalisms is one of the most significant challenges facing modernity. But in the wake of the Enlightenment, shouldn't we be seeing a decline in extreme fundamentalism? If so, then why is it on the rise?

Freud's analysis of religious belief, particularly as reframed by the existential thinkers such as Ernest Becker, provides one answer. If worldviews provide the structures of significance for life and if ideological Others implicitly challenge those structures, we can see how, in the face of pluralism, individuals would seek to engage in worldview defense. Pluralism is *existentially* difficult. The call to tolerate alternative worldviews is implicitly suggesting that all worldviews are equal. This relativizing of worldviews undermines the worldview's ability to function as a source of ultimate meaning and significance. This undermining, existentially speaking, is a scary prospect. So it becomes much easier to double down on the worldview and to consider Others as deviant, ignorant, or evil. At the very least, we consider Others as mistaken. To protect ourselves from anxiety, we tilt toward a dogmatic certainty and become worldview fundamentalists—all driven by an underlying existential fear.

These dynamics, how pluralism breeds fear-based fundamentalism, have been cogently described by the sociologists Peter Berger and Anton Zijderveld (2009). As indicated by Berger and Zijderveld (2009), the modern world "produces plurality. And plurality increases the individual's ability to make choices between and among worldviews" (p. 18). Centuries ago churches could "rely on either cultural taken-for-grantedness or the coercive power of the state to fill its pews" (p. 20). But in the modern world, with its clash of competing worldviews, religious faiths now find themselves competing with each other:

> Pluralization also changes the relations of religious institutions with each other. They now find themselves as competitors in a free, or relatively free, market. Once they give up the project of restoring or creating anew a religious monopoly, they must somehow acknowledge their competition. (p. 21)

All this competition and choice creates the modern experience of relativization, the sense that I am choosing among equality viable alternatives. But this experience of shopping for or choosing a religion undermines the very foundation of faith, the belief that my faith is the source of ultimate truth. True, on first blush this expansion of choice seems to be a good thing, a liberation. But the modern person can become quickly overwhelmed with both the number of choices on offer and how choice itself trivializes the religious project. As Berger and Zijderveld (2009) describe it:

> The relativization that was first experienced as a great unburdening now itself becomes a great burden. The individual now looks back with nostalgia to the lost absolutes of his past; alternatively, he or she searches for new absolutes. The liberation that is now sought is a liberation *from* the burden of relativity, *from* the many choices of the modern condition. (p. 45)

This is the dynamic described above, a retreat into a new absolutism that allows us to escape from the existential burden of a relativizing pluralism. This is the allure of fundamentalism in modernity. Fundamentalism helps us cope with the anxiety caused by the relativizing encounter with Otherness in our pluralistic world. At the end of the day, fundamentalism is embraced for the existential consolation it provides. As Berger and Zijderveld summarize:

> This is the great refusal of relativization. The proponents of the various versions of neo-absolutism have very seductive messages: "Do you feel lost in the 'patchwork' of religious possibilities? Here, surrender to the one true faith that we offer you, and you'll find yourself at peace with the world." Comparable messages are on offer to allay the vertigo of choice in morality, politics, lifestyles. And the message isn't lying: Fanatics *are* more at peace, less torn, than those who struggle daily with the challenges of relativity. This peace, however, comes with a price. (2009, p. 47)

We already know what this price is: worldview defense, the stigmatization of Otherness and difference. These suspicions about out-group members scale up to affect the whole of society. Society becomes ideologically balkanized, with individuals seeking ideological reassurances from the like-minded. These ideological groups and their suspicions about each other make modern societies increasingly unstable and prone to conflict. As Berger and Zijderveld describe it, "The final outcome may be all-out civil strife, between radicalized subcultures and the majority society, and/or between/among the several subcultures themselves" (2009, p. 86).

All this is to confirm the larger point under discussion. Specifically, if religion is going to live up to its full moral and social potential it will need to both diagnose and master the fear-based dynamics that linger beneath the surface of the religious experience. Modern pluralism presents a difficult existential challenge for faith. Beneath bland calls for tolerance among belief systems, there is the threat of relativization which undermines the ultimate legitimacy of faith, effectively obliterating the very source of life meaning for many individuals. As a consequence, many individuals, to cope with this fear, will engage in worldview defense, retreating into an absolutism that stigmatizes out-group members. This is the price religious groups will pay if they don't step back and take Freud seriously. Unself-reflective groups will often retreat into existential illusions, and those illusions will need to be protected from criticism—often violently so.

That said, there is no easy solution here, no quick fix for religious communities wanting to reduce fear-based dogmatism and intolerance among its members. Regardless, the lesson to take away here is that religious communities will find Freud, perhaps surprisingly, to be an important conversation partner. True, Freud's thoroughgoing skepticism will rankle at times. But given the challenges of religious extremism, fundamentalism, and fanaticism facing the world today, Freud's analysis is too important to dismiss. The reflection we see in the mirror Freud holds up to religious experience is not a pretty picture. But we turn away at our own peril.

7.

Having addressed religious readers, let me now turn to address any readers who are skeptical of religion. If religious believers are encouraged to take Freud seriously, the other side of the coin is that Freud does not appear to possess the complete picture when it comes to religious experience. Rather, the evidence appears to support William James's notion of religious varieties. Freud's reductionistic analysis of religious faith should be rejected as a final and comprehensive answer about the motivations of belief. In the end, skeptics of religion who wish to use Freudian critiques of religion, suggesting that all belief reduces to wishful thinking, will need to note that painting with this broad brush isn't supported by the evidence. The religious experience is more sprawling and multifaceted than Freud's simplistic one size fits all analysis.

That said, I think the skeptics of religion, if they have gotten to this point in the book, do have a legitimate concern to level at the argument and analyses I've offered in these pages, particularly if these skeptics are social scientists.

Let me state the problem clearly: I present this book as a dispassionate piece of social scientific investigation, an objective analysis of the rival models of James and Freud regarding the religious experience. And at the end of this analysis I've argued that the data, collected from my laboratory, support the notion of James's religious varieties.

So far so good. The problem comes from the fact that I've also framed this book as a new apologetics, the use of social scientific research to defend the legitimacy and authenticity of religious belief. Compounding this problem is also the fact that I am a confessing Christian.

In short, how can I claim to be doing science when it is clear I have a vested interest in the outcome of these investigations? Am I not biased? Am I not prone to look for data that fit my agenda? The problem is clear: science is corrupted if it becomes apologetical. It is no longer science in that instance, but propaganda.

Let me address this criticism in a couple of different ways.

First, I did characterize this book and the empirical research it contains as a new sort of apologetics. I mainly use that description to point to the radical shift that occurred when suspicious functional accounts of religious belief, like the one Freud offered in *The Future of an Illusion*, began to gain attention and influence. The shift was away from metaphysics, epistemology, and ontology toward issues rooted in psychology, sociology and biology. The question was no longer "Does God exist?" but "Why would people want to believe in God in the first place?" That's a different sort of question requiring different sorts of answers.

In short, my use of the description "new sort of apologetics" was mainly intended to recognize this shift about how the debate about faith has been removed, in many cases, from the realm of theology and been taken up by the life and social sciences. Each day in newspaper, magazine and journal articles we find genetics, neuroscience, anthropology, sociology and psychology all weighing in on the question of faith, its nature, origin and function. Consequently, if there is going to be a defense of faith, it going to have to take place here, in the realm of social and biological research. Here is where, sifting among this data, a new apologetics will have to begin.

Still, we shouldn't be sifting this data with an agenda in mind, with a point to prove. Nor should researchers set out to collect data to fit their preconceived notions. Again, the whole notion of apologetics is misplaced when it comes to science.

That observation is true, but it simply reflects another way this sort of apologetics is "new." Specifically, science is a way of putting theories at *risk*. This is what it means when we say a hypothesis is testable or falsifiable. Consequently, if we are to be data driven in these conversations we need to be willing to admit error and to welcome data points that do not fit our expectations. We have to be willing to admit that our theory is not supported by the evidence. By contrast, our tendency is to assume that apologetics doesn't involve any risk. Apologetical advocates tend to claim that they are in possession of the truth. There is no question, in their minds at least, that they might be mistaken. Science, in contrast, with its data-driven approach seems to be the exact opposite. In the scientific enterprise, our preconceived notions, however cherished, must be let go when the data point us in a different direction. In science we are willing to admit we are wrong. This willingness seems very different from what we see on display in religious polemics.

Or is it? Yes, we are familiar with the caricature of apologetics, the dogmatic advocates who will defend their belief to the last breath, evidence and reason be damned. But is this the proper view of apologetics? Let me suggest that any legitimate apologetics, of whatever stripe, should be epistemically virtuous. That is, the apologetical enterprise should be characterized by an openness to argument, evidence, and persuasion, if only for the simple fact that a position cannot be successfully defended (the goal of any apologist), if the advocate is willfully blind, resistant, or immune to evidence and logic. How would that be a defense? How would that be persuasive?

I want to suggest that the apologetical enterprise, properly understood, has always involved openness to evidence and argument, that it has always involved risk. Religious faith, or anything for that matter, should be defended for as long as the evidence will carry it. And no further.

There is a symmetry here. The skeptic can be just as blind to evidence as the believer. So the best we can ask is for both parties to be transparent about their biases and to approach the evidence and the debate with open minds. The outcome cannot be predicted from the outset. Both sides should be willing to undergo the risk inherent in true and, dare we say, authentic conversation.

8.

So my first response to the charge of bias is simply to suggest that any defense of a position must be commensurate with the evidence. This, I'm suggesting, has always been the proper role of apologetics. A defense that ignores and plays fast and loose with the evidence is no defense at all.

And yet, this doesn't really address the charge of bias: that my data collection, hypothesis formulation, and data interpretation may be, and perhaps likely are, tinged with experimenter bias. How do I respond to that charge?

I have three interrelated responses. First, I'm not sure there is a view from nowhere, a location where scientists are wholly free from their culturally bound perspective. For example, I don't see how a skeptic of religion investigating religious phenomena could escape a similar criticism. Thus, I think the best we can hope for is not to pretend that we have achieved a wholly objective vantage point. The history of science is littered with facts that were once considered as immutable as the law of gravity only to be revealed (in hindsight) as mere prejudice. No, it is best not to pretend to objectivity. It is better to be clear about our social location, to be as transparent as possible about our values and biases.

Once on the table, these potential blinders can be taken into consideration and factored into the picture. In short, if I admit to my biases regarding the authenticity of religious belief I hope that any skeptics of religion, when revisiting the data, would also lay their prejudice just as clearly upon the table.

My second response to a criticism of bias is simply this: let the research process continue. It is a truism in science that published findings need replication. The empirical studies reviewed in Part 3 are, at best, preliminary findings. Much more research is required. Only additional research will settle the question as to whether the Jamesian approach of religious varieties better explains the relationship between religious experience and existential consolation. Currently, there is very little research on this topic. My research is almost alone within the empirical literature in taking up these questions. Consequently, the best way to address the issue of bias would be for additional research to investigate these questions. In fact, one of my hopes in writing this book is to stimulate and encourage just these sorts of research projects among my fellow social scientists.

My third and final response along these lines relates to the two different approaches used by William James and Sigmund Freud in their two seminal works. Freud, as a self-professed outsider to faith, attempted to explain, as he often tried to do, as much of the human experience as he could with a handful of psychoanalytic principles. To this day, the sweep and ambition of psychoanalytic theory is stunning. It is an impressive theory in its scope. And yet, there were times in Freud's career when his confidence in the explanatory power of psychoanalysis outstripped the data. And it appears that religious experience was one of those instances. Again, this is not to say that Freud didn't put his finger on legitimate, psychological dynamics within the religious experience. But Freud's theoretical insistence upon making the whole of the human experience fit within the framework of psychoanalytic theory often blinded him to phenomena that fell outside those theoretical borders.

Contrast Freud's approach with the one used by William James in *The Varieties of Religious Experience*. If Freud's was a top-down approach, the attempt to impose a systematizing theory upon a messy reality, James' approach was decidedly bottom-up. Using his testimonial approach, James gathered the data and then attempted to detect patterns. James was less interested in explanation (a prime concern of Freud) than description, and as complete and as rich a description he could muster. Strictly as a matter of method, then, James was better poised to get on the inside of the religious experience. At the very least, it enabled James to appreciate the sprawling complexity of the religious experience in a way that is missing in *The Future of an Illusion*. Seeking to get on the inside, James was able to see dynamics within the religious experience that largely eluded Freud.

The point in making this contrast is simply this. If research into the religious experience is to continue we will need, going forward, the perspectives of both insiders and outsiders. This is simply good science. If we wish to avoid the scientific mistakes made by Freud, we will need first to follow the lead of William James. Before we can move on to any theoretical speculations concerning the nature and function of religious belief we will need, first, to engage in James's descriptive work. We will need to describe, as richly as possible, the full width and depth of the religious experience. Otherwise, we simply crack off a small bit of the whole. That was Freud's mistake. Wanting to offer a theory that would explain the nature and function of religious belief, he failed to do the requisite descriptive work, largely, I expect, because of his distaste for the subject. And lacking a complete picture of the data, Freud's explanation was, of necessity, limited, simplistic, and less than comprehensive.

All that to say that social scientists who are insiders to faith will play an important role in future scientific research efforts. If we really want to make scientific progress in this area, we will need to make sure that our starting point, the description of the religious experience, is as rich, complex, and accurate as the phenomena we are attempting to understand. Social scientists who are insiders of the religious experience will play an important part in this effort. For it may be very difficult for outsiders, such as Freud, to describe the nuances and complexities of faith. Going forward then, a collaborative effort among social scientists, both insiders and outsiders, is needed. Insiders will be vital to ensuring that the Jamesian task of description is both well-done and accurate. Outsiders will bring to the table the objective distance and skepticism of Freud.

To make any progress, we need both Sigmund Freud *and* William James.

9.

To conclude this book, let us finally turn to a question that has been hovering over these pages.

We have spent a great deal of time and effort across many chapters trying to sort through the existential motivations of religious believers. Time and again we've noted how many religious believers, generally the healthy-minded, are motivated by a need for existential consolation. By contrast, we've also noted evidence that suggests that sick souls appear to eschew existential consolation. Sick souls do not appear to be motivated by a need for solace.

And if that lack of a need for solace is true, we are left with a lingering question: What then motivates the faith of the sick soul? If not for existential consolation, why do sick souls believe in God?

One way to frame this question is to return to the experience of the lament psalms. Specifically, if God is experienced as silent, absent, or antagonistic, why hold onto faith? If, experientially speaking, it appears that God is absent from life, why not draw the conclusion that God doesn't exist? And if doubt is a regular feature of the sick soul experience, why would that doubt not progress to disbelief?

No doubt there are many individuals who have walked this road, moving from faith to doubt to disillusionment to disbelief. And during this transition, the religious experience would look very much like the experience of the sick soul. And this is, incidentally, simply another way to resolve the cognitive dissonance often experienced with faith. We've described in great detail across these pages how many religious believers cope with dissonance, how they retreat into healthy-minded consolation. But another way to resolve the dissonance, an option many take, is simply to walk away from faith. For many former believers, there is a great relief in letting go of God, a relief largely produced by the resolution of cognitive dissonance.

And yet, there seem to be many religious believers, the sick souls, who resist moving in *either* direction. Sick souls resist the retreat into religious illusions as well as the pull toward unbelief. They exist in the murky middle between belief and disbelief, between faith and unfaith. Sick souls resolutely sit with the wreckage and rubble of life, much like the biblical character of Job in the Old Testament, and call out to a God who doesn't seem to care or answer. And we have to ask: Why? Why live with and endure these dissonances and ambiguities? Why suffer in this way? Why not simply let go of faith?

A full answer to this question can't be offered here, mainly because there is very little empirical literature I can cite regarding the motivations of the sick soul. So our answers here will be preliminary and tentative. But let me venture two final and concluding observations that I think will bring us full circle.

I think the sick soul is willing to live in between faith and unfaith, belief and disbelief, because this is the only way they can remain truthful to their lived experience. The pieces of life and the life of faith are not so easily fit together. There are gaps, there are missing pieces, and someone has taken away the puzzle box showing us the grand scheme of things. Or, to use another metaphor, life is experienced as broken glass. Life is experienced as shattered. The puzzle pieces here are shards, bit of brokenness that we try to piece together again into a whole. And as we handle the pieces, we are often cut and wounded. Life resists our attempts at putting the pieces together, intellectually and emotionally.

I can only assume that for the sick souls some piece of the puzzle is their experience of God, the Divine, and the transcendent. The movement toward disbelief is untenable for sick souls because it would involve ignoring these pieces within their life experience. And in a similar way, the overall experience of shattered brokenness also prevents a drift toward healthy-minded consolation, the too easy belief that life makes sense, that the pieces of the puzzle are easily fit together. As a result the sick soul lingers, perhaps for a lifetime, in this ambiguous location, holding onto pieces, God among them, that don't quite fit together.

In addition, while the journey of the sick soul is emotionally difficult, many sick souls may eventually come to embrace one of its particular virtues, so much so that the experience of the sick soul might be actively cultivated to reap this potential benefit. Here the sick soul is a way of believing, a mode of living with faith that is sought as an end in itself.

The logic here should by now be obvious. If a fear-based dogmatism leads to violence and intolerance, the experience of doubt may actually be cultivated to reap ethical and moral benefits. Doubt becomes a moral and spiritual exercise. In this we see how individuals might consciously choose the path of the sick soul despite the emotional cost. While solace is lost, openness to Others is gained. As Berger and Zijderveld (2009) summarize (p. 113): "Sincere and consistent doubt is the source of tolerance."

But this goes beyond mere tolerance. True, by refusing to engage in worldview defense, sick souls are better positioned to approach Others with warmth, curiosity, and a spirit of hospitality. While engaging with Others will cause the sick soul to ask some hard questions about the ultimate truthfulness of their own worldview, the moral benefits here are obvious. But the deeper significance of exposing oneself to the suffering, pain, and ambiguities of life is that the exposure allows one both to see and stand in solidarity with those who are suffering. Thus, the virtues of the sick soul are less about tolerance, although that is no small accomplishment, than about an increased capacity for empathy, compassion, and love. Facing the evil and suffering in life is hard and it raises all sorts of difficult questions for people of faith. But if William James (1902/1987) is correct, the path of the sick soul, as hard as it is, may be in his words "the best key to life's significance, and possibly the only openers of our eyes to the deepest levels of truth."

Perhaps then in the final analysis, faith, dogmatically understood, must be traded for love. Doubts are the burden that believers must carry to keep their eyes opened to the suffering of others. It is as Moltmann (1993) described it, "The more a person believes, the more deeply he experiences pain over the suffering in the world." What, then, might be the ultimate proof of the authenticity of faith? Perhaps it is as simple as St. Paul suggested in the First Epistle to the Corinthians:

"And now these three remain: faith, hope and love. But the greatest of these is love." (1 Corinthians 13:13)

Bibliography

Ainsworth, M. D. S. (1985). Attachment across the lifespan. *Bulletin of the New York Academy of Medicine, 61*, 792–812.

Balmer, R. (2000). The Kinkade crusade. *Christianity Today, 44*(14), 48–55.

Bartholomew, K., & Horowitz, L. M. (1991). Attachment styles in young adults: A test of a four-category model. *Journal of Personality and Social Psychology, 61*, 226–244.

Bassett, K. M., Bassett, R. L., Scott, K., Lovejoy, M., Preston, J., Gavette, H., & Grimm, J. P. (2009). Regarding football and worldview: Is defensiveness the best offense?. *Journal of Psychology and Christianity, 28*, 248–263.

Batson, C. D., & Schoenrade, P. A. (1991). Measuring religion as quest: 2. Reliability concerns. *Journal for the Scientific Study of Religion, 30*, 430–447.

Batson, C. D., Schoenrade, P. A., & Ventis, W. L. (1993). *Religion and the individual: A social-psychological perspective*. New York, NY: Oxford University Press.

Beck, R. (2002, March/April). Summer and winter Christians. *New Wineskins*, 20–22.

Beck, R. (2004). The function of religious belief: Defensive versus existential religion. *Journal of Psychology and Christianity, 23*, 208–218.

Beck, R. (2006a). Communion and complaint: Attachment, object-relations, and triangular love perspectives on relationship with God. *Journal of Psychology and Theology, 34*, 43–52.

Beck, R. (2006b). Defensive versus existential religion: Is religious defensiveness predictive of worldview defense? *Journal of Psychology and Theology, 34*, 142–151.

Beck, R. (2007). The winter experience of faith: Empirical, theological, and theoretical perspectives. *Journal of Psychology and Christianity, 26*, 68–78.

Beck, R. (2009a). Feeling queasy about the Incarnation: Terror management theory, death, and the body of Jesus. *Journal of Psychology and Theology, 36*, 303-312.

Beck, R. (2009b). Profanity: The gnostic affront of the seven words you can never say on television. *Journal of Psychology and Theology, 37*, 294-303.

Beck, R., & McDonald, A. (2004). Attachment to God: The Attachment to God Inventory, tests of working model correspondence, and an exploration of faith group differences. *Journal of Psychology and Theology, 32*, 92–103.

Beck, R., McGregor, D., Woodrow, B., Haugen, A., & Killion, K. (2010). Death, art and the fall: A terror management view of Christian aesthetic judgments. *Journal of Psychology and Christianity, 29*, 301–307.

Beck, R., & Taylor, S. (2008). The emotional burden of monotheism: Satan, theodicy, and relationship with God. *Journal of Psychology and Theology, 36*, 151–160.

Becker, E. (1973). *The denial of death*. New York, NY: Free Press.

Becker, E. (1975). *Escape from evil*. New York, NY: Free Press.

Berger, P. L., & Zijderveld, A. C. (2009). *In praise of doubt: How to have convictions without becoming a fanatic*. New York, NY: HarperOne/HarperCollins.

Bloom, H. (1986, March 23). Freud, the greatest modern writer. *The New York Times*. Retrieved from http://www.nytimes.com/1986/03/23/books/freud-the-greatest-modern-writer.html

Bonhoeffer, D. (1997). *Letters and papers from prison*. New York: Simon & Schuster.

Boyd, G. (2001). *Satan and the problem of evil: Constructing a trinitarian warfare theodicy*. Downers Grove, IL: InterVarsity Press.

Brueggemann, W. (1984). *The message of the psalms: A theological commentary*. Minneapolis, MN: Augsburg Fortress Publishers.

Bultmann, R. (1984). *New Testament and mythology and other basic writings*. Philadelphia, PA: Fortress Press.

Bustard, N. (2006). God is good like no other. In N. Bustard (Ed.), *It was good: Making art to the glory of God* (2nd ed., pp. 17-32). Baltimore, MD: Square Halo Books.

Camus, A. (1955). *The myth of Sisyphus and other essays*. (J. O'Brien, Trans.). New York, NY: Vintage Books.

Chaplin, A. (2006). Beauty transfigured. In N. Bustard (Ed.), *It was good: Making art to the glory of God* (2nd ed., pp. 33–50). Baltimore, MD: Square Halo Books.

Darwin, C. (1859/2003). *On the origin of species*. Rockville, MD: Wildside Press.

Dennett, D. C. (2006). *Breaking the spell: Religion as a natural phenomenon*. New York, NY: Penguin Books.

Eagleton, T. (2009). *Reason, faith, and revolution: Reflections on the God debate*. New Haven, CT: Yale University Press.

Edmundson, M. (2007, September 9). Defender of the faith? *The New York Times*. Retrieved from http://www.nytimes.com/2007/09/09/magazine/09wwln-lede-t.html

Ehrman, B. D. (2003). *The lost Christianities*. New York, NY: Oxford University Press.

Ellison, C. W. (1983). Spiritual well-being: Conceptualization and measurement. *Journal of Psychology and Theology, 11*, 330–340.

Ellison, C. W., & Smith, J. (1991). Toward an integrative measure of health and well-being. *Journal of Psychology and Theology, 19*, 35–48.

Freud, S. (1907/1924). Obsessive actions and religious practices. In J. Strachey (Ed.), *The Standard Edition of the Complete Psychological Works of Sigmund Freud* (Vol. 9, pp. 115-128). New York, NY: W. W. Norton & Company.

Freud, S. (1913/1950). *Totem and taboo*. (J. Strachey, Trans.). New York, NY: W. W. Norton & Company.

Freud, S. (1927/1989). *The future of an illusion*. J. Strachey, (Ed.). New York, NY: W. W. Norton & Company.

Freud, S. (1929/1960). *Civilization and its discontents*. (J. Strachey, Trans.). New York, NY: W. W. Norton & Company.

Freud, S. (1939/1955). *Moses and monotheism*. New York, NY: Vintage Books.

Freud, S. (1989). *The Freud reader*. P. Gay, (Ed.). New York, NY: W. W. Norton & Company.

Fullerton, J. T., & Hunsberger, B. (1982). A unidimensional measure of Christian orthodoxy. *Journal for the Scientific Study of Religion, 21*, 317–326.

Gay, P. (1988). *Freud: A life for our time*. New York, NY: W. W. Norton & Company.

Gay, P. (1999, March 29). Sigmund Freud: Psychoanalyst. *Time*. Retrieved from http://www.time.com/time/magazine/article/0,9171,990609-1,00.html

Goldenberg, J. L., Cox, C. R., Pyszczynski, T., Greenberg, J., & Solomon, S. (2002). Understanding human ambivalence about sex: The effects of stripping sex of meaning. *The Journal of Sex Research, 39*, 310–320.

Goldenberg, J. L., Hart, J., Pyszczynski, T., Warnica, G. M., Landau, M., & Thomas, L. (2004). Ambivalence toward the body: Death, neuroticism, and the flight from physical sensation. *Personality and Social Psychology Bulletin, 32*, 1264–1277.

Goldenberg, J. L., McCoy, S. K., Pyszczynski, T., Greenberg, J., & Solomon, S. (2000). The body as a source of self-esteem: The effect of mortality salience on identification with one's body, interest in sex, and appearance monitoring. *Journal of Personality and Social Psychology, 79*, 118–130.

Goldenberg, J. L., Pyszczynski, T., Greenberg, J., & Solomon, S. (2000). Fleeing the body: A terror management perspective on the problem of human corporeality. *Personality and Social Psychology Review, 4*, 200–218.

Goldenberg, J. L., Pyszczynski, T., Greenberg, J., Solomon, S., Kluck, B., & Cornwall, R. (2001). I am not an animal: Mortality salience, disgust, and the denial of human creatureliness. *Journal of Experimental Psychology: General, 130*, 427–435.

Goldenberg, J. L., Pyszczynski, T., McCoy, S. K., Greenberg, J., & Solomon, S. (1999). Death, sex, love, and neuroticism: Why is sex such a problem? *Journal of Personality and Social Psychology, 77*, 1173–1187.

Gorsuch, R. L., & McPherson, S. E. (1989). Intrinsic/extrinsic measurement: I/E-revised and single-item scales. *Journal for the Scientific Study of Religion, 23*, 348–354.

Greenberg, J., Koole, S., & Pyszczynski, T. (Eds.). (2004). *Handbook of experimental existential psychology*. New York, NY: Guilford Press.

Greenberg, J., Pyszczynski, T., Solomon, S., Rosenblatt, A., Veeder, M., Kirkland, S., & Lyon, D. (1990). Evidence for terror management theory II: The effects of mortality salience on reactions to those who threaten or bolster the cultural worldview. *Journal of Personality and Social Psychology, 58*, 308–318.

Greenberg, J., Simon, L., Pyszczynski, T., Solomon, S., & Chatel, D. (1992). Terror management and tolerance: Does mortality salience always intensify negative reactions to others who threaten one's worldview? *Journal of Personality and Social Psychology, 63*, 212–220.

Greenberg, J., Solomon, S., & Pyszczynski, T. (1997). Terror management theory of self-esteem and cultural worldviews: Empirical assessments and conceptual refinements. In M. Zanna (Ed.), *Advances in experimental social psychology* (Vol. 29, pp. 61–139). San Diego, CA: Academic Press.

Greenberg, J., Solomon, S., Pyszczynski, T., Rosenblatt, A., Burling, J., Lyon, D., . . . Pinel, E. (1992). Why do people need self-esteem? Converging evidence that self-esteem serves an anxiety-buffering function. *Journal of Personality and Social Psychology, 63*, 913-922.

Haidt, J., Koller, S., & Dias, M. (1993). Affect, culture, and morality, or is it wrong to eat your dog? *Journal of Personality and Social Psychology, 65*, 613-628.

Hall, M. E. L., & Thoennes, E. (2006). At home in our bodies: Implications of the incarnation for embodiment. *Christian Scholars Review, 36*, 29-46.

Hall, T. W., Brokaw, B. F., Edwards, K. J., & Pike, P. L. (1998). An empirical exploration of psychoanalysis and religion: Spiritual maturity and object relations development. *Journal for the Scientific Study of Religion, 37*, 302-313.

Hall, T. W., & Edwards, K. J. (1996). The initial development and factor analysis of the Spiritual Assessment Inventory. *Journal of Psychology and Theology, 24*, 233-246.

Hall, T. W., & Edwards, K. J. (2002). The Spiritual Assessment Inventory: A theistic model and measure for assessing spiritual development. *Journal for the Scientific Study of Religion, 41*, 341-357.

Harmon-Jones, E., Simon, L., Greenberg, J., Pyszczynski, T., Solomon, S., & McGregor, H. (1997). Terror management theory and self-esteem: Evidence that increased self-esteem reduced mortality salience effects. *Journal of Personality and Social Psychology, 72*, 24-36.

Harris, S. (2004). *The end of faith: Religion, terror, and the future of reason.* New York, NY: W. W. Norton & Company.

Harris, S. (2008). *Letter to a Christian nation.* New York, NY: Vintage Books.

Hazan, C., & Shaver, P. (1987). Romantic love conceptualized as an attachment process. *Journal of Personality and Social Psychology, 52*, 511-524.

Hazan, C., & Shaver, P. (1990). Love and work: An attachment-theoretical perspective. *Journal of Personality and Social Psychology, 59*, 270–280.

Heim, S. M. (2001). *The depth of the riches: A trinitarian theology of religious ends*. Grand Rapids, MI: Eerdmans.

Heschel, A. J. (1955). *God in search of man: A philosophy of Judaism*. New York, NY: Farrar, Straus, and Giroux.

Hill, P. C., & Hall, T. W. (2002). Relational schemas in processing one's image of God and self. *Journal of Psychology and Christianity, 21*, 365–373.

Hitchens, C. (2007a). *God is not great: How religion poisons everything*. New York, NY: Twelve.

Hitchens, C. (2007b). *The portable atheist: Essential readings for the nonbeliever*. Philadelphia, PA: Da Capo Press.

Hume, D. (1739/2001). *A treatise of human nature*. D. F. Norton and M. Norton, (Eds.). New York, NY: Oxford University Press.

Hume, D. (1779/1947). *Dialogues concerning natural religion*. Upper Saddle River, NJ: Prentice Hall.

James, W. (1987). *Writings, 1902-1910: The varieties of religious experience, pragmatism, a pluralistic universe, the meaning of truth, some problems of philosophy, essays*. New York, NY: Library of America.

Kirkpatrick, L. A. (1999). Attachment and religious representations and behavior. In J. Cassidy & P. R. Shaver (Eds.), *Handbook of attachment: Theory, research, and clinical applications* (pp. 803–822). New York, NY: Guilford Press.

Kolodiejchuk, B. (Ed.). (2007). *Mother Teresa: Come be my light*. New York, NY: Doubleday.

Landau, M. J., Goldenberg, J. L., Greenberg, J., Gillath, O., Solomon, S., Cox, C., . . . Pyszczynski, T. (2006). The Siren's call: Terror management and the threat of men's sexual attraction to women. *Journal of Personality and Social Psychology, 90*, 129–146.

Landau, M. J., Greenberg, J., Solomon, S., Pyszczynski, T., & Martens, A. (2006). Windows into nothingness: Terror management, meaninglessness, and negative reactions to modern art. *Journal of Personality and Social Psychology, 90*, 879–892.

Lee, P. (1987). *Against the Protestant Gnostics*. New York, NY: Oxford University Press.

Marty, M. E. (1997). *A cry of absence: Reflections for the winter of the heart*. Grand Rapids, MI: Eerdmans.

Marx, K. (1843/1970). *Critique of Hegel's "Philosophy of Right"*. J. O'Malley (Ed.). New York, NY: Cambridge University Press.

McDonald, A., Beck, R., Allison, S., & Norsworthy, L. (2005). Attachment to God and parents: Testing the correspondence vs. compensation hypotheses. *Journal of Psychology and Christianity, 24*, 21–28.

McGill, A. C. (1982). *Suffering: A test of theological method*. Eugene, OR: Wipf and Stock.

McGill, A. C. (1987). *Life and death: An American theology*. Eugene, OR: Wipf and Stock.

Miles, J. (2001). *Christ: A crisis in the life of God*. New York, NY: Knopf.

Moltmann, J. (1993). *Trinity and kingdom*. Minneapolis, MN: Fortress Press.

Paley, W. (1802/2010). *Natural theology; or, evidences of the existence and attributes of the deity*. Chillicothe, OH: DeWard Publishing.

Pascal, B. (1669/1958). *Pascal's pensées*. New York, NY: E. P. Dutton & Co., Inc.

Pyszczynski, T., Solomon, S., & Greenberg, J. (2003). *In the wake of 9/11: The psychology of terror*. Washington, DC: American Psychological Association.

Richardson, R. D. (2006). *William James: In the maelstrom of American modernism: A biography*. Boston, MA: Houghton Mifflin.

Ricoeur, P. (1970). *Freud and philosophy: An essay on interpretation*. (D. Savage, Trans.). New Haven, CT: Yale University Press.

Rowatt, W. C., & Kirkpatrick, L. A. (2002). Two dimensions of attachment to God and their relation to affect, religiosity, and personality constructs. *Journal for the Scientific Study of Religion, 41*, 637–651.

Ryken, P. G. (2006). *Art for God's sake: A call to recover the arts*. Phillipsburg, NJ: P&R Publishing.

Solomon, S., Greenberg, J., & Pyszczynski, T. (2004). The cultural animal: Twenty years of terror management theory and research. In J. Greenberg, S. L. Koole, & T. Pyszczynski (Eds.), *Handbook of experimental existential psychology* (pp. 13–34). New York, NY: Guilford Press.

Taylor, C. (2007). *A secular age*. Cambridge, MA: Belknap.

Tillich, P. (1999). *The essential Tillich*. F. F. Church, (Ed.). Chicago, IL: The University of Chicago Press.

Turner, S. (2001). *Imagine: A vision for Christians in the arts*. Downers Grove, IL: InterVarsity Press.

Shakespeare, W. (1623/2009). *Macbeth*. New York, NY: Oxford University Press.

Vail, K., Rothschild, Z. K., Weise, D. R., Solomon, S., Pyszczynski, T., & Greenberg, J. (2010). A terror management analysis of the psychological functions of religion. *Personality and Social Psychology Review, 14*, 84–94.

Van Biema, D. (2007, August 23). Mother Teresa's crisis of faith. *Time*. Retrieved from www.time.com /time/magazine/article/0,9171,1655720,00.html

Yalom, I. D. (1980). *Existential psychotherapy*. New York, NY: Basic.